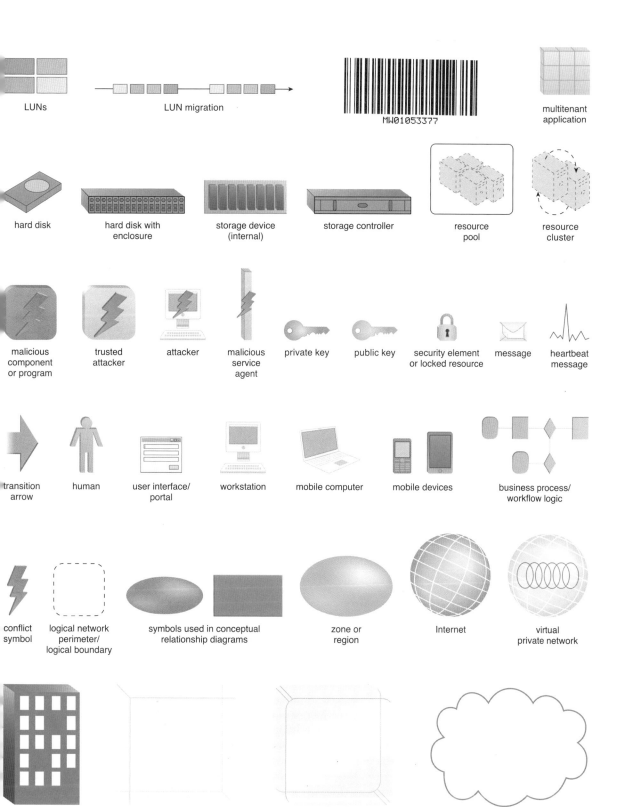

LUNs

LUN migration

MW01053377

multitenant application

hard disk

hard disk with enclosure

storage device (internal)

storage controller

resource pool

resource cluster

malicious component or program

trusted attacker

attacker

malicious service agent

private key

public key

security element or locked resource

message

heartbeat message

transition arrow

human

user interface/ portal

workstation

mobile computer

mobile devices

business process/ workflow logic

conflict symbol

logical network perimeter/ logical boundary

symbols used in conceptual relationship diagrams

zone or region

Internet

virtual private network

organization

general physical boundary

system or program boundary

cloud

Praise for this Book

"Cloud computing, more than most disciplines in IT, suffers from too much talk and not enough practice. Thomas Erl has written a timely book that condenses the theory and buttresses it with real-world examples that demystify this important technology. An important guidebook for your journey into the cloud."

—Scott Morrison, Chief Technology Officer, Layer 7 Technologies

"An excellent, extremely well-written, lucid book that provides a comprehensive picture of cloud computing, covering multiple dimensions of the subject. The case studies presented in the book provide a real-world, practical perspective on leveraging cloud computing in an organization. The book covers a wide range of topics, from technology aspects to the business value provided by cloud computing. This is the best, most comprehensive book on the subject—a must-read for any cloud computing practitioner or anyone who wants to get an in-depth picture of cloud computing concepts and practical implementation."

—Suzanne D'Souza, SOA/BPM Practice Lead, KBACE Technologies

"This book offers a thorough and detailed description of cloud computing concepts, architectures, and technologies. It serves as a great reference for both newcomers and experts and is a must-read for any IT professional interested in cloud computing."

—Andre Tost, Senior Technical Staff Member, IBM Software Group

"This is a great book on the topic of cloud computing. It is impressive how the content spans from taxonomy, technology, and architectural concepts to important business considerations for cloud adoption. It really does provide a holistic view to this technology paradigm."

—Kapil Bakshi, Architecture and Strategy, Cisco Systems Inc.

"I have read every book written by Thomas Erl and *Cloud Computing* is another excellent publication and demonstration of Thomas Erl's rare ability to take the most complex topics and provide critical core concepts and technical information in a logical and understandable way."

—Melanie A. Allison, Principal, Healthcare Technology Practice,
Integrated Consulting Services

"Companies looking to migrate applications or infrastructure to the cloud are often misled by buzzwords and industry hype. This work cuts through the hype and provides a detailed look, from investigation to contract to implementation to termination, at what it takes for an organization to engage with cloud service providers. This book really lays out the benefits and struggles with getting a company to an IaaS, PaaS, or SaaS solution."

—Kevin Davis, Ph.D., Solutions Architect

"Thomas, in his own distinct and erudite style, provides a comprehensive and a definitive book on cloud computing. Just like his previous masterpiece, *Service-Oriented Architecture: Concepts, Technology, and Design*, this book is sure to engage CxOs, cloud architects, and the developer community involved in delivering software assets on the cloud. Thomas and his authoring team have taken great pains in providing great clarity and detail in documenting cloud architectures, cloud delivery models, cloud governance, and economics of cloud, without forgetting to explain the core of cloud computing that revolves around Internet architecture and virtualization. As a reviewer for this outstanding book, I must admit I have learned quite a lot while reviewing the material. A 'must have' book that should adorn everybody's desk!"

—Vijay Srinivasan, Chief Architect - Technology, Cognizant Technology Solutions

"This book provides comprehensive and descriptive vendor-neutral coverage of cloud computing technology, from both technical and business aspects. It provides a deep-down analysis of cloud architectures and mechanisms that capture the real-world moving parts of cloud platforms. Business aspects are elaborated on to give readers a broader perspective on choosing and defining basic cloud computing business models. Thomas Erl's *Cloud Computing: Concepts, Technology & Architecture* is an excellent source of knowledge of fundamental and in-depth coverage of cloud computing."

—Masykur Marhendra Sukmanegara, Communication Media & Technology,
Consulting Workforce Accenture

"The richness and depth of the topics discussed are incredibly impressive. The depth and breadth of the subject matter are such that a reader could become an expert in a short amount of time."

—Jamie Ryan, Solutions Architect, Layer 7 Technologies

"Demystification, rationalization, and structuring of implementation approaches have always been strong parts in each and every one of Thomas Erl's books. This book is no exception. It provides the definitive, essential coverage of cloud computing and, most importantly, presents this content in a very comprehensive manner. Best of all, this book follows the conventions of the previous service technology series titles, making it read like a natural extension of the library. I strongly believe that this will be another best-seller from one of the top-selling IT authors of the past decade."

—Sergey Popov, Senior Enterprise Architect SOA/Security, Liberty Global International

"A must-read for anyone involved in cloud design and decision making! This insightful book provides in-depth, objective, vendor-neutral coverage of cloud computing concepts, architecture models, and technologies. It will prove very valuable to anyone who needs to gain a solid understanding of how cloud environments work and how to design and migrate solutions to clouds."

—Gijs in 't Veld, Chief Architect, Motion10

"A reference book covering a wide range of aspects related to cloud providers and cloud consumers. If you would like to provide or consume a cloud service and need to know how, this is your book. The book has a clear structure to facilitate a good understanding of the various concepts of cloud."

—Roger Stoffers, Solution Architect

"Cloud computing has been around for a few years, yet there is still a lot of confusion around the term and what it can bring to developers and deployers alike. This book is a great way of finding out what's behind the cloud, and not in an abstract or high-level manner: It dives into all of the details that you'd need to know in order to plan for developing applications on cloud and what to look for when using applications or services hosted on a cloud. There are very few books that manage to capture this level of detail about the evolving cloud paradigm as this one does. It's a must for architects and developers alike."

—Dr. Mark Little, Vice President, Red Hat

"This book provides a comprehensive exploration of the concepts and mechanics behind clouds. It's written for anyone interested in delving into the details of how cloud environments function, how they are architected, and how they can impact business. This is the book for any organization seriously considering adopting cloud computing. It will pave the way to establishing your cloud computing roadmap."

—*Damian Maschek, SOA Architect, Deutsche Bahn*

"One of the best books on cloud computing I have ever read. It is complete yet vendor technology neutral and successfully explains the major concepts in a well-structured and disciplined way. It goes through all the definitions and provides many hints for organizations or professionals who are approaching and/or assessing cloud solutions. This book gives a complete list of topics playing fundamental roles in the cloud computing discipline. It goes through a full list of definitions very clearly stated. Diagrams are simple to understand and self-contained. Readers with different skill sets, expertise, and backgrounds will be able to understand the concepts seamlessly."

—*Antonio Bruno, Infrastructure and Estate Manager, UBS AG*

"*Cloud Computing: Concepts, Technology & Architecture* is a comprehensive book that focuses on what cloud computing is really all about…. This book will become the foundation on which many organizations will build successful cloud adoption projects. It is a must-read reference for both IT infrastructure and application architects interested in cloud computing or involved in cloud adoption projects. It contains extremely useful and comprehensive information for those who need to build cloud-based architectures or need to explain it to customers thinking about adopting cloud computing technology in their organization."

—*Johan Kumps, SOA Architect, RealDolmen*

"This book defines the basic terminology and patterns for the topic—a useful reference for the cloud practitioner. Concepts from multitenancy to hypervisor are presented in a succinct and clear manner. The underlying case studies provide wonderful real-worldness."

—*Dr. Thomas Rischbeck, Principal Architect, ipt*

"The book provides a good foundation to cloud services and issues in cloud service design. Chapters highlight key issues that need to be considered in learning how to think in cloud technology terms; this is highly important in today's business and technology environments where cloud computing plays a central role in connecting user services with virtualized resources and applications."

—*Mark Skilton, Director, Office of Strategy and Technology, Global Infrastructure Services, Capgemini*

"The book is well organized and covers basic concepts, technologies, and business models about cloud computing. It defines and explains a comprehensive list of terminologies and glossaries about cloud computing so cloud computing experts can speak and communicate with the same set of standardized language. The book is easy to understand and consistent with early published books from Thomas Erl.… It is a must-read for both beginners and experienced professionals."

—*Jian "Jeff" Zhong, Chief Technology Officer (Acting) and Chief Architect for SOA and Cloud Computing, Futrend Technology Inc.*

"Students of the related specialties can fulfill their educational process with very easily understood materials that are broadly illustrated and clearly described. Professors of different disciplines, from business analysis to IT implementation—even legal and financial monitoring—can use the book as an on-table lecturing manual. IT specialists of all ranks and fields of application will find the book as a practical and useful support for sketching solutions unbound to any particular vendor or brand."

—*Alexander Gromoff, Director of Science & Education, Center of Information Control Technologies, Chairman of BPM Chair in Business Informatics Department, National Research University "Higher School of Economics"*

"*Cloud Computing: Concepts, Technology & Architecture* is a comprehensive compendium of all the relevant information about the transformative cloud technology. Erl's latest title concisely and clearly illustrates the origins and positioning of the cloud paradigm as the next-generation computing model. All the chapters are carefully written and arranged in an easy-to-understand manner. This book will be immeasurably beneficial for business and IT professionals. It is set to shake up and help organize the world of cloud computing."

—*Pethuru Raj, Ph.D., Enterprise Architecture Consultant, Wipro*

"A cloud computing book that will stand out and survive the test of time, even in one of the fastest evolving areas of technology. This book does a great job breaking down the high level of complexity of cloud computing into easy-to-understand pieces. It goes beyond the basic, often repeated, explanations. It examines the fundamental concepts and the components, as well as the mechanisms and architectures that make up cloud computing environments. The approach gradually builds the reader's understanding from the ground up.

"In a rapidly evolving area like cloud computing, it's easy to focus on details and miss the big picture. The focus on concepts and architectural models instead of vendor-specific details allows readers to quickly gain essential knowledge of complex topics. The concepts come together in the last part of the book, which should be required reading for any decision maker evaluating when and how to start a transition to cloud computing. Its thorough, comprehensive coverage of fundamentals and advanced topics makes the book a valuable resource to keep on your desk or your eBook reader, regardless if you're new to the topic or you already have cloud experience.

"I highly recommend the book to those looking to implement or evaluate cloud environments, or simply looking to educate themselves in a field that will shape IT over the next decade."

—*Christoph Schittko, Principal Technology Strategist & Cloud Solution Director, Microsoft*

"*Cloud Computing: Concepts, Technology & Architecture* is an excellent resource for IT professionals and managers who want to learn and understand cloud computing, and who need to select or build cloud systems and solutions. It lays the foundation for cloud concepts, models, technologies, and mechanisms. As the book is vendor-neutral, it will remain valid for many years. We will recommend this book to Oracle customers, partners, and users for their journey toward cloud computing. This book has the potential to become the basis for a cloud computing manifesto, comparable to what was accomplished with the SOA manifesto."

—*Jürgen Kress, Fusion Middleware Partner Adoption, Oracle EMEA*

Cloud Computing

Concepts, Technology & Architecture

Thomas Erl,
Zaigham Mahmood,
and Ricardo Puttini

PRENTICE HALL

UPPER SADDLE RIVER, NJ • BOSTON • INDIANAPOLIS • SAN FRANCISCO

NEW YORK • TORONTO • MONTREAL • LONDON • MUNICH • PARIS • MADRID

CAPE TOWN • SYDNEY • TOKYO • SINGAPORE • MEXICO CITY

Many of the designations used by manufacturers and sellers to distinguish their products are claimed as trademarks. Where those designations appear in this book, and the publisher was aware of a trademark
claim, the designations have been printed with initial capital letters or in
all capitals.

The authors and publisher have taken care in the preparation of this
book, but make no expressed or implied warranty of any kind and
assume no responsibility for errors or omissions. No liability is assumed
for incidental or consequential damages in connection with or arising
out of the use of the information or programs contained herein.

The publisher offers excellent discounts on this book when ordered
in quantity for bulk purchases or special sales, which may include
electronic versions and/or custom covers and content particular to your
business, training goals, marketing focus, and branding interests. For
more information, please contact:

U.S. Corporate and Government Sales
(800) 382-3419
corpsales@pearsontechgroup.com

For sales outside the United States, please contact:

International Sales
international@pearsoned.com

Visit us on the Web: informit.com/ph

The Library of Congress Cataloging-in-Publication data is on file.

Copyright © 2013 Arcitura Education Inc.

All rights reserved. Printed in the United States of America. This publication is protected by copyright, and permission must be obtained from
the publisher prior to any prohibited reproduction, storage in a retrieval
system, or transmission in any form or by any means, electronic,
mechanical, photocopying, recording, or likewise. To obtain permission to use material from this work, please submit a written request
to Pearson Education, Inc., Permissions Department, One Lake Street,
Upper Saddle River, New Jersey 07458, or you may fax your request to
(201) 236-3290.

ISBN-13: 978-0-13-338752-0
ISBN-10: 0-13-338752-6

Text printed in the United States on recycled paper at Courier in
Westford, Massachusetts.

Second Printing: September 2013

Editor-in-Chief
Mark L. Taub

Managing Editor
Kristy Hart

Senior Project Editor
Betsy Gratner

**Copy Editor and
Development Editor**
Maria Lee

Senior Indexer
Cheryl Lenser

Proofreaders
Maria Lee
Williams Woods
Publishing

Publishing Coordinator
Kim Boedigheimer

Research Assistant
Briana Lee

Cover Designer
Thomas Erl

Compositor
Bumpy Design

Photos
Thomas Erl
Dominika Sládkovičová

Graphics
KK Lui
Briana Lee

To my family and friends
—Thomas Erl

To Zoya, Hanya, and Ozair with love
—Zaigham Mahmood

To Silvia, Luiza, Isadora, and Lucas
—Ricardo Puttini

Contents at a Glance

Contents

PART I: FUNDAMENTAL CLOUD COMPUTING

Chapter 4: Fundamental Concepts and Models 51

CHAPTER 5: Cloud-Enabling Technology 79

PART II: CLOUD COMPUTING MECHANISMS

CHAPTER 7: Cloud Infrastructure Mechanisms 139

CHAPTER 8: Specialized Cloud Mechanisms 169

PART III: CLOUD COMPUTING ARCHITECTURE

PART V: APPENDICES

Foreword by Pamela J. Wise-Martinez

The idea of cloud computing isn't new, or overly complicated from a technology resources and internetworking perspective. What's new is the growth and maturity of cloud computing methods, and strategies that enable the goals of business agility.

Looking back, the phrase "utility computing" didn't captivate or create the stir in the information industry as the term "cloud computing" has in recent years. Nevertheless, appreciation of readily available resources has arrived and the utilitarian or servicing features are what are at the heart of *outsourcing* the access of information technology resources and services. In this light, cloud computing represents a flexible, cost-effective, and proven delivery platform for business and consumer information services over the Internet. Cloud computing has become an industry game changer as businesses and information technology leaders realize the potential in *combining and sharing* computing resources as opposed to *building and maintaining* them.

There's seemingly no shortage of views regarding the benefits of cloud computing nor is there a shortage of vendors willing to offer services in either open source or promising commercial solutions. Beyond the hype, there are many aspects of the cloud that have earned new consideration due to their increased service capability and potential efficiencies. The ability to demonstrate transforming results in cloud computing to resolve traditional business problems using information technology management best practices now exists. In the case of economic impacts, the principle of *pay-as-you-go* and *computer agnostic services* are concepts ready for prime time. We can measure performance as well as calculate the economic and environmental effects of cloud computing today.

The architectural change from *client-server* to *service orientation* led to an evolution of composable and reusable code; though the practice had been around for many years, it is now the de facto approach used to lower cost and identify best practices and patterns for increasing business agility. This has advanced the computer software industry's design methods, components, and engineering. Comparatively, the wide acceptance and adoption of cloud computing is revolutionizing information and technology resource management. We now have the ability to outsource hardware and software capabilities on a large-scale to fulfill end-to-end business automation requirements. Marks and Lozano understood this emergence and the need for better software design: *"…we now have the ability to collect, transport, process, store, and access data nearly anywhere in nearly arbitrary volume."* The limitations depend largely on how "cloudy" or cloud-aware the service/component is, and hence the need for better software architecture. (Eric A. Marks and Roberto Lozano [*Executive Guide to Cloud Computing*]).

The reusable evolution through service architecture reinforces a focus on business objectives as opposed to the number of computing platforms to support. As a viable resource management alternative, cloud computing is fundamentally changing the way we think about computing solutions in retail, education, and public sectors. The use of cloud computing architecture and standards are driving unique ways in which computing solutions are delivered, as well as platform diversity to meet bottom-line business objectives.

Thomas Erl's body of work on service technology guided the technology industry through eloquent illustrations and literature over the past decade. Thomas' brilliant efforts on principles, concepts, patterns, and expressions gave the information technology community an *evolved* software architecture approach that now forms a foundation for cloud computing goals to be successfully fulfilled in practice. This is a key assertion, as cloud computing is no longer a far-reaching concept of the future, but rather a dominant information technology service option and resource delivery presence.

Thomas' *Cloud Computing: Concepts, Technology & Architecture* takes the industry beyond the definitions of cloud computing and juxtaposes virtualization, grid, and sustainment strategies as contrasted in day to day operations. Thomas and his team of authors take the reader from beginning to end with the essential elements of cloud computing, its history, innovation, and demand. Through case studies and architectural models they articulate service requirements, infrastructure, security, and outsourcing of salient computing resources.

Thomas again enlightens the industry with poignant analysis and reliable architecture-driven practices and principles. No matter the level of interest or experience, the reader will find clear value in this in-depth, vendor-neutral study of cloud computing.

Pamela J. Wise-Martinez,
Inventor and Chief Architect
Department of Energy, National Nuclear Security Administration

(Disclaimer: The views expressed are the personal views of the author and are not intended to reflect either the views of the U.S. Government, the U.S. Department of Energy, or the National Nuclear Security Administration.)

Acknowledgments

In alphabetical order by last name:

- Ahmed Aamer, AlFaisaliah Group
- Randy Adkins, Modus21
- Melanie Allison, Integrated Consulting Services
- Gabriela Inacio Alves, University of Brasilia
- Marcelo Ancelmo, IBM Rational Software Services
- Kapil Bakshi, Cisco Systems
- Toufic Boubez, Metafor Software
- Antonio Bruno, UBS AG
- Dr. Paul Buhler, Modus21
- Pethuru Raj Cheliah, Wipro
- Kevin Davis, Ph.D.
- Suzanne D'Souza, KBACE Technologies
- Yili Gong, Wuhan University
- Alexander Gromoff, Center of Information Control Technologies
- Chris Haddad, WSO2
- Richard Hill, University of Derby
- Michaela Iorga, Ph.D.
- Johan Kumps, RealDolmen
- Gijs in 't Veld, Motion10
- Masykur Marhendra, Consulting Workforce Accenture
- Damian Maschek, Deutshe Bahn
- Claynor Mazzarolo, IBTI
- Charlie Mead, W3C
- Steve Millidge, C2B2
- Jorge Minguez, Thales Deutschland
- Scott Morrison, Layer 7

- Amin Naserpour, HP
- Vicente Navarro, European Space Agency
- Laura Olson, IBM WebSphere
- Tony Pallas, Intel
- Cesare Pautasso, University of Lugano
- Sergey Popov, Liberty Global International
- Olivier Poupeney, Dreamface Interactive
- Alex Rankov, EMC
- Dan Rosanova, West Monroe Partners
- Jaime Ryan, Layer 7
- Filippos Santas, Credit Suisse
- Christoph Schittko, Microsoft
- Guido Schmutz, Trivadis
- Mark Skilton, Capgemini
- Gary Smith, CloudComputingArchitect.com
- Kevin Spiess
- Vijay Srinivasan, Cognizant
- Daniel Starcevich, Raytheon
- Roger Stoffers, HP
- Andre Toffanello, IBTI
- Andre Tost, IBM Software Group
- Bernd Trops, talend
- Clemens Utschig, Boehringer Ingelheim Pharma
- Ignaz Wanders, Archimiddle
- Philip Wik, Redflex
- Jorge Williams, Rackspace
- Dr. Johannes Maria Zaha
- Jeff Zhong, Futrend Technologies

Special thanks to the CloudSchool.com research and development team that produced the CCP course modules upon which this book is based.

Chapter 1

Introduction

The past couple of decades saw the business-centric concept of outsourcing services and the technology-centric notion of utility computing evolve along relatively parallel streams. When they finally met to form a technology landscape with a compelling business case and seismic impacts on the IT industry as a whole, it became evident that what resultantly was termed and branded as "cloud computing" was more than just another IT trend. It had become an opportunity to further align and advance the goals of the business with the capabilities of technology.

Those who understand this opportunity can seize it to leverage proven and mature components of cloud platforms to not only fulfill existing strategic business goals, but to even inspire businesses to set new objectives and directions based on the extent to which cloud-driven innovation can further help optimize business operations.

The first step to succeeding is education. Cloud computing adoption is not trivial. The cloud computing marketplace is unregulated. And, not all products and technologies branded with "cloud" are, in fact, sufficiently mature to realize or even supportive of realizing actual cloud computing benefits. To add to the confusion, there are different definitions and interpretations of cloud-based models and frameworks floating around IT literature and the IT media space, which leads to different IT professionals acquiring different types of cloud computing expertise.

And then, of course, there is the fact that cloud computing is, at its essence, a form of service provisioning. As with any type of service we intend to hire or outsource (IT-related or otherwise), it is commonly understood that we will be confronted with a marketplace comprised of service providers of varying quality and reliability. Some may offer attractive rates and terms, but may have unproven business histories or highly proprietary environments. Others may have a solid business background, but may demand higher rates and less flexible terms. Others yet, may simply be insincere or temporary business ventures that unexpectedly disappear or are acquired within a short period of time.

Back to the importance of getting educated. There is no greater danger to a business than approaching cloud computing adoption with ignorance. The magnitude of a failed adoption effort not only correspondingly impacts IT departments, but can actually regress a business to a point where it finds itself steps behind from where it was prior to the adoption—and, perhaps, even more steps behind competitors that have been successful at achieving their goals in the meantime.

Cloud computing has much to offer but its roadmap is riddled with pitfalls, ambiguities, and mistruths. The best way to navigate this landscape is to chart each part of the journey by making educated decisions about how and to what extent your project should proceed. The scope of an adoption is equally important to its approach, and both of these aspects need to be determined by business requirements. Not by a product vendor, not by a cloud vendor, and not by self-proclaimed cloud experts. Your organization's business goals must be fulfilled in a concrete and measurable manner with each completed phase of the adoption. This validates your scope, your approach, and the overall direction of the project. In other words, it keeps your project aligned.

Gaining a vendor-neutral understanding of cloud computing from an industry perspective empowers you with the clarity necessary to determine what is factually cloud-related and what is not, as well as what is relevant to your business requirements and what is not. With this information you can establish criteria that will allow you to filter out the parts of the cloud computing product and service provider marketplaces to focus on what has the most potential to help you and your business to succeed. We developed this book to assist you with this goal.

—**Thomas Erl**

1.1 Objectives of This Book

This book is the result of more than two years of research and analysis of the commercial cloud computing industry, cloud computing vendor platforms, and further innovation and contributions made by cloud computing industry standards organizations and practitioners. The purpose of this book is to break down proven and mature cloud computing technologies and practices into a series of well-defined concepts, models, and technology mechanisms and architectures. The resulting chapters establish concrete, academic coverage of fundamental aspects of cloud computing concepts and technologies. The range of topics covered is documented using vendor-neutral terms and descriptions, carefully defined to ensure full alignment with the cloud computing industry as a whole.

1.2 What This Book Does Not Cover

Due to the vendor-neutral basis of this book, it does not contain any significant coverage
of cloud computing vendor products, services, or technologies. This book is complementary to other titles that provide product-specific coverage and to vendor product
literature itself. If you are new to the commercial cloud computing landscape, you are
encouraged to use this book as a starting point before proceeding to books and courses
that are proprietary to vendor product lines.

1.3 Who This Book Is For

This book is aimed at the following target audience:

- IT practitioners and professionals who require vendor-neutral coverage of cloud
  computing technologies, concepts, mechanisms, and models

- IT managers and decision makers who seek clarity regarding the business and
  technological implications of cloud computing

- professors and students and educational institutions that require well-researched
  and well-defined academic coverage of fundamental cloud computing topics

- business managers who need to assess the potential economic gains and viability
  of adopting cloud computing resources

- technology architects and developers who want to understand the different moving parts that comprise contemporary cloud platforms

1.4 How This Book Is Organized

The book begins with Chapters 1 and 2 providing introductory content and background
information for the case studies. All subsequent chapters are organized into the following parts:

- Part I: Fundamental Cloud Computing

- Part II: Cloud Computing Mechanisms

- Part III: Cloud Computing Architecture

- Part IV: Working with Clouds

- Part V: Appendices

Part I: Fundamental Cloud Computing

The four chapters in this part cover introductory topics in preparation for all subsequent chapters. Note that Chapters 3 and 4 do not contain case study content.

Chapter 3: Understanding Cloud Computing

Following a brief history of cloud computing and a discussion of business drivers and technology innovations, basic terminology and concepts are introduced, along with descriptions of common benefits and challenges of cloud computing adoption.

Chapter 4: Fundamental Concepts and Models

Cloud delivery and cloud deployment models are discussed in detail, following sections that establish common cloud characteristics and roles and boundaries.

Chapter 5: Cloud-Enabling Technology

Contemporary technologies that realize modern-day cloud computing platforms and innovations are discussed, including data centers, virtualization, and Web-based technologies.

Chapter 6: Fundamental Cloud Security

Security topics and concepts relevant and distinct to cloud computing are introduced, including descriptions of common cloud security threats and attacks.

Part II: Cloud Computing Mechanisms

Technology mechanisms represent well-defined IT artifacts that are established within an IT industry and commonly distinct to a certain computing model or platform. The technology-centric nature of cloud computing requires the establishment of a formal level of mechanisms to be able to explore how solutions can be assembled via different combinations of mechanism implementations.

This part formally documents 20 technology mechanisms that are used within cloud environments to enable generic and specialized forms of functionality. Each mechanism description is accompanied by a case study example that demonstrates its usage. The utilization of the mechanisms is further explored throughout the technology architectures covered in Part III.

Chapter 7: Cloud Infrastructure Mechanisms

Technology mechanisms foundational to cloud platforms are covered, including Logical Network Perimeter, Virtual Server, Cloud Storage Device, Cloud Usage Monitor, Resource Replication, and Ready-Made Environment.

Chapter 8: Specialized Cloud Mechanisms

A range of specialized technology mechanisms is described, including Automated Scaling Listener, Load Balancer, SLA Monitor, Pay-Per-Use Monitor, Audit Monitor, Failover System, Hypervisor, Resource Cluster, Multi-Device Broker, and State Management Database.

Chapter 9: Cloud Management Mechanisms

Mechanisms that enable the hands-on administration and management of cloud-based IT resources are explained, including Remote Administration System, Resource Management System, SLA Management System, and Billing Management System.

Chapter 10: Cloud Security Mechanisms

Security mechanisms that can be used to counter and prevent the threats described in Chapter 6 are covered, including Encryption, Hashing, Digital Signatures, Public Key Infrastructures (PKI), Identity and Access Management (IAM) Systems, Single Sign-On (SSO), Cloud-Based Security Groups, and Hardened Virtual Server Images.

Part III: Cloud Computing Architecture

Technology architecture within the realm of cloud computing introduces requirements and considerations that manifest themselves in broadly scoped architectural layers and numerous distinct architectural models.

This set of chapters builds upon the coverage of cloud computing mechanisms from Part II by formally documenting 29 cloud-based technology architectures and scenarios in which different combinations of the mechanisms are documented in relation to fundamental, advanced, and specialized cloud architectures.

Chapter 11: Fundamental Cloud Architectures

Fundamental cloud architectural models establish baseline functions and capabilities. The architectures covered in this chapter are Workload Distribution, Resource Pooling, Dynamic Scalability, Elastic Resource Capacity, Service Load Balancing, Cloud Bursting, Elastic Disk Provisioning, and Redundant Storage.

Chapter 12: Advanced Cloud Architectures

Advanced cloud architectural models establish sophisticated and complex environments, several of which directly build upon fundamental models. The architectures covered in this chapter are Hypervisor Clustering, Load Balanced Virtual Server Instances, Non-Disruptive Service Relocation, Zero Downtime, Cloud Balancing, Resource Reservation, Dynamic Failure Detection and Recovery, Bare-Metal Provisioning, Rapid Provisioning, and Storage Workload Management.

Chapter 13: Specialized Cloud Architectures

Specialized cloud architectural models address distinct functional areas. The architectures covered in this chapter are Direct I/O Access, Direct LUN Access, Dynamic Data Normalization, Elastic Network Capacity, Cross-Storage Device Vertical Tiering, Intra-Storage Device Vertical Data Tiering, Load-Balanced Virtual Switches, Multipath Resource Access, Persistent Virtual Network Configuration, Redundant Physical Connection for Virtual Servers, and Storage Maintenance Window. Note that this chapter does not contain a case study example.

Part IV: Working with Clouds

Cloud computing technologies and environments can be adopted to varying extents. An organization can migrate select IT resources to a cloud, while keeping all other IT resources on-premise—or it can form significant dependencies on a cloud platform by migrating larger amounts of IT resources or even using the cloud environment to create them.

For any organization, it is important to assess a potential adoption from a practical and business-centric perspective in order to pinpoint the most common factors that pertain to financial investments, business impact, and various legal considerations. This set of chapters explores these and other topics related to the real-world considerations of working with cloud-based environments.

Chapter 14: Cloud Delivery Model Considerations

Cloud environments need to be built and evolved by cloud providers in response to cloud consumer requirements. Cloud consumers can use clouds to create or migrate IT resources to, subsequent to their assuming administrative responsibilities. This chapter provides a technical understanding of cloud delivery models from both the provider and consumer perspectives, each of which offers revealing insights into the inner workings and architectural layers of cloud environments.

Chapter 15: Cost Metrics and Pricing Models

Cost metrics for network, server, storage, and software usage are described, along with various formulas for calculating integration and ownership costs related to cloud environments. The chapter concludes with a discussion of cost management topics as they relate to common business terms used by cloud provider vendors.

Chapter 16: Service Quality Metrics and SLAs

Service level agreements establish the guarantees and usage terms for cloud services and are often determined by the business terms agreed upon by cloud consumers and cloud providers. This chapter provides detailed insight into how cloud provider guarantees are expressed and structured via SLAs, along with metrics and formulas for calculating common SLA values, such as availability, reliability, performance, scalability, and resiliency.

Part V: Appendices

Appendix A: Case Study Conclusions

The individual storylines of the case studies are concluded and the results of each organization's cloud computing adoption efforts are summarized.

Appendix B: Industry Standards Organizations

This appendix describes industry standards organizations and efforts in support of the cloud computing industry.

Appendix C: Mapping Mechanisms to Characteristics

A table is provided, mapping cloud characteristics to the cloud computing mechanisms that can help realize the characteristics.

Appendix D: Data Center Facilities (TIA-942)

A brief overview and breakdown of common data center facilities in reference to the TIA-942 Telecommunications Infrastructure Standard for Data Centers.

Appendix E: Cloud-Adapted Risk Management Framework

An overview of the Cloud-Adapted Risk Management Framework (CRMF) that is part of the NIST Cloud Computing Security Reference Architecture.

Appendix F: Cloud Provisioning Contracts

The actual agreements signed between cloud provider vendors and cloud consumer organizations are distinct legal contracts that encompass a range of specific terms and considerations. This appendix highlights the typical parts of a cloud provisioning contract, and provides further guidelines.

Appendix G: Cloud Business Case Template

This appendix provides a checklist of items that can be used as a starting point for assembling a business case for the adoption of cloud computing.

1.5 Conventions

Symbols and Figures

This book contains a series of diagrams that are referred to as *figures*. The primary symbols used throughout the figures are individually described in the symbol legend located on the inside of the book cover. Full-color, high-resolution versions of all figures in this book can be viewed and downloaded at www.servicetechbooks.com/cloud/figures and www.informit.com/title/9780133387520.

Summary of Key Points

For quick reference purposes, each of the sections within Chapters 3 through 6 in Part I, "Fundamental Cloud Computing," concludes with a *Summary of Key Points* sub-section that concisely highlights the primary statements made within the section, in bullet list format.

1.6 Additional Information

These sections provide supplementary information and resources for the *Prentice Hall Service Technology Series from Thomas Erl*.

Updates, Errata, and Resources (www.servicetechbooks.com)

Information about other series titles and various supporting resources can be found at the official book series Web site: www.servicetechbooks.com. You are encouraged to visit this site regularly to check for content changes and corrections.

Referenced Specifications (www.servicetechspecs.com)

This site provides a central portal to the original specification documents created and maintained by primary standards organizations, with a section dedicated exclusively to cloud computing industry standards.

The Service Technology Magazine (www.servicetechmag.com)

The Service Technology Magazine is a monthly publication provided by Arcitura Education Inc. and Prentice Hall and is officially associated with the *Prentice Hall Service Technology Series from Thomas Erl. The Service Technology Magazine* is dedicated to publishing specialized articles, case studies, and papers by industry experts and professionals.

International Service Technology Symposium (www.servicetechsymposium.com)

This site is dedicated to the International Service Technology Symposium conference series. These events are held throughout the world and frequently feature authors from the *Prentice Hall Service Technology Series from Thomas Erl.*

What Is Cloud? (www.whatiscloud.com)

A quick reference site comprised of excerpts from this book to provide coverage of fundamental cloud computing topics.

What Is REST? (www.whatisrest.com)

This Web site provides a concise overview of REST architecture and constraints. REST services are referenced in Chapter 5 of this book as one of the possible implementation mediums for cloud services.

Cloud Computing Design Patterns (www.cloudpatterns.org)

The cloud computing design patterns master catalog is published on this site. The mechanisms described in this book are referenced as implementation options for various design patterns that represent established practices and technology feature-sets.

Service-Orientation (www.serviceorientation.com)

This site provide papers, book excerpts, and various content dedicated to describing and defining the service-orientation paradigm, associated principles, and the service-oriented technology architectural model.

CloudSchool.com™ Certified Cloud (CCP) Professional (www.cloudschool.com)

The official site for the Cloud Certified Professional (CCP) curriculum dedicated to specialized areas of cloud computing, including technology, architecture, governance, security, capacity, virtualization, and storage.

SOASchool.com® SOA Certified (SOACP) Professional (www.soaschool.com)

The official site for the SOA Certified Professional (SOACP) curriculum dedicated to specialized areas of service-oriented architecture and service-orientation, including analysis, architecture, governance, security, development, and quality assurance.

Notification Service

To be automatically notified of new book releases in this series, new supplementary content for this title, or key changes to the aforementioned resource sites, use the notification form at www.servicetechbooks.com or send a blank e-mail to notify@arcitura.com.

Chapter 2

Case Study Background

Case study examples provide scenarios in which organizations assess, use, and manage cloud computing models and technologies. Three organizations from different industries are presented for analysis in this book, each of which has distinctive business, technological, and architectural objectives that are introduced in this chapter.

The organizations presented for case study are:

- Advanced Telecom Networks (ATN) – a global company that supplies network equipment to the telecommunications industry

- DTGOV – a public organization that specializes in IT infrastructure and technology services for public sector organizations

- Innovartus Technologies Inc. – a medium-sized company that develops virtual toys and educational entertainment products for children

Most chapters after Part I include one or more *Case Study Example* sections. A conclusion to the storylines is provided in Appendix A.

2.1 Case Study #1: ATN

ATN is a company that provides network equipment to telecommunications industries across the globe. Over the years, ATN has grown considerably and their product portfolio has expanded to accommodate several acquisitions, including companies that specialize in infrastructure components for Internet, GSM, and cellular providers. ATN is now a leading supplier of a diverse range of telecommunications infrastructure.

In recent years, market pressure has been increasing. ATN has begun looking for ways to increase its competitiveness and efficiency by taking advantage of new technologies, especially those that can assist in cost reduction.

Technical Infrastructure and Environment

ATN's various acquisitions have resulted in a highly complex and heterogeneous IT landscape. A cohesive consolidation program was not applied to the IT environment after each acquisition round, resulting in similar applications running concurrently and an increase in maintenance costs. In 2010, ATN merged with a major European telecommunications supplier, adding another applications portfolio to its inventory. The IT complexity snowballed into a serious obstruction and became a source of critical concern to ATN's board of directors.

Business Goals and New Strategy

ATN management decided to pursue a consolidation initiative and outsource applications maintenance and operations overseas. This lowered costs but unfortunately did not address their overall operational inefficiency. Applications still had overlapping functions that could not be easily consolidated. It eventually became apparent that outsourcing was insufficient as consolidation became a possibility only if the architecture of the entire IT landscape changed.

As a result, ATN decided to explore the potential of adopting cloud computing. However, subsequent to their initial inquiries they became overwhelmed by the plenitude of cloud providers and cloud-based products.

Roadmap and Implementation Strategy

ATN is unsure of how to choose the right set of cloud computing technologies and vendors—many solutions appear to still be immature and new cloud-based offerings continue to emerge in the market.

A preliminary cloud computing adoption roadmap is discussed to address a number of key points:

- *IT Strategy* – The adoption of cloud computing needs to promote optimization of the current IT framework, and produce both lower short-term investments and consistent long-term cost reduction.

- *Business Benefits* – ATN needs to evaluate which of the current applications and IT infrastructure can leverage cloud computing technology to achieve the desired optimization and cost reductions. Additional cloud computing benefits such as greater business agility, scalability, and reliability need to be realized to promote business value.

- *Technology Considerations* – Criteria need to be established to help choose the most appropriate cloud delivery and deployment models and cloud vendors and products.

- *Cloud Security* – The risks associated with migrating applications and data to the cloud must be determined.

ATN fears that they might lose control over their applications and data if entrusted to cloud providers, leading to incompliance with internal policies and telecom market regulations. They also wonder how their existing legacy applications would be integrated into the new cloud-based domain.

To define a succinct plan of action, ATN hires an independent IT consulting company called CloudEnhance, who are well recognized for their technology architecture expertise in the transition and integration of cloud computing IT resources. CloudEnhance consultants begin by suggesting an appraisal process comprised of five steps:

1. A brief evaluation of existing applications to measures factors, such as complexity, business-criticality, usage frequency, and number of active users. The identified factors are then placed in a hierarchy of priority to help determine the most suitable candidate applications for migration to a cloud environment.

2. A more detailed evaluation of each selected application using a proprietary assessment tool.

3. The development of a target application architecture that exhibits the interaction between cloud-based applications, their integration with ATN's existing infrastructure and legacy systems, and their development and deployment processes.

4. The authoring of a preliminary business case that documents projected cost savings based on performance indicators, such as cost of cloud readiness, effort for application transformation and interaction, ease of migration and implementation, and various potential long-term benefits.

5. The development of a detailed project plan for a pilot application.

ATN proceeds with the process and resultantly builds its first prototype by focusing on an application that automates a low-risk business area. During this project ATN ports several of the business area's smaller applications that were running on different technologies over to a PaaS platform. Based on positive results and feedback received for the prototype project, ATN decides to embark on a strategic initiative to garner similar benefits for other areas of the company.

2.2 Case Study #2: DTGOV

DTGOV is a public company that was created in the early 1980s by the Ministry of Social Security. The decentralization of the ministry's IT operations to a public company under private law gave DTGOV an autonomous management structure with significant flexibility to govern and evolve its IT enterprise.

At the time of its creation, DTGOV had approximately 1,000 employees, operational branches in 60 localities nation-wide, and operated two mainframe-based data centers. Over time, DTGOV has expanded to more than 3,000 employees and branch offices in more than 300 localities, with three data centers running both mainframe and low-level platform environments. Its main services are related to processing social security benefits across the country.

DTGOV has enlarged its customer portfolio in the last two decades. It now serves other public-sector organizations and provides basic IT infrastructure and services, such as server hosting and server colocation. Some of its customers have also outsourced the operation, maintenance, and development of applications to DTGOV.

DTGOV has sizable customer contracts that encompass various IT resources and services. However, these contracts, services, and associated service levels are not standardized— negotiated service provisioning conditions are typically customized for each customer individually. DTGOV's operations are resultantly becoming increasingly complex and difficult to manage, which has led to inefficiencies and inflated costs.

The DTGOV board realized, some time ago, that the overall company structure could be improved by standardizing its services portfolio, which implies the reengineering of both IT operational and management models. This process has started with the standardization of the hardware platform through the creation of a clearly defined technological lifecycle, a consolidated procurement policy, and the establishment of new acquisition practices.

Technical Infrastructure and Environment

DTGOV operates three data centers: one is exclusively dedicated to low-level platform servers while the other two have both mainframe and low-level platforms. The mainframe systems are reserved for the Ministry of Social Security and therefore not available for outsourcing.

The data center infrastructure occupies approximately 20,000 square feet of computer room space and hosts more than 100,000 servers with different hardware configurations. The total storage capacity is approximately 10,000 terabytes. DTGOV's network has redundant high-speed data links connecting the data centers in a full mesh topology. Their Internet connectivity is considered to be provider-independent since their network interconnects all of the major national telecom carriers.

Server consolidation and virtualization projects have been in place for five years, considerably decreasing the diversity of hardware platforms. As a result, systematic tracking of the investments and operational costs related to the hardware platform has revealed significant improvement. However, there is still remarkable diversity in their software platforms and configurations due to customer service customization requirements.

Business Goals and New Strategy

A chief strategic objective of the standardization of DTGOV's service portfolio is to achieve increased levels of cost effectiveness and operational optimization. An internal executive-level commission was established to define the directions, goals, and strategic roadmap for this initiative. The commission has identified cloud computing as a guidance option and an opportunity for further diversification and improvement of services and customer portfolios.

The roadmap addresses the following key points:

- *Business Benefits* – Concrete business benefits associated with the standardization of service portfolios under the umbrella of cloud computing delivery models need to be defined. For example, how can the optimization of IT infrastructure and operational models result in direct and measurable cost reductions?

- *Service Portfolio* – Which services should become cloud-based, and which customers should they be extended to?

- *Technical Challenges* – The limitations of the current technology infrastructure in relation to the runtime processing requirements of cloud computing models must be understood and documented. Existing infrastructure must be leveraged to whatever extent possible to optimize up-front costs assumed by the development of the cloud-based service offerings.

- *Pricing and SLAs* – An appropriate contract, pricing, and service quality strategy needs to be defined. Suitable pricing and service-level agreements (SLAs) must be determined to support the initiative.

One outstanding concern relates to changes to the current format of contracts and how they may impact business. Many customers may not want to—or may not be prepared to—adopt cloud contracting and service delivery models. This becomes even more critical when considering the fact that 90% of DTGOV's current customer portfolio is comprised of public organizations that typically do not have the autonomy or the agility to switch operating methods on such short notice. Therefore, the migration process is expected to be long term, which may become risky if the roadmap is not properly and clearly defined. A further outstanding issue pertains to IT contract regulations in the public sector—existing regulations may become irrelevant or unclear when applied to cloud technologies.

Roadmap and Implementation Strategy

Several assessment activities were initiated to address the aforementioned issues. The first was a survey of existing customers to probe their level of understanding, on-going initiatives, and plans regarding cloud computing. Most of the respondents were aware of and knowledgeable about cloud computing trends, which was considered a positive finding.

An investigation of the service portfolio revealed clearly identified infrastructure services relating to hosting and colocation. Technical expertise and infrastructure were also evaluated, determining that data center operation and management are key areas of expertise of DTGOV IT staff.

With these findings, the commission decided to:

1. choose IaaS as the target delivery platform to start the cloud computing provisioning initiative

2. hire a consulting firm with sufficient cloud provider expertise and experience to correctly identify and rectify any business and technical issues that may afflict the initiative

3. deploy new hardware resources with a uniform platform into two different data centers, aiming to establish a new, reliable environment to use for the provisioning of initial IaaS-hosted services

4. identify three customers that plan to acquire cloud-based services in order to establish pilot projects and define contractual conditions, pricing, and service-level policies and models

5. evaluate service provisioning of the three chosen customers for the initial period of six months before publicly offering the service to other customers

As the pilot project proceeds, a new Web-based management environment is released to allow for the self-provisioning of virtual servers, as well as SLA and financial tracking functionality in realtime. The pilot projects are considered highly successful, leading to the next step of opening the cloud-based services to other customers.

2.3 Case Study #3: Innovartus Technologies Inc.

The primary business line of Innovartus Technologies Inc. is the development of virtual toys and educational entertainment products for children. These services are provided through a Web portal that employs a role-playing model to create customized virtual games for PCs and mobile devices. The games allow users to create and manipulate virtual toys (cars, dolls, pets) that can be outfitted with virtual accessories that are obtained by completing simple educational quests. The main demographic is children under 12 years. Innovartus further has a social network environment that enables users to exchange items and collaborate with others. All of these activities can be monitored and tracked by the parents, who can also participate in a game by creating specific quests for their children.

The most valuable and revolutionary feature of Innovartus' applications is an experimental end-user interface that is based on natural interface concepts. Users can interact via voice commands, simple gestures that are captured with a Webcam, and directly by touching tablet screens.

The Innovartus portal has always been cloud-based. It was originally developed via a PaaS platform and has been hosted by the same cloud provider ever since. However, recently this environment has revealed several technical limitations that impact features of Innovartus' user interface programming frameworks.

Technical Infrastructure and Environment

Many of Innovartus' other office automation solutions, such as shared file repositories and various productivity tools, are also cloud-based. The on-premise corporate IT environment is relatively small, comprised mainly of work area devices, laptops, and graphic design workstations.

Business Goals and Strategy

Innovartus has been diversifying the functionality of the IT resources that are used for their Web-based and mobile applications. The company has also increased efforts to internationalize their applications; both the Web site and the mobile applications are currently offered in five different languages.

Roadmap and Implementation Strategy

Innovartus intends to continue building upon its cloud-based solutions; however, the current cloud hosting environment has limitations that need to be overcome:

- scalability needs to be improved to accommodate increased and less predictable cloud consumer interaction

- service levels need to be improved to avoid outages that are currently more frequent than expected

- cost effectiveness needs to be improved, as leasing rates are higher with the current cloud provider when compared to others

These and other factors have led Innovartus to decide to migrate to a larger, more globally established cloud provider.

The roadmap for this migration project includes:

- a technical and economic report about the risks and impacts of the planned migration

- a decision tree and a rigorous study initiative focused on the criteria for selecting the new cloud provider

- portability assessments of applications to determine how much of each existing cloud service architecture is proprietary to the current cloud provider's environment

Innovartus is further concerned about how and to what extent the current cloud provider will support and cooperate with the migration process.

Fundamental Cloud Computing

The upcoming chapters establish concepts and terminology that are referenced throughout subsequent chapters and parts in this book. It is recommended that Chapters 3 and 4 be reviewed, even for those already familiar with cloud computing fundamentals. Sections in Chapters 5 and 6 can be selectively skipped by those already familiar with the corresponding technology and security topics.

Chapter 3

Understanding Cloud Computing

This is the first of two chapters that provide an overview of introductory cloud computing topics. It begins with a brief history of cloud computing along with short descriptions of its business and technology drivers. This is followed by definitions of basic concepts and terminology, in addition to explanations of the primary benefits and challenges of cloud computing adoption.

3.1 Origins and Influences

A Brief History

The idea of computing in a "cloud" traces back to the origins of utility computing, a concept that computer scientist John McCarthy publicly proposed in 1961:

> *"If computers of the kind I have advocated become the computers of the future, then computing may someday be organized as a public utility just as the telephone system is a public utility. … The computer utility could become the basis of a new and important industry."*

In 1969, Leonard Kleinrock, a chief scientist of the Advanced Research Projects Agency Network or ARPANET project that seeded the Internet, stated:

> *"As of now, computer networks are still in their infancy, but as they grow up and become sophisticated, we will probably see the spread of 'computer utilities' …".*

The general public has been leveraging forms of Internet-based computer utilities since the mid-1990s through various incarnations of search engines (Yahoo!, Google), e-mail services (Hotmail, Gmail), open publishing platforms (MySpace, Facebook, YouTube), and other types of social media (Twitter, LinkedIn). Though consumer-centric, these services popularized and validated core concepts that form the basis of modern-day cloud computing.

In the late 1990s, Salesforce.com pioneered the notion of bringing remotely provisioned services into the enterprise. In 2002, Amazon.com launched the Amazon Web Services (AWS) platform, a suite of enterprise-oriented services that provide remotely provisioned storage, computing resources, and business functionality.

A slightly different evocation of the term "Network Cloud" or "Cloud" was introduced in the early 1990s throughout the networking industry. It referred to an abstraction layer derived in the delivery methods of data across heterogeneous public and semi-public networks that were primarily packet-switched, although cellular networks used the "Cloud" term as well. The networking method at this point supported the transmission of data from one end-point (local network) to the "Cloud" (wide area network) and then further decomposed to another intended end-point. This is relevant, as the networking industry still references the use of this term, and is considered an early adopter of the concepts that underlie utility computing.

It wasn't until 2006 that the term "cloud computing" emerged in the commercial arena. It was during this time that Amazon launched its Elastic Compute Cloud (EC2) services that enabled organizations to "lease" computing capacity and processing power to run their enterprise applications. Google Apps also began providing browser-based enterprise applications in the same year, and three years later, the Google App Engine became another historic milestone.

Definitions

A Gartner report listing cloud computing at the top of its strategic technology areas further reaffirmed its prominence as an industry trend by announcing its formal definition as:

> "...a style of computing in which scalable and elastic IT-enabled capabilities are delivered as a service to external customers using Internet technologies."

This is a slight revision of Gartner's original definition from 2008, in which "massively scalable" was used instead of "scalable and elastic." This acknowledges the importance of scalability in relation to the ability to scale vertically and not just to enormous proportions.

Forrester Research provided its own definition of cloud computing as:

> "...a standardized IT capability (services, software, or infrastructure) delivered via Internet technologies in a pay-per-use, self-service way."

The definition that received industry-wide acceptance was composed by the National Institute of Standards and Technology (NIST). NIST published its original definition back in 2009, followed by a revised version after further review and industry input that was published in September of 2011:

> *"Cloud computing is a model for enabling ubiquitous, convenient, on-demand network access to a shared pool of configurable computing resources (e.g., networks, servers, storage, applications, and services) that can be rapidly provisioned and released with minimal management effort or service provider interaction. This cloud model is composed of five essential characteristics, three service models, and four deployment models."*

This book provides a more concise definition:

> *"Cloud computing is a specialized form of distributed computing that introduces utilization models for remotely provisioning scalable and measured resources."*

This simplified definition is in line with all of the preceding definition variations that were put forth by other organizations within the cloud computing industry. The characteristics, service models, and deployment models referenced in the NIST definition are further covered in Chapter 4.

Business Drivers

Before delving into the layers of technologies that underlie clouds, the motivations that led to their creation by industry leaders must first be understood. Several of the primary business drivers that fostered modern cloud-based technology are presented in this section.

The origins and inspirations of many of the characteristics, models, and mechanisms covered throughout subsequent chapters can be traced back to the upcoming business drivers. It is important to note that these influences shaped clouds and the overall cloud computing market from both ends. They have motivated organizations to adopt cloud computing in support of their business automation requirements. They have correspondingly motivated other organizations to become providers of cloud environments and cloud technology vendors in order to create and meet the demand to fulfill consumer needs.

Capacity Planning

Capacity planning is the process of determining and fulfilling future demands of an organization's IT resources, products, and services. Within this context, *capacity* represents the maximum amount of work that an IT resource is capable of delivering in a given period of time. A discrepancy between the capacity of an IT resource and its demand can result in a system becoming either inefficient (over-provisioning) or unable to fulfill user needs (under-provisioning). Capacity planning is focused on minimizing this discrepancy to achieve predictable efficiency and performance.

Different capacity planning strategies exist:

- *Lead Strategy* – adding capacity to an IT resource in anticipation of demand

- *Lag Strategy* – adding capacity when the IT resource reaches its full capacity

- *Match Strategy* – adding IT resource capacity in small increments, as demand increases

Planning for capacity can be challenging because it requires estimating usage load fluctuations. There is a constant need to balance peak usage requirements without unnecessary over-expenditure on infrastructure. An example is outfitting IT infrastructure to accommodate maximum usage loads which can impose unreasonable financial investments. In such cases, moderating investments can result in under-provisioning, leading to transaction losses and other usage limitations from lowered usage thresholds.

Cost Reduction

A direct alignment between IT costs and business performance can be difficult to maintain. The growth of IT environments often corresponds to the assessment of their maximum usage requirements. This can make the support of new and expanded business automations an ever-increasing investment. Much of this required investment is funneled into infrastructure expansion because the usage potential of a given automation solution will always be limited by the processing power of its underlying infrastructure.

Two costs need to be accounted for: the cost of acquiring new infrastructure, and the cost of its ongoing ownership. Operational overhead represents a considerable share of IT budgets, often exceeding up-front investment costs.

Common forms of infrastructure-related operating overhead include the following:

- technical personnel required to keep the environment operational

- upgrades and patches that introduce additional testing and deployment cycles

- utility bills and capital expense investments for power and cooling

- security and access control measures that need to be maintained and enforced to protect infrastructure resources

- administrative and accounts staff that may be required to keep track of licenses and support arrangements

The on-going ownership of internal technology infrastructure can encompass burdensome responsibilities that impose compound impacts on corporate budgets. An IT department can consequently become a significant—and at times overwhelming—drain on the business, potentially inhibiting its responsiveness, profitability, and overall evolution.

Organizational Agility

Businesses need the ability to adapt and evolve to successfully face change caused by both internal and external factors. Organizational agility is the measure of an organization's responsiveness to change.

An IT enterprise often needs to respond to business change by scaling its IT resources beyond the scope of what was previously predicted or planned for. For example, infrastructure may be subject to limitations that prevent the organization from responding to usage fluctuations—even when anticipated—if previous capacity planning efforts were restricted by inadequate budgets.

In other cases, changing business needs and priorities may require IT resources to be more available and reliable than before. Even if sufficient infrastructure is in place for an organization to support anticipated usage volumes, the nature of the usage may generate runtime exceptions that bring down hosting servers. Due to a lack of reliability controls within the infrastructure, responsiveness to consumer or customer requirements may be reduced to a point whereby a business' overall continuity is threatened.

On a broader scale, the up-front investments and infrastructure ownership costs that are required to enable new or expanded business automation solutions may themselves be prohibitive enough for a business to settle for IT infrastructure of less-than-ideal quality, thereby decreasing its ability to meet real-world requirements.

Worse yet, the business may decide against proceeding with an automation solution altogether upon review of its infrastructure budget, because it simply cannot afford to. This form of inability to respond can inhibit an organization from keeping up with market demands, competitive pressures, and its own strategic business goals.

Technology Innovations

Established technologies are often used as inspiration and, at times, the actual foundations upon which new technology innovations are derived and built. This section briefly describes the pre-existing technologies considered to be the primary influences on cloud computing.

Clustering

A cluster is a group of independent IT resources that are interconnected and work as a single system. System failure rates are reduced while availability and reliability are increased, since redundancy and failover features are inherent to the cluster.

A general prerequisite of hardware clustering is that its component systems have reasonably identical hardware and operating systems to provide similar performance levels when one failed component is to be replaced by another. Component devices that form a cluster are kept in synchronization through dedicated, high-speed communication links.

The basic concept of built-in redundancy and failover is core to cloud platforms. Clustering technology is explored further in Chapter 8 as part of the *Resource Cluster* mechanism description.

Grid Computing

A computing grid (or "computational grid") provides a platform in which computing resources are organized into one or more logical pools. These pools are collectively coordinated to provide a high performance distributed grid, sometimes referred to as a "super virtual computer." Grid computing differs from clustering in that grid systems are much more loosely coupled and distributed. As a result, grid computing systems can involve computing resources that are heterogeneous and geographically dispersed, which is generally not possible with cluster computing-based systems.

Grid computing has been an on-going research area in computing science since the early 1990s. The technological advancements achieved by grid computing projects have influenced various aspects of cloud computing platforms and mechanisms, specifically in relation to common feature-sets such as networked access, resource pooling, and scalability and resiliency. These types of features can be established by both grid computing and cloud computing, in their own distinctive approaches.

For example, grid computing is based on a middleware layer that is deployed on computing resources. These IT resources participate in a grid pool that implements a series of workload distribution and coordination functions. This middle tier can contain load balancing logic, failover controls, and autonomic configuration management, each having previously inspired similar—and several more sophisticated—cloud computing technologies. It is for this reason that some classify cloud computing as a descendant of earlier grid computing initiatives.

Virtualization

Virtualization represents a technology platform used for the creation of virtual instances of IT resources. A layer of virtualization software allows physical IT resources to provide multiple virtual images of themselves so that their underlying processing capabilities can be shared by multiple users.

Prior to the advent of virtualization technologies, software was limited to residing on and being coupled with static hardware environments. The virtualization process severs this software-hardware dependency, as hardware requirements can be simulated by emulation software running in virtualized environments.

Established virtualization technologies can be traced to several cloud characteristics and cloud computing mechanisms, having inspired many of their core features. As cloud computing evolved, a generation of *modern* virtualization technologies emerged to overcome the performance, reliability, and scalability limitations of traditional virtualization platforms.

As a foundation of contemporary cloud technology, modern virtualization provides a variety of virtualization types and technology layers that are discussed separately in Chapter 5.

Technology Innovations vs. Enabling Technologies

It is essential to highlight several other areas of technology that continue to contribute to modern-day cloud-based platforms. These are distinguished as *cloud-enabling technologies*, the following of which are covered in Chapter 5:

- Broadband Networks and Internet Architecture
- Data Center Technology
- (Modern) Virtualization Technology
- Web Technology
- Multitenant Technology
- Service Technology

Each of these cloud-enabling technologies existed in some form prior to the formal advent of cloud computing. Some were refined further, and on occasion even redefined, as a result of the subsequent evolution of cloud computing.

SUMMARY OF KEY POINTS

- The primary business drivers that exposed the need for cloud computing and led to its formation include capacity planning, cost reduction, and organizational agility.

- The primary technology innovations that influenced and inspired key distinguishing features and aspects of cloud computing include clustering, grid computing, and traditional forms of virtualization.

3.2 Basic Concepts and Terminology

This section establishes a set of basic terms that represent the fundamental concepts and aspects pertaining to the notion of a cloud and its most primitive artifacts.

Cloud

A *cloud* refers to a distinct IT environment that is designed for the purpose of remotely provisioning scalable and measured IT resources. The term originated as a metaphor for the Internet which is, in essence, a network of networks providing remote access to a set of decentralized IT resources. Prior to cloud computing becoming its own formalized IT industry segment, the symbol of a cloud was commonly used to represent the Internet in a variety of specifications and mainstream documentation of Web-based architectures. This same symbol is now used to specifically represent the boundary of a cloud environment, as shown in Figure 3.1.

Figure 3.1

The symbol used to denote the boundary of a cloud environment.

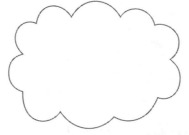

It is important to distinguish the term "cloud" and the cloud symbol from the Internet. As a specific environment used to remotely provision IT resources, a cloud has a finite boundary. There are many individual clouds that are accessible via the Internet.

Whereas the Internet provides open access to many Web-based IT resources, a cloud is typically privately owned and offers access to IT resources that is metered.

Much of the Internet is dedicated to the access of content-based IT resources published via the World Wide Web. IT resources provided by cloud environments, on the other hand, are dedicated to supplying back-end processing capabilities and user-based access to these capabilities. Another key distinction is that it is not necessary for clouds to be Web-based even if they are commonly based on Internet protocols and technologies. Protocols refer to standards and methods that allow computers to communicate with each other in a pre-defined and structured manner. A cloud can be based on the use of any protocols that allow for the remote access to its IT resources.

> **NOTE**
>
> Diagrams in this book depict the Internet using the globe symbol.

IT Resource

An *IT resource* is a physical or virtual IT-related artifact that can be either software-based, such as a virtual server or a custom software program, or hardware-based, such as a physical server or a network device (Figure 3.2).

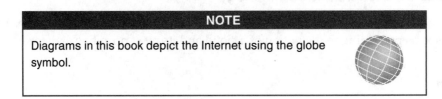

Figure 3.2
Examples of common IT resources and their corresponding symbols.

Figure 3.3 illustrates how the cloud symbol can be used to define a boundary for a cloud-based environment that hosts and provisions a set of IT resources. The displayed IT resources are consequently considered to be cloud-based IT resources.

Figure 3.3

A cloud is hosting eight IT resources: three virtual servers, two cloud services, and three storage devices.

Technology architectures and various interaction scenarios involving IT resources are illustrated in diagrams like the one shown in Figure 3.3. It is important to note the following points when studying and working with these diagrams:

- The IT resources shown within the boundary of a given cloud symbol usually do not represent all of the available IT resources hosted by that cloud. Subsets of IT resources are generally highlighted to demonstrate a particular topic.

- Focusing on the relevant aspects of a topic requires many of these diagrams to intentionally provide abstracted views of the underlying technology architectures. This means that only a portion of the actual technical details are shown.

Furthermore, some diagrams will display IT resources outside of the cloud symbol. This convention is used to indicate IT resources that are not cloud-based.

NOTE

The virtual server IT resource displayed in Figure 3.2 is further discussed in Chapters 5 and 7. Physical servers are sometimes referred to as *physical hosts* (or just *hosts*) in reference to the fact that they are responsible for hosting virtual servers.

On-Premise

As a distinct and remotely accessible environment, a cloud represents an option for the deployment of IT resources. An IT resource that is hosted in a conventional IT enterprise within an organizational boundary (that does not specifically represent a cloud) is considered to be located on the premises of the IT enterprise, or *on-premise* for short. In other words, the term "on-premise" is another way of stating "on the premises of a controlled IT environment that is not cloud-based." This term is used to qualify an IT resource as an alternative to "cloud-based." An IT resource that is on-premise cannot be cloud-based, and vice-versa.

Note the following key points:

- An on-premise IT resource can access and interact with a cloud-based IT resource.

- An on-premise IT resource can be moved to a cloud, thereby changing it to a cloud-based IT resource.

- Redundant deployments of an IT resource can exist in both on-premise and cloud-based environments.

If the distinction between on-premise and cloud-based IT resources is confusing in relation to private clouds (described in the *Cloud Deployment Models* section of Chapter 4), then an alternative qualifier can be used.

Cloud Consumers and Cloud Providers

The party that provides cloud-based IT resources is the *cloud provider*. The party that uses cloud-based IT resources is the *cloud consumer*. These terms represent roles usually assumed by organizations in relation to clouds and corresponding cloud provisioning contracts. These roles are formally defined in Chapter 4, as part of the *Roles and Boundaries* section.

Scaling

Scaling, from an IT resource perspective, represents the ability of the IT resource to handle increased or decreased usage demands.

The following are types of scaling:

- *Horizontal Scaling* – scaling out and scaling in
- *Vertical Scaling* – scaling up and scaling down

The next two sections briefly describe each.

Horizontal Scaling

The allocating or releasing of IT resources that are of the same type is referred to as *horizontal scaling* (Figure 3.4). The horizontal allocation of resources is referred to as *scaling out* and the horizontal releasing of resources is referred to as *scaling in*. Horizontal scaling is a common form of scaling within cloud environments.

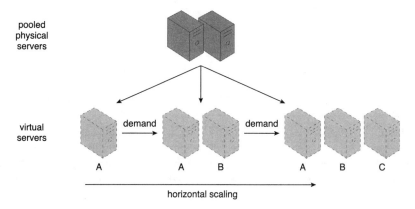

Figure 3.4

An IT resource (Virtual Server A) is scaled out by adding more of the same IT resources (Virtual Servers B and C).

Vertical Scaling

When an existing IT resource is replaced by another with higher or lower capacity, *vertical scaling* is considered to have occurred (Figure 3.5). Specifically, the replacing of an IT resource with another that has a higher capacity is referred to as *scaling up* and the replacing an IT resource with another that has a lower capacity is considered *scaling down*. Vertical scaling is less common in cloud environments due to the downtime required while the replacement is taking place.

Figure 3.5

An IT resource (a virtual server with two CPUs) is scaled up by replacing it with a more powerful IT resource with increased capacity for data storage (a physical server with four CPUs).

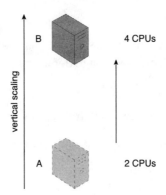

B   4 CPUs

A   2 CPUs

Table 3.1 provides a brief overview of common pros and cons associated with horizontal and vertical scaling.

Horizontal Scaling	Vertical Scaling
less expensive (through commodity hardware components)	more expensive (specialized servers)
IT resources instantly available	IT resources normally instantly available
resource replication and automated scaling	additional setup is normally needed
additional IT resources needed	no additional IT resources needed
not limited by hardware capacity	limited by maximum hardware capacity

Table 3.1

A comparison of horizontal and vertical scaling.

Cloud Service

Although a cloud is a remotely accessible environment, not all IT resources residing within a cloud can be made available for remote access. For example, a database or a physical server deployed within a cloud may only be accessible by other IT resources that are within the same cloud. A software program with a published API may be deployed specifically to enable access by remote clients.

A *cloud service* is any IT resource that is made remotely accessible via a cloud. Unlike other IT fields that fall under the service technology umbrella—such as service-oriented architecture—the term "service" within the context of cloud computing is especially broad. A cloud service can exist as a simple Web-based software program with a technical interface invoked via the use of a messaging protocol, or as a remote access point for administrative tools or larger environments and other IT resources.

In Figure 3.6, the yellow circle symbol is used to represent the cloud service as a simple Web-based software program. A different IT resource symbol may be used in the latter case, depending on the nature of the access that is provided by the cloud service.

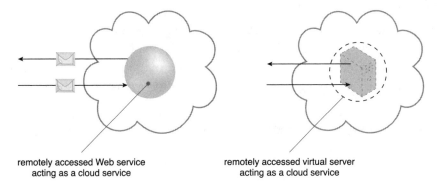

remotely accessed Web service
acting as a cloud service

remotely accessed virtual server
acting as a cloud service

Figure 3.6

A cloud service with a published technical interface is being accessed by a consumer outside of the cloud (left). A cloud service that exists as a virtual server is also being accessed from outside of the cloud's boundary (right). The cloud service on the left is likely being invoked by a consumer program that was designed to access the cloud service's published technical interface. The cloud service on the right may be accessed by a human user that has remotely logged on to the virtual server.

The driving motivation behind cloud computing is to provide IT resources as services that encapsulate other IT resources, while offering functions for clients to use and leverage remotely. A multitude of models for generic types of cloud services have emerged, most of which are labeled with the "as-a-service" suffix.

> **NOTE**
>
> Cloud service usage conditions are typically expressed in a service-level agreement (SLA) that is the human-readable part of a service contract between a cloud provider and cloud consumer that describes QoS features, behaviors, and limitations of a cloud-based service or other provisions.

An SLA provides details of various measurable characteristics related to IT outcomes, such as uptime, security characteristics, and other specific QoS features, including availability, reliability, and performance. Since the implementation of a service is hidden from the cloud consumer, an SLA becomes a critical specification. SLAs are covered in detail in Chapter 16.

Cloud Service Consumer

The *cloud service consumer* is a temporary runtime role assumed by a software program when it accesses a cloud service.

As shown in Figure 3.7, common types of cloud service consumers can include software programs and services capable of remotely accessing cloud services with published service contracts, as well as workstations, laptops and mobile devices running software capable of remotely accessing other IT resources positioned as cloud services.

Figure 3.7

Examples of cloud service consumers. Depending on the nature of a given diagram, an artifact labeled as a cloud service consumer may be a software program or a hardware device (in which case it is implied that it is running a software program capable of acting as a cloud service consumer).

3.3 Goals and Benefits

The common benefits associated with adopting cloud computing are explained in this section.

> **NOTE**
>
> The following sections make reference to the terms "public cloud" and "private cloud." These terms are described in the *Cloud Deployment Models* section in Chapter 4.

Reduced Investments and Proportional Costs

Similar to a product wholesaler that purchases goods in bulk for lower price points, public cloud providers base their business model on the mass-acquisition of IT resources that are then made available to cloud consumers via attractively priced leasing packages. This opens the door for organizations to gain access to powerful infrastructure without having to purchase it themselves.

The most common economic rationale for investing in cloud-based IT resources is in the reduction or outright elimination of up-front IT investments, namely hardware and software purchases and ownership costs. A cloud's Measured Usage characteristic represents a feature-set that allows measured operational expenditures (directly related to business performance) to replace anticipated capital expenditures. This is also referred to as *proportional costs*.

This elimination or minimization of up-front financial commitments allows enterprises to start small and accordingly increase IT resource allocation as required. Moreover, the reduction of up-front capital expenses allows for the capital to be redirected to the core business investment. In its most basic form, opportunities to decrease costs are derived from the deployment and operation of large-scale data centers by major cloud providers. Such data centers are commonly located in destinations where real estate, IT professionals, and network bandwidth can be obtained at lower costs, resulting in both capital and operational savings.

The same rationale applies to operating systems, middleware or platform software, and application software. Pooled IT resources are made available to and shared by multiple cloud consumers, resulting in increased or even maximum possible utilization. Operational costs and inefficiencies can be further reduced by applying proven practices and patterns for optimizing cloud architectures, their management, and their governance.

Common measurable benefits to cloud consumers include:

- On-demand access to pay-as-you-go computing resources on a short-term basis (such as processors by the hour), and the ability to release these computing resources when they are no longer needed.

- The perception of having unlimited computing resources that are available on demand, thereby reducing the need to prepare for provisioning.

- The ability to add or remove IT resources at a fine-grained level, such as modifying available storage disk space by single gigabyte increments.

- Abstraction of the infrastructure so applications are not locked into devices or locations and can be easily moved if needed.

For example, a company with sizable batch-centric tasks can complete them as quickly as their application software can scale. Using 100 servers for one hour costs the same as using one server for 100 hours. This "elasticity" of IT resources, achieved without requiring steep initial investments to create a large-scale computing infrastructure, can be extremely compelling.

Despite the ease with which many identify the financial benefits of cloud computing, the actual economics can be complex to calculate and assess. The decision to proceed with a cloud computing adoption strategy will involve much more than a simple comparison between the cost of leasing and the cost of purchasing. For example, the financial benefits of dynamic scaling and the risk transference of both over-provisioning (under-utilization) and under-provisioning (over-utilization) must also be accounted for. Chapter 15 explores common criteria and formulas for performing detailed financial comparisons and assessments.

NOTE

Another area of cost savings offered by clouds is the "as-a-service" usage model, whereby technical and operational implementation details of IT resource provisioning are abstracted from cloud consumers and packaged into "ready-to-use" or "off-the-shelf" solutions. These services-based products can simplify and expedite the development, deployment, and administration of IT resources when compared to performing equivalent tasks with on-premise solutions. The resulting savings in time and required IT expertise can be significant and can contribute to the justification of adopting cloud computing.

Increased Scalability

By providing pools of IT resources, along with tools and technologies designed to leverage them collectively, clouds can instantly and dynamically allocate IT resources to cloud consumers, on-demand or via the cloud consumer's direct configuration. This empowers cloud consumers to scale their cloud-based IT resources to accommodate processing fluctuations and peaks automatically or manually. Similarly, cloud-based IT resources can be released (automatically or manually) as processing demands decrease.

A simple example of usage demand fluctuations throughout a 24 hour period is provided in Figure 3.8.

Figure 3.8

An example of an organization's changing demand for an IT resource over the course of a day.

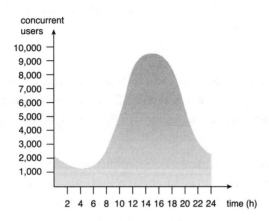

The inherent, built-in feature of clouds to provide flexible levels of scalability to IT resources is directly related to the aforementioned proportional costs benefit. Besides the evident financial gain to the automated reduction of scaling, the ability of IT resources to always meet and fulfill unpredictable usage demands avoids potential loss of business that can occur when usage thresholds are met.

> **NOTE**
>
> When associating the benefit of Increased Scalability with the capacity planning strategies introduced earlier in the *Business Drivers* section, the Lag and Match Strategies are generally more applicable due to a cloud's ability to scale IT resources on-demand.

Increased Availability and Reliability

The availability and reliability of IT resources are directly associated with tangible business benefits. Outages limit the time an IT resource can be "open for business" for its customers, thereby limiting its usage and revenue generating potential. Runtime failures that are not immediately corrected can have a more significant impact during high-volume usage periods. Not only is the IT resource unable to respond to customer requests, its unexpected failure can decrease overall customer confidence.

A hallmark of the typical cloud environment is its intrinsic ability to provide extensive support for increasing the availability of a cloud-based IT resource to minimize or even eliminate outages, and for increasing its reliability so as to minimize the impact of runtime failure conditions.

Specifically:

- An IT resource with increased availability is accessible for longer periods of time (for example, 22 hours out of a 24 hour day). Cloud providers generally offer "resilient" IT resources for which they are able to guarantee high levels of availability.

- An IT resource with increased reliability is able to better avoid and recover from exception conditions. The modular architecture of cloud environments provides extensive failover support that increases reliability.

It is important that organizations carefully examine the SLAs offered by cloud providers when considering the leasing of cloud-based services and IT resources. Although many cloud environments are capable of offering remarkably high levels of availability and reliability, it comes down to the guarantees made in the SLA that typically represent their actual contractual obligations.

SUMMARY OF KEY POINTS

- Cloud environments are comprised of highly extensive infrastructure that offers pools of IT resources that can be leased using a pay-for-use model whereby only the actual usage of the IT resources is billable. When compared to equivalent on-premise environments, clouds provide the potential for reduced initial investments and operational costs proportional to measured usage.

- The inherent ability of a cloud to scale IT resources enables organizations to accommodate unpredictable usage fluctuations without being limited by pre-defined thresholds that may turn away usage requests from customers. Conversely, the ability of a cloud to decrease required scaling is a feature that relates directly to the proportional costs benefit.

- By leveraging cloud environments to make IT resources highly available and reliable, organizations are able to increase quality-of-service guarantees to customers and further reduce or avoid potential loss of business resulting from unanticipated runtime failures.

3.4 Risks and Challenges

Several of the most critical cloud computing challenges pertaining mostly to cloud consumers that use IT resources located in public clouds are presented and examined.

Increased Security Vulnerabilities

The moving of business data to the cloud means that the responsibility over data security becomes shared with the cloud provider. The remote usage of IT resources requires an expansion of trust boundaries by the cloud consumer to include the external cloud. It can be difficult to establish a security architecture that spans such a trust boundary without introducing vulnerabilities, unless cloud consumers and cloud providers happen to support the same or compatible security frameworks—which is unlikely with public clouds.

Another consequence of overlapping trust boundaries relates to the cloud provider's privileged access to cloud consumer data. The extent to which the data is secure is now limited to the security controls and policies applied by both the cloud consumer and cloud provider. Furthermore, there can be overlapping trust boundaries from different cloud consumers due to the fact that cloud-based IT resources are commonly shared.

The overlapping of trust boundaries and the increased exposure of data can provide malicious cloud consumers (human and automated) with greater opportunities to attack IT resources and steal or damage business data. Figure 3.9 illustrates a scenario whereby two organizations accessing the same cloud service are required to extend their respective trust boundaries to the cloud, resulting in overlapping trust boundaries. It can be challenging for the cloud provider to offer security mechanisms that accommodate the security requirements of both cloud service consumers.

Overlapping trust boundaries is a security threat that is discussed in more detail in Chapter 6.

Reduced Operational Governance Control

Cloud consumers are usually allotted a level of governance control that is lower than that over on-premise IT resources. This can introduce risks associated with how the cloud provider operates its cloud, as well as the external connections that are required for communication between the cloud and the cloud consumer.

trust boundary of Organization X

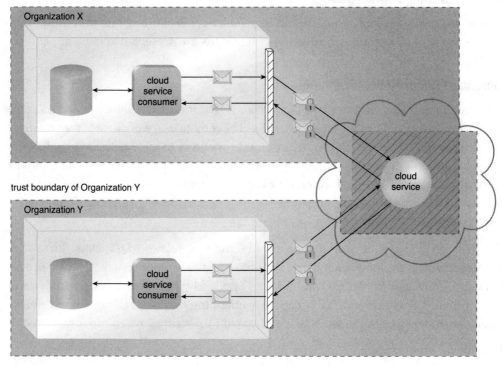

Figure 3.9
The shaded area with diagonal lines indicates the overlap of two organizations' trust boundaries.

Consider the following examples:

- An unreliable cloud provider may not maintain the guarantees it makes in the SLAs that were published for its cloud services. This can jeopardize the quality of the cloud consumer solutions that rely on these cloud services.

- Longer geographic distances between the cloud consumer and cloud provider can require additional network hops that introduce fluctuating latency and potential bandwidth constraints.

The latter scenario is illustrated in Figure 3.10.

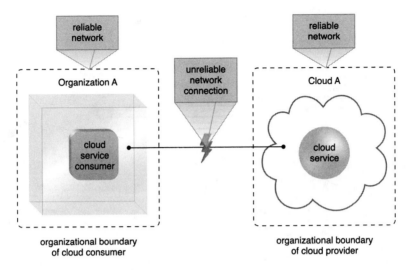

Figure 3.10

An unreliable network connection compromises the quality of communication between cloud consumer and cloud provider environments.

Legal contracts, when combined with SLAs, technology inspections, and monitoring, can mitigate governance risks and issues. A cloud governance system is established through SLAs, given the "as-a-service" nature of cloud computing. A cloud consumer must keep track of the actual service level being offered and the other warranties that are made by the cloud provider.

Note that different cloud delivery models offer varying degrees of operational control granted to cloud consumers, as further explained in Chapter 4.

Limited Portability Between Cloud Providers

Due to a lack of established industry standards within the cloud computing industry, public clouds are commonly proprietary to various extents. For cloud consumers that have custom-built solutions with dependencies on these proprietary environments, it can be challenging to move from one cloud provider to another.

Portability is a measure used to determine the impact of moving cloud consumer IT resources and data between clouds (Figure 3.11).

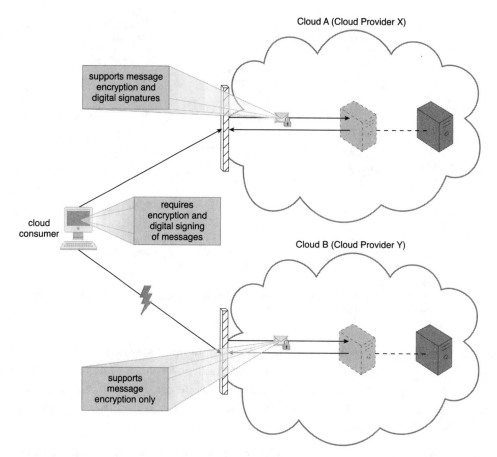

Figure 3.11
A cloud consumer's application has a decreased level of portability when assessing a potential migration from Cloud A to Cloud B, because the cloud provider of Cloud B does not support the same security technologies as Cloud A.

Multi-Regional Compliance and Legal Issues

Third-party cloud providers will frequently establish data centers in affordable or convenient geographical locations. Cloud consumers will often not be aware of the physical location of their IT resources and data when hosted by public clouds. For some organizations, this can pose serious legal concerns pertaining to industry or government regulations that specify data privacy and storage policies. For example, some UK laws require personal data belonging to UK citizens to be kept within the United Kingdom.

Another potential legal issue pertains to the accessibility and disclosure of data. Countries have laws that require some types of data to be disclosed to certain government agencies or to the subject of the data. For example, a European cloud consumer's data that is located in the U.S. can be more easily accessed by government agencies (due to the U.S. Patriot Act) when compared to data located in many European Union countries.

Most regulatory frameworks recognize that cloud consumer organizations are ultimately responsible for the security, integrity, and storage of their own data, even when it is held by an external cloud provider.

SUMMARY OF KEY POINTS

- Cloud environments can introduce distinct security challenges, some of which pertain to overlapping trust boundaries imposed by a cloud provider sharing IT resources with multiple cloud consumers.

- A cloud consumer's operational governance can be limited within cloud environments due to the control exercised by a cloud provider over its platforms.

- The portability of cloud-based IT resources can be inhibited by dependencies upon proprietary characteristics imposed by a cloud.

- The geographical location of data and IT resources can be out of a cloud consumer's control when hosted by a third-party cloud provider. This can introduce various legal and regulatory compliance concerns.

Chapter 4

Fundamental Concepts and Models

The upcoming sections cover introductory topic areas pertaining to the fundamental models used to categorize and define clouds and their most common service offerings, along with definitions of organizational roles and the specific set of characteristics that collectively distinguish a cloud.

4.1 Roles and Boundaries

Organizations and humans can assume different types of pre-defined roles depending on how they relate to and/or interact with a cloud and its hosted IT resources. Each of the upcoming roles participates in and carries out responsibilities in relation to cloud-based activity. The following sections define these roles and identify their main interactions.

Cloud Provider

The organization that provides cloud-based IT resources is the *cloud provider*. When assuming the role of cloud provider, an organization is responsible for making cloud services available to cloud consumers, as per agreed upon SLA guarantees. The cloud provider is further tasked with any required management and administrative duties to ensure the on-going operation of the overall cloud infrastructure.

Cloud providers normally own the IT resources that are made available for lease by cloud consumers; however, some cloud providers also "resell" IT resources leased from other cloud providers.

Cloud Consumer

A *cloud consumer* is an organization (or a human) that has a formal contract or arrangement with a cloud provider to use IT resources made available by the cloud provider. Specifically, the cloud consumer uses a cloud service consumer to access a cloud service (Figure 4.1).

The figures in this book do not always explicitly label symbols as "cloud consumers." Instead, it is generally implied that organizations or humans shown remotely accessing cloud-based IT resources are considered cloud consumers.

Figure 4.1

A cloud consumer (Organization A) interacts with a cloud service from a cloud provider (that owns Cloud A). Within Organization A, the cloud service consumer is being used to access the cloud service.

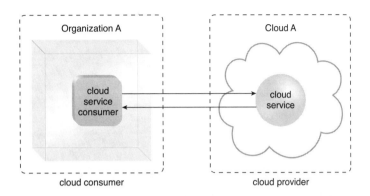

NOTE

When depicting interaction scenarios between cloud-based IT resources and consumer organizations, there are no strict rules as to how the terms "cloud service consumer" and "cloud consumer" are used in this book. The former is usually used to label software programs or applications that programmatically interface with a cloud service's technical contract or API. The latter term is more broad in that it can be used to label an organization, an individual accessing a user-interface, or a software program that assumes the role of cloud consumer when interacting with a cloud, a cloud-based IT resource, or a cloud provider. The broad applicability of the "cloud consumer" term is intentional as it allows it to be used in figures that explore different types of consumer-provider relationships within different technical and business contexts.

Cloud Service Owner

The person or organization that legally owns a cloud service is called a *cloud service owner*. The cloud service owner can be the cloud consumer, or the cloud provider that owns the cloud within which the cloud service resides.

For example, either the cloud consumer of Cloud X or the cloud provider of Cloud X could own Cloud Service A (Figures 4.2 and 4.3).

Note that a cloud consumer that owns a cloud service hosted by a third-party cloud does not necessarily need to be the user (or consumer) of the cloud service. Several cloud consumer organizations develop and deploy cloud services in clouds owned by other parties for the purpose of making the cloud services available to the general public.

The reason a cloud service owner is not called a cloud resource owner is because the cloud service owner role only applies to cloud services (which, as explained in Chapter 3, are externally accessible IT resources that reside in a cloud).

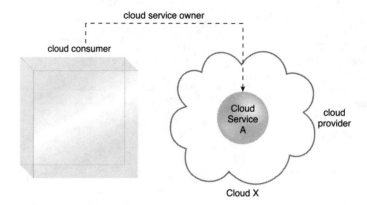

Figure 4.2

A cloud consumer can be a cloud service owner when it deploys its own service in a cloud.

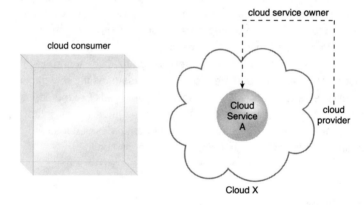

Figure 4.3

A cloud provider becomes a cloud service owner if it deploys its own cloud service, typically for other cloud consumers to use.

Cloud Resource Administrator

A *cloud resource administrator* is the person or organization responsible for administering a cloud-based IT resource (including cloud services). The cloud resource administrator can be (or belong to) the cloud consumer or cloud provider of the cloud within which the cloud service resides. Alternatively, it can be (or belong to) a third-party organization contracted to administer the cloud-based IT resource.

For example, a cloud service owner can contract a cloud resource administrator to administer a cloud service (Figures 4.4 and 4.5).

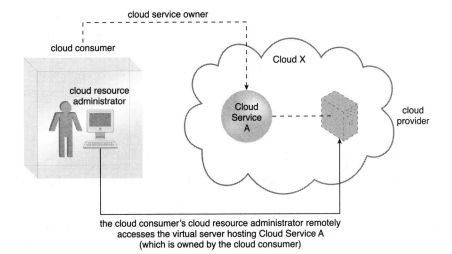

the cloud consumer's cloud resource administrator remotely
accesses the virtual server hosting Cloud Service A
(which is owned by the cloud consumer)

Figure 4.4

A cloud resource administrator can be with a cloud consumer organization and administer remotely
accessible IT resources that belong to the cloud consumer.

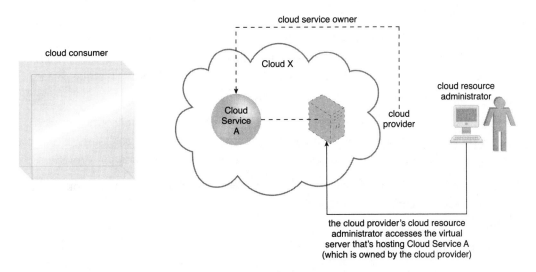

the cloud provider's cloud resource
administrator accesses the virtual
server that's hosting Cloud Service A
(which is owned by the cloud provider)

Figure 4.5

A cloud resource administrator can be with a cloud provider organization for which it can administer the cloud provider's
internally and externally available IT resources.

The reason a cloud resource administrator is not referred to as a "cloud service administrator" is because this role may be responsible for administering cloud-based IT resources that don't exist as cloud services. For example, if the cloud resource administrator belongs to (or is contracted by) the cloud provider, IT resources not made remotely accessible may be administered by this role (and these types of IT resources are not classified as cloud services).

Additional Roles

The NIST Cloud Computing Reference Architecture defines the following supplementary roles:

- *Cloud Auditor* – A third-party (often accredited) that conducts independent assessments of cloud environments assumes the role of the *cloud auditor*. The typical responsibilities associated with this role include the evaluation of security controls, privacy impacts, and performance. The main purpose of the cloud auditor role is to provide an unbiased assessment (and possible endorsement) of a cloud environment to help strengthen the trust relationship between cloud consumers and cloud providers.

- *Cloud Broker* – This role is assumed by a party that assumes the responsibility of managing and negotiating the usage of cloud services between cloud consumers and cloud providers. Mediation services provided by *cloud brokers* include service intermediation, aggregation, and arbitrage.

- *Cloud Carrier* – The party responsible for providing the wire-level connectivity between cloud consumers and cloud providers assumes the role of the *cloud carrier*. This role is often assumed by network and telecommunication providers.

While each is legitimate, most architectural scenarios covered in this book do not include these roles.

Organizational Boundary

An *organizational boundary* represents the physical perimeter that surrounds a set of IT resources that are owned and governed by an organization. The organizational boundary does not represent the boundary of an actual organization, only an organizational set of IT assets and IT resources. Similarly, clouds have an organizational boundary (Figure 4.6).

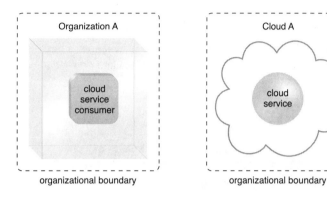

Figure 4.6

Organizational boundaries of a cloud consumer (left), and a cloud provider (right), represented by a broken line notation.

Trust Boundary

When an organization assumes the role of cloud consumer to access cloud-based IT resources, it needs to extend its trust beyond the physical boundary of the organization to include parts of the cloud environment.

A *trust boundary* is a logical perimeter that typically spans beyond physical boundaries to represent the extent to which IT resources are trusted (Figure 4.7). When analyzing cloud environments, the trust boundary is most frequently associated with the trust issued by the organization acting as the cloud consumer.

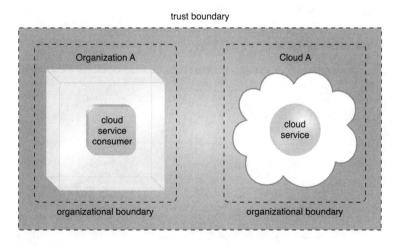

Figure 4.7

An extended trust boundary encompasses the organizational boundaries of the cloud provider and the cloud consumer.

NOTE

Another type of boundary relevant to cloud environments is the logical network perimeter. This type of boundary is classified as a cloud computing mechanism and is covered in Chapter 7.

SUMMARY OF KEY POINTS

- Common roles associated with cloud-based interaction and relationships include the cloud provider, cloud consumer, cloud service owner, and cloud resource administrator.

- An organizational boundary represents the physical scope of IT resources owned and governed by an organization. A trust boundary is the logical perimeter that encompasses the IT resources trusted by an organization.

4.2 Cloud Characteristics

An IT environment requires a specific set of characteristics to enable the remote provisioning of scalable and measured IT resources in an effective manner. These characteristics need to exist to a meaningful extent for the IT environment to be considered an effective cloud.

The following six specific characteristics are common to the majority of cloud environments:

- on-demand usage
- ubiquitous access
- multitenancy (and resource pooling)
- elasticity
- measured usage
- resiliency

Cloud providers and cloud consumers can assess these characteristics individually and collectively to measure the value offering of a given cloud platform. Although cloud-based services and IT resources will inherit and exhibit individual characteristics to varying extents, usually the greater the degree to which they are supported and utilized, the greater the resulting value proposition.

> **NOTE**
>
> The NIST definition of cloud computing defines only five characteristics; resiliency is excluded. Resiliency has emerged as an aspect of significant importance and its common level of support constitutes its necessary inclusion as a common cloud characteristic.

On-Demand Usage

A cloud consumer can unilaterally access cloud-based IT resources giving the cloud consumer the freedom to self-provision these IT resources. Once configured, usage of the self-provisioned IT resources can be automated, requiring no further human involvement by the cloud consumer or cloud provider. This results in an *on-demand usage* environment. Also known as "on-demand self-service usage," this characteristic enables the service-based and usage-driven features found in mainstream clouds.

Ubiquitous Access

Ubiquitous access represents the ability for a cloud service to be widely accessible. Establishing ubiquitous access for a cloud service can require support for a range of devices, transport protocols, interfaces, and security technologies. To enable this level of access generally requires that the cloud service architecture be tailored to the particular needs of different cloud service consumers.

Multitenancy (and Resource Pooling)

The characteristic of a software program that enables an instance of the program to serve different consumers (tenants) whereby each is isolated from the other, is referred to as *multitenancy*. A cloud provider pools its IT resources to serve multiple cloud service consumers by using multitenancy models that frequently rely on the use of virtualization technologies. Through the use of multitenancy technology, IT resources can be dynamically assigned and reassigned, according to cloud service consumer demands.

Resource pooling allows cloud providers to pool large-scale IT resources to serve multiple cloud consumers. Different physical and virtual IT resources are dynamically assigned and reassigned according to cloud consumer demand, typically followed by execution through statistical multiplexing. Resource pooling is commonly achieved through multitenancy technology, and therefore encompassed by this multitenancy characteristic. See the *Resource Pooling Architecture* section in Chapter 11 for a more detailed explanation.

Figures 4.8 and 4.9 illustrate the difference between single-tenant and multitenant environments.

Figure 4.8

In a single-tenant environment, each cloud consumer has a separate IT resource instance.

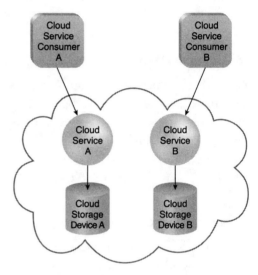

Figure 4.9

In a multitenant environment, a single instance of an IT resource, such as a cloud storage device, serves multiple consumers.

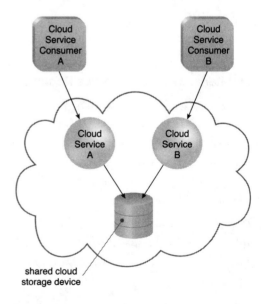

As illustrated in Figure 4.9, multitenancy allows several cloud consumers to use the same IT resource or its instance while each remains unaware that it may be used by others.

Elasticity

Elasticity is the automated ability of a cloud to transparently scale IT resources, as required in response to runtime conditions or as pre-determined by the cloud consumer or cloud provider. Elasticity is often considered a core justification for the adoption of cloud computing, primarily due to the fact that it is closely associated with the Reduced Investment and Proportional Costs benefit. Cloud providers with vast IT resources can offer the greatest range of elasticity.

Measured Usage

The *measured usage* characteristic represents the ability of a cloud platform to keep track of the usage of its IT resources, primarily by cloud consumers. Based on what is measured, the cloud provider can charge a cloud consumer only for the IT resources actually used and/or for the timeframe during which access to the IT resources was granted. In this context, measured usage is closely related to the on-demand characteristic.

Measured usage is not limited to tracking statistics for billing purposes. It also encompasses the general monitoring of IT resources and related usage reporting (for both cloud provider and cloud consumers). Therefore, measured usage is also relevant to clouds that do not charge for usage (which may be applicable to the private cloud deployment model described in the upcoming *Cloud Deployment Models* section).

Resiliency

Resilient computing is a form of failover that distributes redundant implementations of IT resources across physical locations. IT resources can be pre-configured so that if one becomes deficient, processing is automatically handed over to another redundant implementation. Within cloud computing, the characteristic of *resiliency* can refer to redundant IT resources within the same cloud (but in different physical locations) or across multiple clouds. Cloud consumers can increase both the reliability and availability of their applications by leveraging the resiliency of cloud-based IT resources (Figure 4.10).

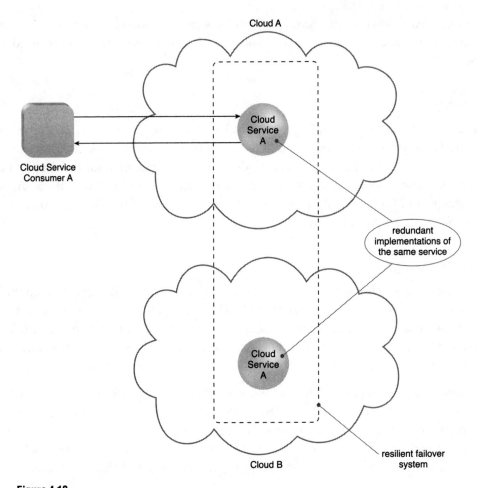

Figure 4.10

A resilient system in which Cloud B hosts a redundant implementation of Cloud Service A to provide failover in case Cloud Service A on Cloud A becomes unavailable.

SUMMARY OF KEY POINTS

- On-demand usage is the ability of a cloud consumer to self-provision and use necessary cloud-based services without requiring cloud provider interaction. This characteristic is related to measured usage, which represents the ability of a cloud to measure the usage of its IT resources.

- Ubiquitous access allows cloud-based services to be accessed by diverse cloud service consumers, while multitenancy is the ability of a single instance of an IT resource to transparently serve multiple cloud consumers simultaneously.

- The elasticity characteristic represents the ability of a cloud to transparently and automatically scale IT resources out or in. Resiliency pertains to a cloud's inherent failover features.

4.3 Cloud Delivery Models

A *cloud delivery model* represents a specific, pre-packaged combination of IT resources offered by a cloud provider. Three common cloud delivery models have become widely established and formalized:

- Infrastructure-as-a-Service (IaaS)

- Platform-as-a-Service (PaaS)

- Software-as-a-Service (SaaS)

These three models are interrelated in how the scope of one can encompass that of another, as explored in the *Combining Cloud Delivery Models* section later in this chapter.

NOTE

Many specialized variations of the three base cloud delivery models have emerged, each comprised of a distinct combination of IT resources. Some examples include:

- Storage-as-a-Service

- Database-as-a-Service

- Security-as-a-Service

- Communication-as-a-Service

- Integration-as-a-Service

- Testing-as-a-Service

- Process-as-a-Service

Note also that a cloud delivery model can be referred to as a cloud service delivery model because each model is classified as a different type of cloud service offering.

Infrastructure-as-a-Service (IaaS)

The IaaS delivery model represents a self-contained IT environment comprised of infrastructure-centric IT resources that can be accessed and managed via cloud service-based interfaces and tools. This environment can include hardware, network, connectivity, operating systems, and other "raw" IT resources. In contrast to traditional hosting or outsourcing environments, with IaaS, IT resources are typically virtualized and packaged into bundles that simplify up-front runtime scaling and customization of the infrastructure.

The general purpose of an IaaS environment is to provide cloud consumers with a high level of control and responsibility over its configuration and utilization. The IT resources provided by IaaS are generally not pre-configured, placing the administrative responsibility directly upon the cloud consumer. This model is therefore used by cloud consumers that require a high level of control over the cloud-based environment they intend to create.

Sometimes cloud providers will contract IaaS offerings from other cloud providers in order to scale their own cloud environments. The types and brands of the IT resources provided by IaaS products offered by different cloud providers can vary. IT resources available through IaaS environments are generally offered as freshly initialized virtual instances. A central and primary IT resource within a typical IaaS environment is the virtual server. Virtual servers are leased by specifying server hardware requirements, such as processor capacity, memory, and local storage space, as shown in Figure 4.11.

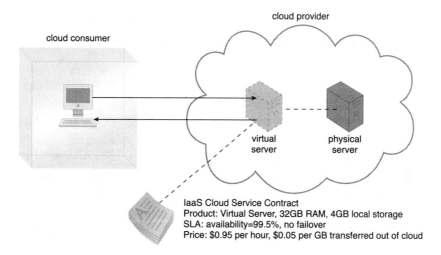

cloud provider

cloud consumer

virtual
server

physical
server

IaaS Cloud Service Contract
Product: Virtual Server, 32GB RAM, 4GB local storage
SLA: availability=99.5%, no failover
Price: $0.95 per hour, $0.05 per GB transferred out of cloud

Figure 4.11

A cloud consumer is using a virtual server within an IaaS environment. Cloud consumers are provided
with a range of contractual guarantees by the cloud provider, pertaining to characteristics such as
capacity, performance, and availability.

Platform-as-a-Service (PaaS)

The PaaS delivery model represents a pre-defined "ready-to-use" environment typically
comprised of already deployed and configured IT resources. Specifically, PaaS relies on
(and is primarily defined by) the usage of a ready-made environment that establishes a
set of pre-packaged products and tools used to support the entire delivery lifecycle of
custom applications.

Common reasons a cloud consumer would use and invest in a PaaS environment
include:

- The cloud consumer wants to extend on-premise environments into the cloud for
  scalability and economic purposes.

- The cloud consumer uses the ready-made environment to entirely substitute an
  on-premise environment.

- The cloud consumer wants to become a cloud provider and deploys its own cloud
  services to be made available to other external cloud consumers.

By working within a ready-made platform, the cloud consumer is spared the administrative burden of setting up and maintaining the bare infrastructure IT resources provided

via the IaaS model. Conversely, the cloud consumer is granted a lower level of control over the underlying IT resources that host and provision the platform (Figure 4.12).

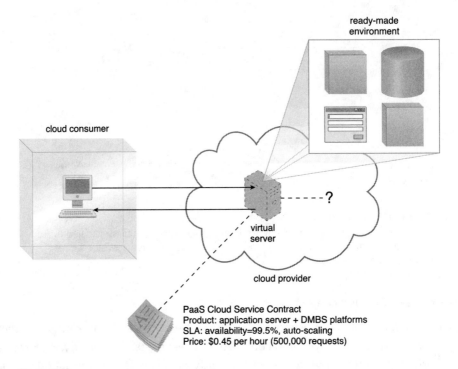

Figure 4.12

A cloud consumer is accessing a ready-made PaaS environment. The question mark indicates that the cloud consumer is intentionally shielded from the implementation details of the platform.

PaaS products are available with different development stacks. For example, Google App Engine offers a Java and Python-based environment.

The ready-made environment is further described as a cloud computing mechanism in Chapter 7.

Software-as-a-Service (SaaS)

A software program positioned as a shared cloud service and made available as a "product" or generic utility represents the typical profile of a SaaS offering. The SaaS delivery model is typically used to make a reusable cloud service widely available (often commercially) to a range of cloud consumers. An entire marketplace exists around SaaS products that can be leased and used for different purposes and via different terms (Figure 4.13).

A cloud consumer is generally granted very limited administrative control over a SaaS implementation. It is most often provisioned by the cloud provider, but it can be legally owned by whichever entity assumes the cloud service owner role. For example, an organization acting as a cloud consumer while using and working with a PaaS environment can build a cloud service that it decides to deploy in that same environment as a SaaS offering. The same organization then effectively assumes the cloud provider role as the SaaS-based cloud service is made available to other organizations that act as cloud consumers when using that cloud service.

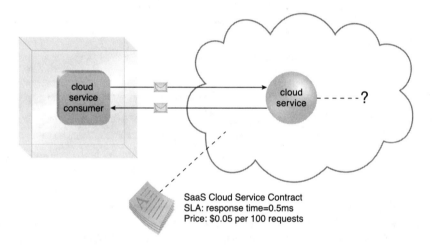

Figure 4.13

The cloud service consumer is given access the cloud service contract, but not to any underlying IT resources or implementation details.

Comparing Cloud Delivery Models

Provided in this section are three tables that compare different aspects of cloud delivery model usage and implementation. Table 4.1 contrasts control levels and Table 4.2 compares typical responsibilities and usage.

Cloud Delivery Model	Typical Level of Control Granted to Cloud Consumer	Typical Functionality Made Available to Cloud Consumer
SaaS	usage and usage-related configuration	access to front-end user-interface
PaaS	limited administrative	moderate level of administrative control over IT resources relevant to cloud consumer's usage of platform
IaaS	full administrative	full access to virtualized infrastructure-related IT resources and, possibly, to underlying physical IT resources

Table 4.1

A comparison of typical cloud delivery model control levels.

Cloud Delivery Model	Common Cloud Consumer Activities	Common Cloud Provider Activities
SaaS	uses and configures cloud service	implements, manages, and maintains cloud service monitors usage by cloud consumers
PaaS	develops, tests, deploys, and manages cloud services and cloud-based solutions	pre-configures platform and provisions underlying infrastructure, middleware, and other needed IT resources, as necessary monitors usage by cloud consumers
IaaS	sets up and configures bare infrastructure, and installs, manages, and monitors any needed software	provisions and manages the physical processing, storage, networking, and hosting required monitors usage by cloud consumers

Table 4.2

Typical activities carried out by cloud consumers and cloud providers in relation to the cloud delivery models.

Combining Cloud Delivery Models

The three base cloud delivery models comprise a natural provisioning hierarchy, allowing for opportunities for the combined application of the models to be explored. The upcoming sections briefly highlight considerations pertaining to two common combinations.

IaaS + PaaS

A PaaS environment will be built upon an underlying infrastructure comparable to the physical and virtual servers and other IT resources provided in an IaaS environment. Figure 4.14 shows how these two models can conceptually be combined into a simple layered architecture.

A cloud provider would not normally need to provision an IaaS environment from its own cloud in order to make a PaaS environment available to cloud consumers. So how would the architectural view provided by Figure 4.15 be useful or applicable? Let's say that the cloud provider offering the PaaS environment chose to lease an IaaS environment from a *different* cloud provider.

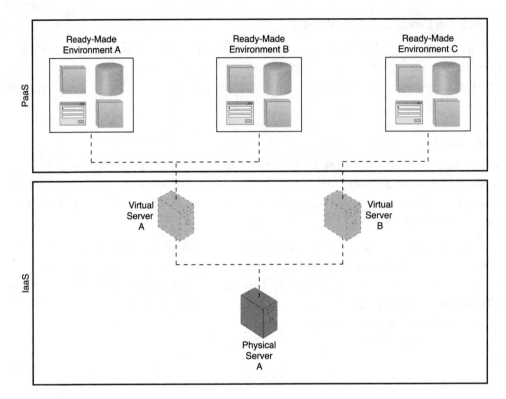

Figure 4.14

A PaaS environment based on the IT resources provided by an underlying IaaS environment.

The motivation for such an arrangement may be influenced by economics or maybe because the first cloud provider is close to exceeding its existing capacity by serving other cloud consumers. Or, perhaps a particular cloud consumer imposes a legal requirement for data to be physically stored in a specific region (different from where the first cloud provider's cloud resides), as illustrated in Figure 4.15.

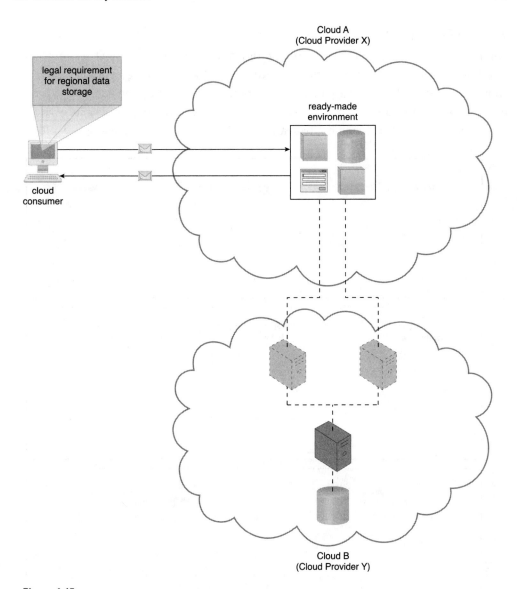

Figure 4.15

An example of a contract between Cloud Providers X and Y, in which services offered by Cloud Provider X are physically hosted on virtual servers belonging to Cloud Provider Y. Sensitive data that is legally required to stay in a specific region is physically kept in Cloud B, which is physically located in that region.

IaaS + PaaS + SaaS

All three cloud delivery models can be combined to establish layers of IT resources that build upon each other. For example, by adding on to the preceding layered architecture shown in Figure 4.15, the ready-made environment provided by the PaaS environment can be used by the cloud consumer organization to develop and deploy its own SaaS cloud services that it can then make available as commercial products (Figure 4.16).

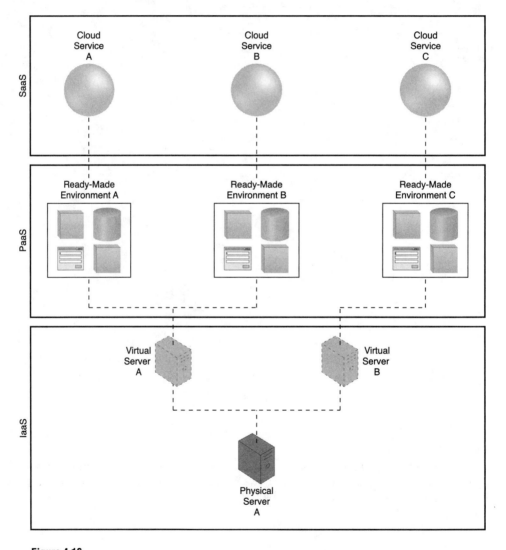

Figure 4.16

A simple layered view of an architecture comprised of IaaS and PaaS environments hosting three SaaS cloud service implementations.

SUMMARY OF KEY POINTS

- The IaaS cloud delivery model offers cloud consumers a high level of administrative control over "raw" infrastructure-based IT resources.

- The PaaS cloud delivery model enables a cloud provider to offer a pre-configured environment that cloud consumers can use to build and deploy cloud services and solutions, albeit with decreased administrative control.

- SaaS is a cloud delivery model for shared cloud services that can be positioned as commercialized products hosted by clouds.

- Different combinations of IaaS, PaaS, and SaaS are possible, depending on how cloud consumers and cloud providers choose to leverage the natural hierarchy established by these base cloud delivery models.

4.4 Cloud Deployment Models

A cloud deployment model represents a specific type of cloud environment, primarily distinguished by ownership, size, and access.

There are four common cloud deployment models:

- Public cloud

- Community cloud

- Private cloud

- Hybrid cloud

The following sections describe each.

Public Clouds

A *public cloud* is a publicly accessible cloud environment owned by a third-party cloud provider. The IT resources on public clouds are usually provisioned via the previously described cloud delivery models and are generally offered to cloud consumers at a cost or are commercialized via other avenues (such as advertisement).

The cloud provider is responsible for the creation and on-going maintenance of the public cloud and its IT resources. Many of the scenarios and architectures explored in upcoming chapters involve public clouds and the relationship between the providers and consumers of IT resources via public clouds.

Figure 4.17 shows a partial view of the public cloud landscape, highlighting some of the primary vendors in the marketplace.

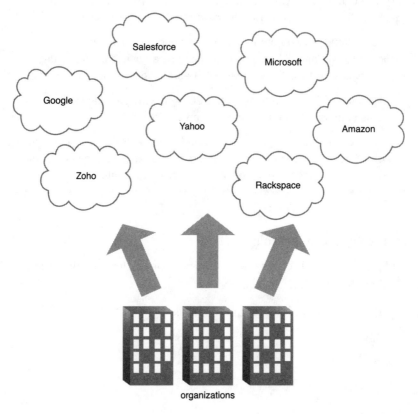

Figure 4.17

Organizations act as cloud consumers when accessing cloud services and IT resources made available by different cloud providers.

Community Clouds

A community cloud is similar to a public cloud except that its access is limited to a specific community of cloud consumers. The community cloud may be jointly owned by the community members or by a third-party cloud provider that provisions a public cloud with limited access. The member cloud consumers of the community typically share the responsibility for defining and evolving the community cloud (Figure 4.18).

Membership in the community does not necessarily guarantee access to or control of all the cloud's IT resources. Parties outside the community are generally not granted access unless allowed by the community.

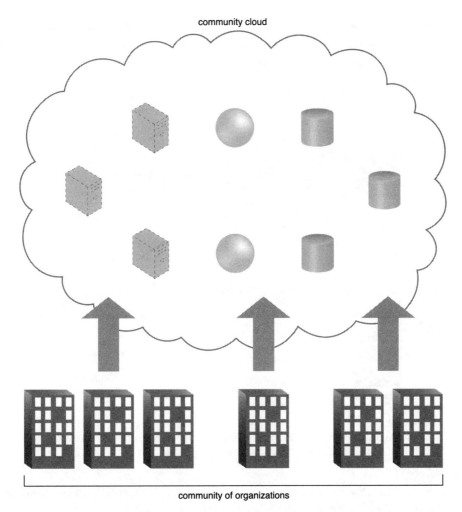

Figure 4.18
An example of a "community" of organizations accessing IT resources from a community cloud.

Private Clouds

A private cloud is owned by a single organization. Private clouds enable an organization to use cloud computing technology as a means of centralizing access to IT resources
by different parts, locations, or departments of the organization. When a private cloud
exists as a controlled environment, the problems described in the *Risks and Challenges*
section from Chapter 3 do not tend to apply.

The use of a private cloud can change how organizational and trust boundaries are defined and applied. The actual administration of a private cloud environment may be carried out by internal or outsourced staff.

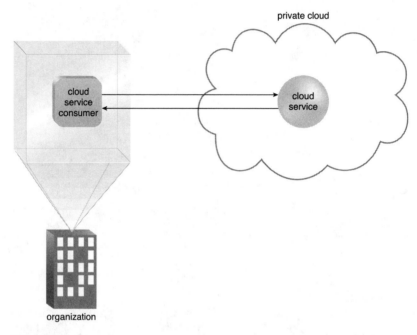

Figure 4.19

A cloud service consumer in the organization's on-premise environment accesses a cloud service hosted on the same organization's private cloud via a virtual private network.

With a private cloud, the same organization is technically both the cloud consumer and cloud provider (Figure 4.19). In order to differentiate these roles:

- a separate organizational department typically assumes the responsibility for provisioning the cloud (and therefore assumes the cloud provider role)

- departments requiring access to the private cloud assume the cloud consumer role

It is important to use the terms "on-premise" and "cloud-based" correctly within the context of a private cloud. Even though the private cloud may physically reside on the organization's premises, IT resources it hosts are still considered "cloud-based" as long as they are made remotely accessible to cloud consumers. IT resources hosted outside of the private cloud by the departments acting as cloud consumers are therefore considered "on-premise" in relation to the private cloud-based IT resources.

Hybrid Clouds

A hybrid cloud is a cloud environment comprised of two or more different cloud deployment models. For example, a cloud consumer may choose to deploy cloud services processing sensitive data to a private cloud and other, less sensitive cloud services to a public cloud. The result of this combination is a hybrid deployment model (Figure 4.20).

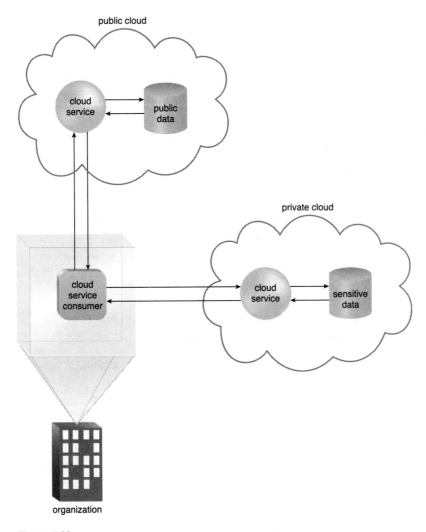

Figure 4.20

An organization using a hybrid cloud architecture that utilizes both a private and public cloud.

Hybrid deployment architectures can be complex and challenging to create and maintain due to the potential disparity in cloud environments and the fact that management responsibilities are typically split between the private cloud provider organization and the public cloud provider.

Other Cloud Deployment Models

Additional variations of the four base cloud deployment models can exist. Examples include:

- *Virtual Private Cloud* – Also known as a "dedicated cloud" or "hosted cloud," this model results in a self-contained cloud environment hosted and managed by a public cloud provider, and made available to a cloud consumer.

- *Inter-Cloud* – This model is based on an architecture comprised of two or more inter-connected clouds.

SUMMARY OF KEY POINTS

- A public cloud is owned by a third party and generally offers commercialized cloud services and IT resources to cloud consumer organizations.

- A private cloud is owned by an individual organization and resides within the organization's premises.

- A community cloud is normally limited for access by a group of cloud consumers that may also share responsibility in its ownership.

- A hybrid cloud is a combination of two or more other cloud deployment models.

Chapter 5

Cloud-Enabling Technology

Modern-day clouds are underpinned by a set of primary technology components that collectively enable key features and characteristics associated with contemporary cloud computing. The following such technologies are covered in this section:

- Broadband Networks and Internet Architecture
- Data Center Technology
- Virtualization Technology
- Web Technology
- Multitenant Technology
- Service Technology

Each existed and matured prior to the advent of cloud computing, although cloud computing advancements helped further evolve select areas of these cloud-enabling technologies.

5.1 Broadband Networks and Internet Architecture

All clouds must be connected to a network. This inevitable requirement forms an inherent dependency on internetworking.

Internetworks, or the Internet, allow for the remote provisioning of IT resources and are directly supportive of ubiquitous network access. Cloud consumers have the option of accessing the cloud using only private and dedicated network links in LANs, although most clouds are Internet-enabled. The potential of cloud platforms therefore generally grows in parallel with advancements in Internet connectivity and service quality.

Internet Service Providers (ISPs)

Established and deployed by ISPs, the Internet's largest backbone networks are strategically interconnected by core routers that connect the world's multinational networks. As shown in Figure 5.1, an ISP network interconnects to other ISP networks and various organizations.

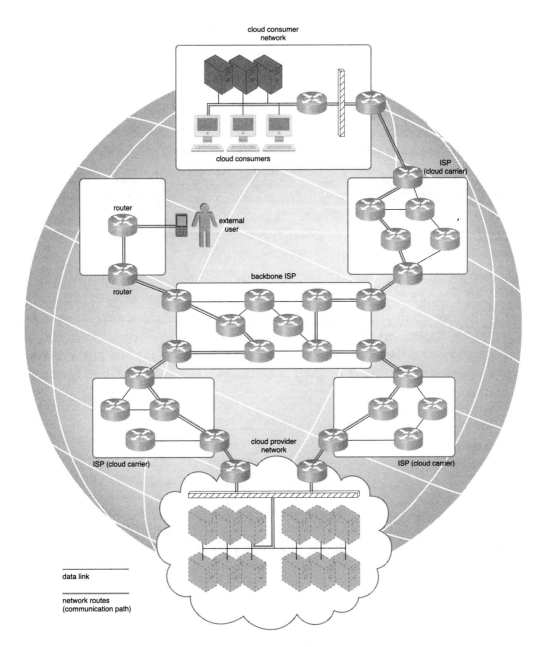

Figure 5.1

Messages travel over dynamic network routes in this ISP internetworking configuration.

The concept of the Internet was based on a decentralized provisioning and management model. ISPs can freely deploy, operate, and manage their networks in addition to selecting partner ISPs for interconnection. No centralized entity comprehensively governs the Internet, although bodies like the Internet Corporation for Assigned Names and Numbers (ICANN) supervise and coordinate Internet communications.

Governmental and regulatory laws dictate the service provisioning conditions for organizations and ISPs both within and outside of national borders. Certain realms of the Internet still require the demarcation of national jurisdiction and legal boundaries.

The Internet's topology has become a dynamic and complex aggregate of ISPs that are highly interconnected via its core protocols. Smaller branches extend from these major nodes of interconnection, branching outwards through smaller networks until eventually reaching every Internet-enabled electronic device.

Worldwide connectivity is enabled through a hierarchical topology composed of Tiers 1, 2, and 3 (Figure 5.2). The core Tier 1 is made of large-scale, international cloud providers that oversee massive interconnected global networks, which are connected to Tier 2's large regional providers. The interconnected ISPs of Tier 2 connect with Tier 1 providers, as well as the local ISPs of Tier 3. Cloud consumers and cloud providers can connect directly using a Tier 1 provider, since any operational ISP can enable Internet connection.

Figure 5.2

An abstraction of the internetworking structure of the Internet.

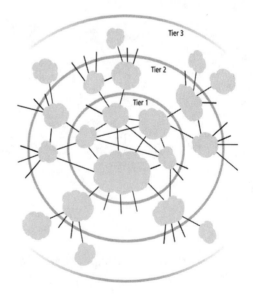

The communication links and routers of the Internet and ISP networks are IT resources that are distributed among countless traffic generation paths. Two fundamental components used to construct the internetworking architecture are *connectionless packet switching* (datagram networks) and *router-based interconnectivity*.

Connectionless Packet Switching (Datagram Networks)

End-to-end (sender-receiver pair) data flows are divided into packets of a limited size that are received and processed through network switches and routers, then queued and forwarded from one intermediary node to the next. Each packet carries the necessary location information, such as the Internet Protocol (IP) or Media Access Control (MAC) address, to be processed and routed at every source, intermediary, and destination node.

Router-Based Interconnectivity

A router is a device that is connected to multiple networks through which it forwards packets. Even when successive packets are part of the same data flow, routers process and forward each packet individually while maintaining the network topology information that locates the next node on the communication path between the source and destination nodes. Routers manage network traffic and gauge the most efficient hop for packet delivery, since they are privy to both the packet source and packet destination.

The basic mechanics of internetworking are illustrated in Figure 5.3, in which a message is coalesced from an incoming group of disordered packets. The depicted router receives and forwards packets from multiple data flows.

The communication path that connects a cloud consumer with its cloud provider may involve multiple ISP networks. The Internet's mesh structure connects Internet hosts (endpoint systems) using multiple alternative network routes that are determined at runtime. Communication can therefore be sustained even during simultaneous network failures, although using multiple network paths can cause routing fluctuations and latency.

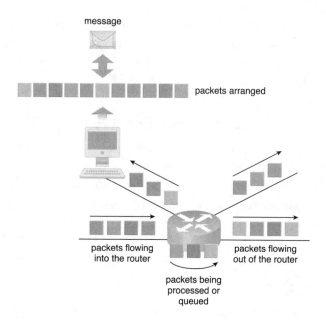

Figure 5.3

Packets traveling through the Internet are directed by a router that arranges them into a message.

This applies to ISPs that implement the Internet's internetworking layer and interact with other network technologies, as follows:

Physical Network

IP packets are transmitted through underlying physical networks that connect adjacent nodes, such as Ethernet, ATM network, and the 3G mobile HSDPA. Physical networks comprise a data link layer that controls data transfer between neighboring nodes, and a physical layer that transmits data bits through both wired and wireless media.

Transport Layer Protocol

Transport layer protocols, such as the Transmission Control Protocol (TCP) and User Datagram Protocol (UDP), use the IP to provide standardized, end-to-end communication support that facilitates the navigation of data packets across the Internet.

Application Layer Protocol

Protocols such as HTTP, SMTP for e-mail, BitTorrent for P2P, and SIP for IP telephony use transport layer protocols to standardize and enable specific data packet transferring methods over the Internet. Many other protocols also fulfill application-centric requirements and use either TCP/IP or UDP as their primary method of data transferring across the Internet and LANs.

Figure 5.4 presents the Internet Reference Model and the protocol stack.

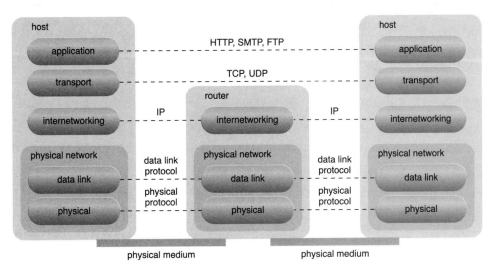

Figure 5.4

A generic view of the Internet reference model and protocol stack.

Technical and Business Considerations

Connectivity Issues

In traditional, on-premise deployment models, enterprise applications and various IT solutions are commonly hosted on centralized servers and storage devices residing in the organization's own data center. End-user devices, such as smartphones and laptops, access the data center through the corporate network, which provides uninterrupted Internet connectivity.

TCP/IP facilitates both Internet access and on-premise data exchange over LANs (Figure 5.5). Although not commonly referred to as a cloud model, this configuration has been implemented numerous times for medium and large on-premise networks.

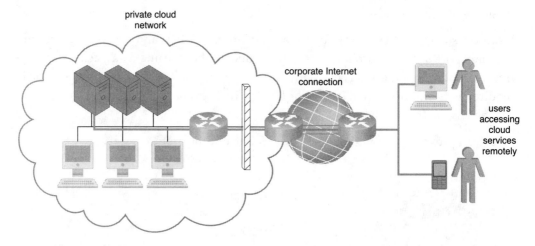

Figure 5.5

The internetworking architecture of a private cloud. The physical IT resources that constitute the cloud are located and managed within the organization.

Organizations using this deployment model can directly access the network traffic to and from the Internet and usually have complete control over and can safeguard their corporate networks using firewalls and monitoring software. These organizations also assume the responsibility of deploying, operating, and maintaining their IT resources and Internet connectivity.

End-user devices that are connected to the network through the Internet can be granted continuous access to centralized servers and applications in the cloud (Figure 5.6).

A salient cloud feature that applies to end-user functionality is how centralized IT resources can be accessed using the same network protocols regardless of whether they reside inside or outside of a corporate network. Whether IT resources are on-premise or Internet-based dictates how internal versus external end-users access services, even if the end-users themselves are not concerned with the physical location of cloud-based IT resources (Table 5.1).

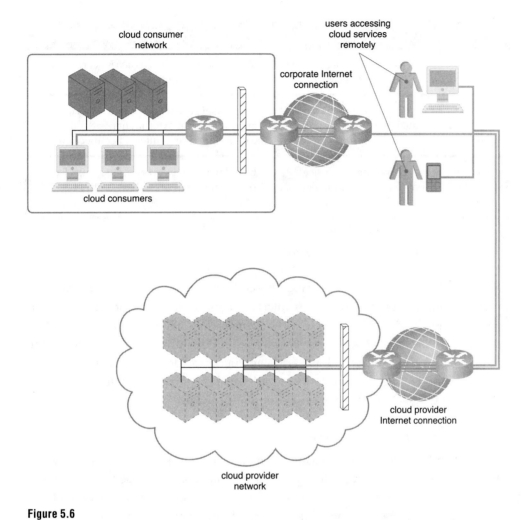

Figure 5.6

The internetworking architecture of an Internet-based cloud deployment model. The Internet is the connecting agent between non-proximate cloud consumers, roaming end-users, and the cloud provider's own network.

On-Premise IT Resources	Cloud-Based IT Resources
internal end-user devices access corporate IT services through the corporate network	internal end-user devices access corporate IT services through an Internet connection
internal users access corporate IT services through the corporate Internet connection while roaming in external networks	internal users access corporate IT services while roaming in external networks through the cloud provider's Internet connection
external users access corporate IT services through the corporate Internet connection	external users access corporate IT services through the cloud provider's Internet connection

Table 5.1

A comparison of on-premise and cloud-based internetworking.

Cloud providers can easily configure cloud-based IT resources to be accessible for both external and internal users through an Internet connection (as previously shown in Figure 5.6). This internetworking architecture benefits internal users that require ubiquitous access to corporate IT solutions, as well as cloud consumers that need to provide Internet-based services to external users. Major cloud providers offer Internet connectivity that is superior to the connectivity of individual organizations, resulting in additional network usage charges as part of their pricing model.

Network Bandwidth and Latency Issues

In addition to being affected by the bandwidth of the data link that connects networks to ISPs, end-to-end bandwidth is determined by the transmission capacity of the shared data links that connect intermediary nodes. ISPs need to use broadband network technology to implement the core network required to guarantee end-to-end connectivity. This type of bandwidth is constantly increasing, as Web acceleration technologies, such as dynamic caching, compression, and pre-fetching, continue to improve end-user connectivity.

Also referred to as time delay, *latency* is the amount of time it takes a packet to travel from one data node to another. Latency increases with every intermediary node on the data packet's path. Transmission queues in the network infrastructure can result in heavy load conditions that also increase network latency. Networks are dependent on traffic conditions in shared nodes, making Internet latency highly variable and often unpredictable.

Packet networks with "best effort" quality-of-service (QoS) typically transmit packets on a first-come/first-serve basis. Data flows that use congested network paths suffer service-level degradation in the form of bandwidth reduction, latency increase, or packet loss when traffic is not prioritized.

The nature of packet switching allows data packets to choose routes dynamically as they travel through the Internet's network infrastructure. End-to-end QoS can be impacted as a result of this dynamic selecting, since the travel speed of data packets is susceptible to conditions like network congestion and is therefore non-uniform.

IT solutions need to be assessed against business requirements that are affected by network bandwidth and latency, which are inherent to cloud interconnection. Bandwidth is critical for applications that require substantial amounts of data to be transferred to and from the cloud, while latency is critical for applications with a business requirement of swift response times.

Cloud Carrier and Cloud Provider Selection

The service levels of Internet connections between cloud consumers and cloud providers are determined by their ISPs, which are usually different and therefore include multiple ISP networks in their paths. QoS management across multiple ISPs is difficult to achieve in practice, requiring collaboration of the cloud carriers on both sides to ensure that their end-to-end service levels are sufficient for business requirements.

Cloud consumers and cloud providers may need to use multiple cloud carriers in order to achieve the necessary level of connectivity and reliability for their cloud applications, resulting in additional costs. Cloud adoption can therefore be easier for applications with more relaxed latency and bandwidth requirements.

SUMMARY OF KEY POINTS

- Cloud consumers and cloud providers typically use the Internet to communicate, which is based on a decentralized provisioning and management model and is not controlled by any centralized entities.

- The main components of internetworking architecture are connectionless packet switching and router-based interconnectivity, which use network routers and switches. Network bandwidth and latency are characteristics that influence QoS, which is heavily impacted by network congestion.

5.2 Data Center Technology

Grouping IT resources in close proximity with one another, rather than having them geographically dispersed, allows for power sharing, higher efficiency in shared IT resource usage, and improved accessibility for IT personnel. These are the advantages that naturally popularized the data center concept. Modern data centers exist as specialized IT infrastructure used to house centralized IT resources, such as servers, databases, networking and telecommunication devices, and software systems.

Data centers are typically comprised of the following technologies and components:

Virtualization

Data centers consist of both physical and virtualized IT resources. The physical IT resource layer refers to the facility infrastructure that houses computing/networking systems and equipment, together with hardware systems and their operating systems (Figure 5.7). The resource abstraction and control of the virtualization layer is comprised of operational and management tools that are often based on virtualization platforms that abstract the physical computing and networking IT resources as virtualized components that are easier to allocate, operate, release, monitor, and control.

Virtualization components are discussed separately in the upcoming *Virtualization Technology* section.

Standardization and Modularity

Data centers are built upon standardized commodity hardware and designed with modular architectures, aggregating multiple identical building blocks of facility infrastructure and equipment to support scalability, growth, and speedy hardware replacements. Modularity and standardization are key requirements for reducing investment and operational costs as they enable economies of scale for the procurement, acquisition, deployment, operation, and maintenance processes.

Common virtualization strategies and the constantly improving capacity and performance of physical devices both favor IT resource consolidation, since fewer physical components are needed to support complex configurations. Consolidated IT resources can serve different systems and be shared among different cloud consumers.

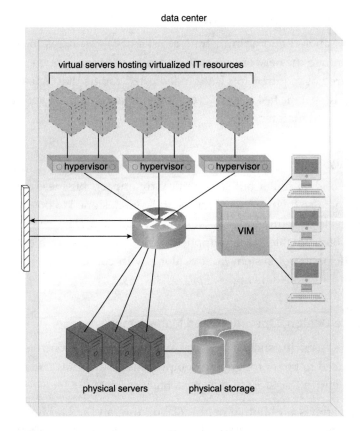

Figure 5.7
The common components of a data center working together to provide virtualized
IT resources supported by physical IT resources.

Automation

Data centers have specialized platforms that automate tasks like provisioning,
configuration, patching, and monitoring without supervision. Advances in data
center management platforms and tools leverage autonomic computing technologies to enable self-configuration and self-recovery. Autonomic computing is
briefly discussed in Appendix H: Emerging Technologies (available online only at
www.servicetechbooks.com/cloud).

Remote Operation and Management

Most of the operational and administrative tasks of IT resources in data centers are commanded through the network's remote consoles and management systems. Technical personnel are not required to visit the dedicated rooms that house servers, except to perform highly specific tasks, such as equipment handling and cabling or hardware-level installation and maintenance.

High Availability

Since any form of data center outage significantly impacts business continuity for the organizations that use their services, data centers are designed to operate with increasingly higher levels of redundancy to sustain availability. Data centers usually have redundant, uninterruptable power supplies, cabling, and environmental control subsystems in anticipation of system failure, along with communication links and clustered hardware for load balancing.

Security-Aware Design, Operation, and Management

Requirements for security, such as physical and logical access controls and data recovery strategies, need to be thorough and comprehensive for data centers, since they are centralized structures that store and process business data.

Due to the sometimes prohibitive nature of building and operating on-premise data centers, outsourcing data center-based IT resources has been a common industry practice for decades. However, the outsourcing models often required long-term consumer commitment and usually could not provide elasticity, issues that a typical cloud can address via inherent features, such as ubiquitous access, on-demand provisioning, rapid elasticity, and pay-per-use.

Facilities

Data center facilities are custom-designed locations that are outfitted with specialized computing, storage, and network equipment. These facilities have several functional layout areas, as well as various power supplies, cabling, and environmental control stations that regulate heating, ventilation, air conditioning, fire protection, and other related subsystems.

The site and layout of a given data center facility are typically demarcated into segregated spaces. Appendix D provides a breakdown of the common rooms and utilities found in data centers.

Computing Hardware

Much of the heavy processing in data centers is often executed by standardized commodity servers that have substantial computing power and storage capacity. Several computing hardware technologies are integrated into these modular servers, such as:

- rackmount form factor server design composed of standardized racks with interconnects for power, network, and internal cooling

- support for different hardware processing architectures, such as x86-32bits, x86-64, and RISC

- a power-efficient multi-core CPU architecture that houses hundreds of processing cores in a space as small as a single unit of standardized racks

- redundant and hot-swappable components, such as hard disks, power supplies, network interfaces, and storage controller cards

Computing architectures such as blade server technologies use rack-embedded physical interconnections (blade enclosures), fabrics (switches), and shared power supply units and cooling fans. The interconnections enhance inter-component networking and management while optimizing physical space and power. These systems typically support individual server hot-swapping, scaling, replacement, and maintenance, which benefits the deployment of fault-tolerant systems that are based on computer clusters.

Contemporary computing hardware platforms generally support industry-standard and proprietary operational and management software systems that configure, monitor, and control hardware IT resources from remote management consoles. With a properly established management console, a single operator can oversee hundreds to thousands of physical servers, virtual servers, and other IT resources.

Storage Hardware

Data centers have specialized storage systems that maintain enormous amounts of digital information in order to fulfill considerable storage capacity needs. These storage systems are containers housing numerous hard disks that are organized into arrays.

Storage systems usually involve the following technologies:

- *Hard Disk Arrays* – These arrays inherently divide and replicate data among multiple physical drives, and increase performance and redundancy by including spare disks. This technology is often implemented using redundant arrays of independent disks (RAID) schemes, which are typically realized through hardware disk array controllers.

- *I/O Caching* – This is generally performed through hard disk array controllers, which enhance disk access times and performance by data caching.

- *Hot-Swappable Hard Disks* – These can be safely removed from arrays without requiring prior powering down.

- *Storage Virtualization* – This is realized through the use of virtualized hard disks and storage sharing.

- *Fast Data Replication Mechanisms* – These include *snapshotting*, which is saving a virtual machine's memory into a hypervisor-readable file for future reloading, and *volume cloning*, which is copying virtual or physical hard disk volumes and partitions.

Storage systems encompass tertiary redundancies, such as robotized tape libraries, which are used as backup and recovery systems that typically rely on removable media. This type of system can exist as a networked IT resource or direct-attached storage (DAS), in which a storage system is directly connected to the computing IT resource using a host bus adapter (HBA). In the former case, the storage system is connected to one or more IT resources through a network.

Networked storage devices usually fall into one of the following categories:

- *Storage Area Network (SAN)* – Physical data storage media are connected through a dedicated network and provide block-level data storage access using industry standard protocols, such as the Small Computer System Interface (SCSI).

- *Network-Attached Storage (NAS)* – Hard drive arrays are contained and managed by this dedicated device, which connects through a network and facilitates access to data using file-centric data access protocols like the Network File System (NFS) or Server Message Block (SMB).

NAS, SAN, and other more advanced storage system options provide fault tolerance in many components through controller redundancy, cooling redundancy, and hard disk arrays that use RAID storage technology.

Network Hardware

Data centers require extensive network hardware in order to enable multiple levels of connectivity. For a simplified version of networking infrastructure, the data center is broken down into five network subsystems, followed by a summary of the most common elements used for their implementation.

Carrier and External Networks Interconnection

A subsystem related to the internetworking infrastructure, this interconnection is usually comprised of backbone routers that provide routing between external WAN connections and the data center's LAN, as well as perimeter network security devices such as firewalls and VPN gateways.

Web-Tier Load Balancing and Acceleration

This subsystem comprises Web acceleration devices, such as XML pre-processors, encryption/decryption appliances, and layer 7 switching devices that perform content-aware routing.

LAN Fabric

The LAN fabric constitutes the internal LAN and provides high-performance and redundant connectivity for all of the data center's network-enabled IT resources. It is often implemented with multiple network switches that facilitate network communications and operate at speeds of up to ten gigabits per second. These advanced network switches can also perform several virtualization functions, such as LAN segregation into VLANs, link aggregation, controlled routing between networks, load balancing, and failover.

SAN Fabric

Related to the implementation of storage area networks (SANs) that provide connectivity between servers and storage systems, the SAN fabric is usually implemented with Fibre Channel (FC), Fibre Channel over Ethernet (FCoE), and InfiniBand network switches.

NAS Gateways

This subsystem supplies attachment points for NAS-based storage devices and implements protocol conversion hardware that facilitates data transmission between SAN and NAS devices.

Data center network technologies have operational requirements for scalability and high availability that are fulfilled by employing redundant and/or fault-tolerant configurations. These five network subsystems improve data center redundancy and reliability to ensure that they have enough IT resources to maintain a certain level of service even in the face of multiple failures.

Ultra high-speed network optical links can be used to aggregate individual gigabit-per-second channels into single optical fibers using multiplexing technologies like dense wavelength-division multiplexing (DWDM). Spread over multiple locations and used to interconnect server farms, storage systems, and replicated data centers, optical links improve transfer speeds and resiliency.

Other Considerations

IT hardware is subject to rapid technological obsolescence, with lifecycles that typically last between five to seven years. The on-going need to replace equipment frequently results in a mix of hardware whose heterogeneity can complicate the entire data center's operations and management (although this can be partially mitigated through virtualization).

Security is another major issue when considering the role of the data center and the vast quantities of data contained within its doors. Even with extensive security precautions in place, housing data exclusively at one data center facility means much more can be compromised by a successful security incursion than if data was distributed across individual unlinked components.

SUMMARY OF KEY POINTS

- A data center is a specialized IT infrastructure that houses centralized IT resources, such as servers, databases, and software systems.

- Data center IT hardware is typically comprised of standardized commodity servers of increased computing power and storage capacity, while storage system technologies include disk arrays and storage virtualization. Technologies used to increase storage capacity include DAS, SAN, and NAS.

- Computing hardware technologies include rackmounted server arrays and multi-core CPU architectures, while specialized high-capacity network hardware and technology, such as content-aware routing, LAN and SAN fabrics, and NAS gateways, are used to improve network connectivity.

5.3 Virtualization Technology

Virtualization is the process of converting a physical IT resource into a virtual IT resource.

Most types of IT resources can be virtualized, including:

- *Servers* – A physical server can be abstracted into a virtual server.

- *Storage* – A physical storage device can be abstracted into a virtual storage device or a virtual disk.

- *Network* – Physical routers and switches can be abstracted into logical network fabrics, such as VLANs.

- *Power* – A physical UPS and power distribution units can be abstracted into what are commonly referred to as virtual UPSs.

This section focuses on the creation and deployment of virtual servers through server virtualization technology.

> **NOTE**
>
> The terms *virtual server* and *virtual machine (VM)* are used synonymously throughout this book.

The first step in creating a new virtual server through virtualization software is the allocation of physical IT resources, followed by the installation of an operating system. Virtual servers use their own guest operating systems, which are independent of the operating system in which they were created.

Both the guest operating system and the application software running on the virtual server are unaware of the virtualization process, meaning these virtualized IT resources are installed and executed as if they were running on a separate physical server. This uniformity of execution that allows programs to run on physical systems as they would on virtual systems is a vital characteristic of virtualization. Guest operating systems typically require seamless usage of software products and applications that do not need to be customized, configured, or patched in order to run in a virtualized environment.

Virtualization software runs on a physical server called a *host* or *physical host*, whose underlying hardware is made accessible by the virtualization software. The virtualization software functionality encompasses system services that are specifically related to virtual machine management and not normally found on standard operating systems. This is why this software is sometimes referred to as a virtual machine manager or a virtual machine monitor (VMM), but most commonly known as a *hypervisor*. (The hypervisor is formally described as a cloud computing mechanism in Chapter 8.)

Hardware Independence

The installation of an operating system's configuration and application software in a unique IT hardware platform results in many software-hardware dependencies. In a non-virtualized environment, the operating system is configured for specific hardware models and requires reconfiguration if these IT resources need to be modified.

Virtualization is a conversion process that translates unique IT hardware into emulated and standardized software-based copies. Through hardware independence, virtual servers can easily be moved to another virtualization host, automatically resolving multiple hardware-software incompatibility issues. As a result, cloning and manipulating virtual IT resources is much easier than duplicating physical hardware. The architectural models explored in Part III of this book provide numerous examples of this.

Server Consolidation

The coordination function that is provided by the virtualization software allows multiple virtual servers to be simultaneously created in the same virtualization host. Virtualization technology enables different virtual servers to share one physical server. This process is called *server consolidation* and is commonly used to increase hardware utilization, load balancing, and optimization of available IT resources. The resulting flexibility is such that different virtual servers can run different guest operating systems on the same host.

This fundamental capability directly supports common cloud features, such as on-demand usage, resource pooling, elasticity, scalability, and resiliency.

Resource Replication

Virtual servers are created as virtual disk images that contain binary file copies of hard disk content. These virtual disk images are accessible to the host's operating system, meaning simple file operations, such as copy, move, and paste, can be used to replicate, migrate, and back up the virtual server. This ease of manipulation and replication is one of the most salient features of virtualization technology as it enables:

- The creation of standardized virtual machine images commonly configured to include virtual hardware capabilities, guest operating systems, and additional application software, for pre-packaging in virtual disk images in support of instantaneous deployment.

- Increased agility in the migration and deployment of a virtual machine's new instances by being able to rapidly scale out and up.

- The ability to roll back, which is the instantaneous creation of VM snapshots by saving the state of the virtual server's memory and hard disk image to a host-based file. (Operators can easily revert to these snapshots and restore the virtual machine to its prior state.)

- The support of business continuity with efficient backup and restoration procedures, as well as the creation of multiple instances of critical IT resources and applications.

Operating System-Based Virtualization

Operating system-based virtualization is the installation of virtualization software in a pre-existing operating system, which is called the *host operating system* (Figure 5.8). For example, a user whose workstation is installed with a specific version of Windows wants to generate virtual servers and installs virtualization software into the host operating system like any other program. This user needs to use this application to generate and operate one or more virtual servers. The user needs to use virtualization software to enable direct access to any of the generated virtual servers. Since the host operating system can provide hardware devices with the necessary support, operating system virtualization can rectify hardware compatibility issues even if the hardware driver is not available to the virtualization software.

Hardware independence that is enabled by virtualization allows hardware IT resources to be more flexibly used. For example, consider a scenario in which the host operating system has the software necessary for controlling five network adapters that are available to the physical computer. The virtualization software can make the five network adapters available to the virtual server, even if the virtualized operating system is incapable of physically housing five network adapters.

Figure 5.8

The different logical layers of operating system-based virtualization, in which the VM is first installed into a full host operating system and subsequently used to generate virtual machines.

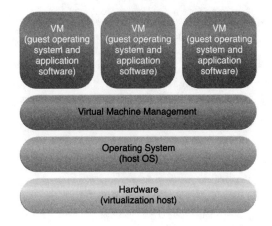

Virtualization software translates hardware IT resources that require unique software for operation into virtualized IT resources that are compatible with a range of operating systems. Since the host operating system is a complete operating system in itself, many operating system-based services that are available as administration tools can be used to manage the physical host.

Examples of such services include:

- Backup and Recovery
- Integration to Directory Services
- Security Management

Operating system-based virtualization can introduce demands and issues related to performance overhead such as:

- The host operating system consumes CPU, memory, and other hardware IT resources.
- Hardware-related calls from guest operating systems need to traverse several layers to and from the hardware, which decreases overall performance.
- Licenses are usually required for host operating systems, in addition to individual licenses for each of their guest operating systems.

A concern with operating system-based virtualization is the processing overhead required to run the virtualization software and host operating systems. Implementing a virtualization layer will negatively affect overall system performance. Estimating, monitoring, and managing the resulting impact can be challenging because it requires expertise in system workloads, software and hardware environments, and sophisticated monitoring tools.

Hardware-Based Virtualization

This option represents the installation of virtualization software directly on the physical host hardware so as to bypass the host operating system, which is presumably engaged with operating system-based virtualization (Figure 5.9). Allowing the virtual servers to interact with hardware without requiring intermediary action from the host operating system generally makes hardware-based virtualization more efficient.

Figure 5.9

The different logical layers of hardware-based virtualization, which does not require another host operating system.

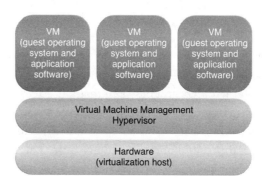

Virtualization software is typically referred to as a *hypervisor* for this type of processing. A hypervisor has a simple user-interface that requires a negligible amount of storage space. It exists as a thin layer of software that handles hardware management functions to establish a virtualization management layer. Device drivers and system services are optimized for the provisioning of virtual servers, although many standard operating system functions are not implemented. This type of virtualization system is essentially used to optimize performance overhead inherent to the coordination that enables multiple virtual servers to interact with the same hardware platform.

One of the main issues of hardware-based virtualization concerns compatibility with hardware devices. The virtualization layer is designed to communicate directly with the host hardware, meaning all of the associated device drivers and support software need to be compatible with the hypervisor. Hardware device drivers may not be as available to hypervisor platforms as they are to operating systems. Host management and administration features may further not include the range of advanced functions that are common to operating systems.

Virtualization Management

Many administrative tasks can be performed more easily using virtual servers as opposed to using their physical counterparts. Modern virtualization software provides several advanced management functions that can automate administration tasks and reduce the overall operational burden on virtualized IT resources.

Virtualized IT resource management is often supported by *virtualization infrastructure management (VIM)* tools that collectively manage virtual IT resources and rely on a centralized management module, otherwise known as a controller, that runs on a dedicated computer. VIMs are commonly encompassed by the resource management system mechanism described in Chapter 9.

Other Considerations

- *Performance Overhead* – Virtualization may not be ideal for complex systems that have high workloads with little use for resource sharing and replication. A poorly formulated virtualization plan can result in excessive performance overhead. A common strategy used to rectify the overhead issue is a technique called para-virtualization, which presents a software interface to the virtual machines that is not identical to that of the underlying hardware. The software interface has instead been modified to reduce the guest operating system's processing overhead, which is more difficult to manage. A major drawback of this approach is the need to adapt the guest operating system to the para-virtualization API, which can impair the use of standard guest operating systems while decreasing solution portability.

- *Special Hardware Compatibility* – Many hardware vendors that distribute specialized hardware may not have device driver versions that are compatible with virtualization software. Conversely, the software itself may be incompatible with recently released hardware versions. These types of incompatibility issues can be resolved using established commodity hardware platforms and mature virtualization software products.

- *Portability* – The programmatic and management interfaces that establish administration environments for a virtualization program to operate with various virtualization solutions can introduce portability gaps due to incompatibilities. Initiatives such as the Open Virtualization Format (OVF) for the standardization of virtual disk image formats are dedicated to alleviating this concern.

SUMMARY OF KEY POINTS

- Server virtualization is the process of abstracting IT hardware into virtual servers using virtualization software.

- Virtualization provides hardware independence, server consolidation, and resource replication, and further supports resource pooling and elastic scalability.

- Virtual servers are realized through either operating system-based or hardware-based virtualization.

5.4 Web Technology

Due to cloud computing's fundamental reliance on internetworking, Web browser universality, and the ease of Web-based service development, Web technology is generally used as both the implementation medium and the management interface for cloud services.

This section introduces the primary Web technologies and discusses their relationship to cloud services.

RESOURCES VS. IT RESOURCES

Artifacts accessible via the World Wide Web are referred to as *resources* or *Web resources*. This is a more generic term than IT resources, which was introduced and defined in Chapter 3. An IT resource, within the context of cloud computing, represents a physical or virtual IT-related artifact that can be software or hardware-based. A resource on the Web, however, can represent a wide range of artifacts accessible via the World Wide Web. For example, a JPG image file accessed via a Web browser is considered a resource. For examples of common IT resources, see the *IT Resource* section in Chapter 3.

Furthermore, the term resource may be used in a broader sense to refer to general types of processable artifacts that may not exist as stand-alone IT resources. For example, CPUs and RAM memory are types of resources that are grouped into resource pools (as explained in Chapter 8) and can be allocated to actual IT resources.

Basic Web Technology

The World Wide Web is a system of interlinked IT resources that are accessed through the Internet. The two basic components of the Web are the Web browser client and the Web server. Other components, such as proxies, caching services, gateways, and load balancers, are used to improve Web application characteristics such as scalability and security. These additional components reside in a layered architecture that is positioned between the client and the server.

Three fundamental elements comprise the technology architecture of the Web:

- *Uniform Resource Locator (URL)* – A standard syntax used for creating identifiers that point to Web-based resources, the URL is often structured using a logical network location.

- *Hypertext Transfer Protocol (HTTP)* – This is the primary communications protocol used to exchange content and data throughout the World Wide Web. URLs are typically transmitted via HTTP.

- *Markup Languages (HTML, XML)* – Markup languages provide a lightweight means of expressing Web-centric data and metadata. The two primary markup languages are HTML (which is used to express the presentation of Web pages) and XML (which allows for the definition of vocabularies used to associate meaning to Web-based data via metadata).

For example, a Web browser can request to execute an action like read, write, update, or delete on a Web resource on the Internet, and proceed to identify and locate the Web resource through its URL. The request is sent using HTTP to the resource host, which is also identified by a URL. The Web server locates the Web resource and performs the requested operation, which is followed by a response being sent back to the client. The response may be comprised of content that includes HTML and XML statements.

Web resources are represented as *hypermedia* as opposed to hypertext, meaning media such as graphics, audio, video, plain text, and URLs can be referenced collectively in a single document. Some types of hypermedia resources cannot be rendered without additional software or Web browser plug-ins.

Web Applications

A distributed application that uses Web-based technologies (and generally relies on Web browsers for the presentation of user-interfaces) is typically considered a *Web application*. These applications can be found in all kinds of cloud-based environments due to their high accessibility.

Figure 5.10 presents a common architectural abstraction for Web applications that is based on the basic three-tier model. The first tier is called the *presentation layer*, which represents the user-interface. The middle tier is the *application layer* that implements application logic, while the third tier is the *data layer* that is comprised of persistent data stores.

Figure 5.10

The three basic architectural tiers of Web applications.

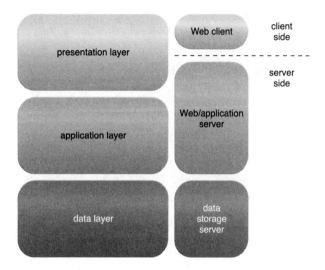

The presentation layer has components on both the client and server-side. Web servers receive client requests and retrieve requested resources directly as static Web content and indirectly as dynamic Web content, which is generated according to the application logic. Web servers interact with application servers in order to execute the requested application logic, which then typically involves interaction with one or more underlying databases.

PaaS ready-made environments enable cloud consumers to develop and deploy Web applications. Typical PaaS offerings have separate instances of the Web server, application server, and data storage server environments.

NOTE

For more information about URLs, HTTP, HTML, and XML, visit www.servicetechspecs.com.

SUMMARY OF KEY POINTS

- Web technology is very commonly used for cloud service implementations and for front-ends used to remotely manage cloud-based IT resources.

- Fundamental technologies of Web architecture include the URL, HTTP, HTML, and XML.

5.5 Multitenant Technology

The multitenant application design was created to enable multiple users (tenants) to access the same application logic simultaneously. Each tenant has its own view of the application that it uses, administers, and customizes as a dedicated instance of the software while remaining unaware of other tenants that are using the same application.

Multitenant applications ensure that tenants do not have access to data and configuration information that is not their own. Tenants can individually customize features of the application, such as:

- *User Interface* – Tenants can define a specialized "look and feel" for their application interface.

- *Business Process* – Tenants can customize the rules, logic, and workflows of the business processes that are implemented in the application.

- *Data Model* – Tenants can extend the data schema of the application to include, exclude, or rename fields in the application data structures.

- *Access Control* – Tenants can independently control the access rights for users and groups.

Multitenant application architecture is often significantly more complex than that of single-tenant applications. Multitenant applications need to support the sharing of various artifacts by multiple users (including portals, data schemas, middleware, and databases), while maintaining security levels that segregate individual tenant operational environments.

Common characteristics of multitenant applications include:

- *Usage Isolation* – The usage behavior of one tenant does not affect the application availability and performance of other tenants.

- *Data Security* – Tenants cannot access data that belongs to other tenants.

- *Recovery* – Backup and restore procedures are separately executed for the data of each tenant.

- *Application Upgrades* – Tenants are not negatively affected by the synchronous upgrading of shared software artifacts.

- *Scalability* – The application can scale to accommodate increases in usage by existing tenants and/or increases in the number of tenants.

- *Metered Usage* – Tenants are charged only for the application processing and features that are actually consumed.

- *Data Tier Isolation* – Tenants can have individual databases, tables, and/or schemas isolated from other tenants. Alternatively, databases, tables, and/or schemas can be designed to be intentionally shared by tenants.

A multitenant application that is being concurrently used by two different tenants is illustrated in Figure 5.11. This type of application is typical with SaaS implementations.

Figure 5.11

A multitenant application that is serving multiple cloud service consumers simultaneously.

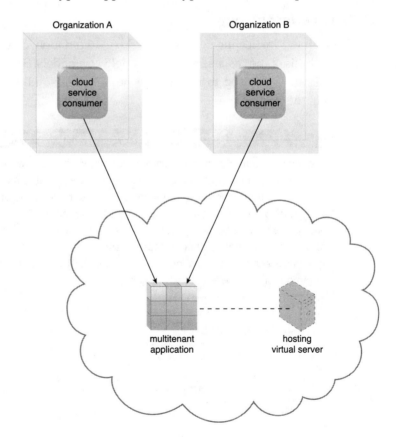

MULTITENANCY VS. VIRTUALIZATION

Multitenancy is sometimes mistaken for virtualization because the concept of multiple tenants is similar to the concept of virtualized instances.

The differences lie in what is multiplied within a physical server acting as a host:

- With virtualization: Multiple virtual copies of the server environment can be hosted by a single physical server. Each copy can be provided to different users, can be configured independently, and can contain its own operating systems and applications.

- With multitenancy: A physical or virtual server hosting an application is designed to allow usage by multiple different users. Each user feels as though they have exclusive usage of the application.

5.6 Service Technology

The field of service technology is a keystone foundation of cloud computing that formed the basis of the "as-a-service" cloud delivery models. Several prominent service technologies that are used to realize and build upon cloud-based environments are described in this section.

ABOUT WEB-BASED SERVICES

Reliant on the use of standardized protocols, *Web-based services* are self-contained units of logic that support interoperable machine-to-machine interaction over a network. These services are generally designed to communicate via non-proprietary technologies in accordance with industry standards and conventions. Because their sole function is to process data between computers, these services expose APIs and do not have user interfaces. Web services and REST services represent two common forms of Web-based services.

Web Services

Also commonly prefixed with "SOAP-based," Web services represent an established and common medium for sophisticated, Web-based service logic. Along with XML, the core technologies behind Web services are represented by the following industry standards:

- *Web Service Description Language (WSDL)* – This markup language is used to create a WSDL definition that defines the application programming interface (API) of a Web service, including its individual operations (functions) and each operation's input and output messages.

- *XML Schema Definition Language (XML Schema)* – Messages exchanged by Web services must be expressed using XML. XML schemas are created to define the data structure of the XML-based input and output messages exchanged by Web services. XML schemas can be directly linked to or embedded within WSDL definitions.

- *SOAP* – Formerly known as the Simple Object Access Protocol, this standard defines a common messaging format used for request and response messages exchanged by Web services. SOAP messages are comprised of body and header sections. The former houses the main message content and the latter is used to contain metadata that can be processed at runtime.

- *Universal Description, Discovery, and Integration (UDDI)* – This standard regulates service registries in which WSDL definitions can be published as part of a service catalog for discovery purposes.

These four technologies collectively form the first generation of Web service technologies (Figure 5.12). A comprehensive set of second-generation Web service technologies (commonly referred to as WS-*) has been developed to address various additional functional areas, such as security, reliability, transactions, routing, and business process automation.

> **NOTE**
>
> To learn more about Web service technologies, read *Web Service Contract Design & Versioning for SOA* from the *Prentice Hall Service Technology Series from Thomas Erl*. This title covers first and second-generation Web service standards in technical detail. See www.servicetechbooks.com/wsc for more information.

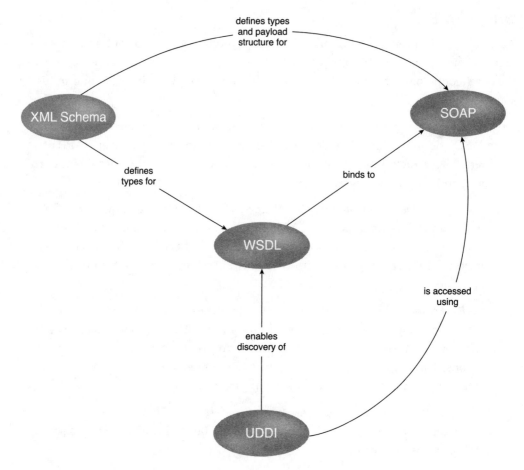

Figure 5.12

An overview of how first-generation Web service technologies commonly relate to each other.

REST Services

REST services are designed according to a set of constraints that shape the service architecture to emulate the properties of the World Wide Web, resulting in service implementations that rely on the use of core Web technologies (described in the *Web Technology* section).

Unlike Web services, REST services do not have individual technical interfaces but instead share a common technical interface that is known as the uniform contract, which is typically established via the use of HTTP methods.

The six REST design constraints are:

- Client-Server

- Stateless

- Cache

- Interface/Uniform Contract

- Layered System

- Code-On-Demand

Each design constraint is described in detail at www.whatisrest.com.

NOTE

To learn more about REST services read *SOA with REST: Principles, Patterns & Constraints for Building Enterprise Solutions with REST* from the *Prentice Hall Service Technology Series from Thomas Erl*. See www.servicetechbooks.com/rest for details.

Service Agents

Service agents are event-driven programs designed to intercept messages at runtime. There are active and passive service agents, both of which are common in cloud environments. Active service agents perform an action upon intercepting and reading the contents of a message. The action typically requires making changes to the message contents (most commonly message header data and less commonly the body content) or changes to the message path itself. Passive service agents, on the other hand, do not change message contents. Instead, they read the message and may then capture certain parts of its contents, usually for monitoring, logging, or reporting purposes.

Cloud-based environments rely heavily on the use of system-level and custom service agents to perform much of the runtime monitoring and measuring required to ensure that features, such as elastic scaling and pay-for-use billing, can be carried out instantaneously.

Several of the mechanisms described in Part II of this book exist as, or rely on the use of, service agents.

Service Middleware

Falling under the umbrella of service technology is the large market of middleware platforms that evolved from messaging-oriented middleware (MOM) platforms used primarily to facilitate integration, to sophisticated service middleware platforms designed
to accommodate complex service compositions.

The two most common types of middleware platforms relevant to services computing
are the enterprise service bus (ESB) and the orchestration platform. The ESB encompasses a range of intermediary processing features, including service brokerage, routing, and message queuing. Orchestration environments are designed to host and execute
workflow logic that drives the runtime composition of services.

Both forms of service middleware can be deployed and operated within cloud-based
environments.

SUMMARY OF KEY POINTS

- Web-based services, such as Web services and REST services, rely
  on non-proprietary communications and technical interface definitions
  to establish standardized communications frameworks based on Web
  technology.

- Service agents provide event-driven runtime processing that can be applied
  to numerous functional areas within clouds. Many are deployed automatically as part of operating systems and cloud-based products.

- Service middleware, such as ESBs and orchestration platforms, can be
  deployed on clouds.

5.7 CASE STUDY EXAMPLE

DTGOV has assembled cloud-aware infrastructures in each of its data centers, which are comprised of the following components:

• Tier-3 facility infrastructure, which provides redundant configurations for all of the central subsystems in the data center facility layer.

• Redundant connections with utility service providers that have installed local capacity for power generation and water supply that activates in the event of general failure.

• An internetwork that supplies an ultra-high bandwidth interconnection between the three data centers through dedicated links.

• Redundant Internet connections in each data center to multiple ISPs and the .GOV extranet, which interconnects DTGOV with its main government clients.

• Standardized hardware of higher aggregated capacity that is abstracted by a cloud-aware virtualization platform.

Physical servers are organized on server racks, each of which has two redundant top-of-rack router switches (layer 3) that are connected to each physical server. These router switches are interconnected to LAN core-switches that have been configured as a cluster. The core-switches connect to routers that supply internetworking capabilities and firewalls that provide network access control capabilities. Figure 5.13 illustrates the physical layout of the server network connections inside of the data center.

A separate network that connects the storage systems and servers is installed with clustered storage area network (SAN) switches and similar redundant connections to various devices (Figure 5.14).

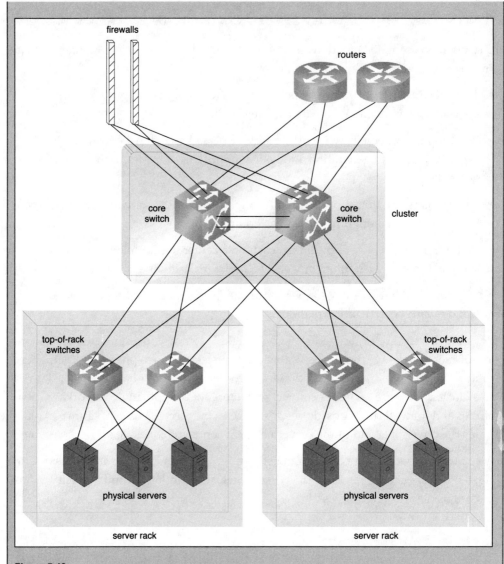

Figure 5.13
A view of the server network connections inside the DTGOV data center.

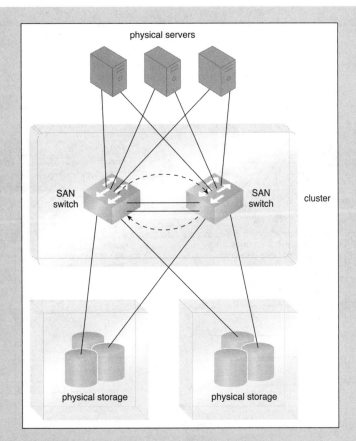

Figure 5.14
A view of the storage system network connections inside the DTGOV data center.

Figure 5.15 illustrates an internetworking architecture that is established between every data center pair within the DTGOV corporate infrastructure.

As shown in Figures 5.14 and 5.15, combining interconnected physical IT resources with virtualized IT resources on the physical layer enables the dynamic and well-managed configuration and allocation of virtual IT resources.

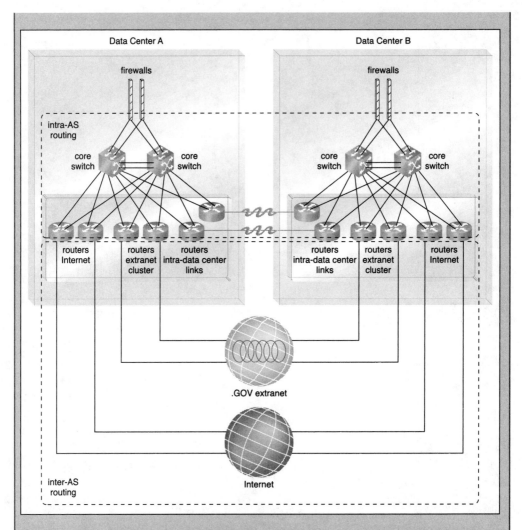

Figure 5.15

The internetworking setup between two data centers that is similarly implemented between every pair of DTGOV data centers. The DTGOV internetwork is designed to be an autonomous system (AS) on the Internet, meaning the links interconnecting the data centers with the LANs define the intra-AS routing domain. The interconnections to external ISPs are controlled through inter-AS routing technology, which shapes Internet traffic and enables flexible configurations for load-balancing and failover.

Chapter 6

Fundamental Cloud Security

This chapter introduces terms and concepts that address basic information security within clouds, and then concludes by defining a set of threats and attacks common to public cloud environments. The cloud security mechanisms covered in Chapter 10 establish the security controls used to counter these threats.

6.1 Basic Terms and Concepts

Information security is a complex ensemble of techniques, technologies, regulations, and behaviors that collaboratively protect the integrity of and access to computer systems and data. IT security measures aim to defend against threats and interference that arise from both malicious intent and unintentional user error.

The upcoming sections define fundamental security terms relevant to cloud computing and describe associated concepts.

Confidentiality

Confidentiality is the characteristic of something being made accessible only to authorized parties (Figure 6.1). Within cloud environments, confidentiality primarily pertains to restricting access to data in transit and storage.

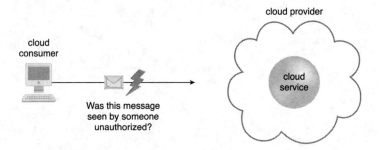

Figure 6.1

The message issued by the cloud consumer to the cloud service is considered confidential only if it is not accessed or read by an unauthorized party.

Integrity

Integrity is the characteristic of not having been altered by an unauthorized party (Figure 6.2). An important issue that concerns data integrity in the cloud is whether a cloud consumer can be guaranteed that the data it transmits to a cloud service matches the data received by that cloud service. Integrity can extend to how data is stored, processed, and retrieved by cloud services and cloud-based IT resources.

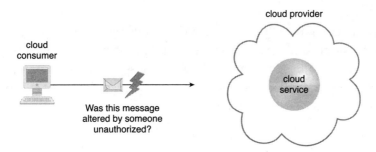

Figure 6.2

The message issued by the cloud consumer to the cloud service is considered to have integrity if it has not been altered.

Authenticity

Authenticity is the characteristic of something having been provided by an authorized source. This concept encompasses non-repudiation, which is the inability of a party to deny or challenge the authentication of an interaction. Authentication in non-repudiable interactions provides proof that these interactions are uniquely linked to an authorized source. For example, a user may not be able to access a non-repudiable file after its receipt without also generating a record of this access.

Availability

Availability is the characteristic of being accessible and usable during a specified time period. In typical cloud environments, the availability of cloud services can be a responsibility that is shared by the cloud provider and the cloud carrier. The availability of a cloud-based solution that extends to cloud service consumers is further shared by the cloud consumer.

Threat

A *threat* is a potential security violation that can challenge defenses in an attempt to breach privacy and/or cause harm. Both manually and automatically instigated threats are designed to exploit known weaknesses, also referred to as vulnerabilities. A threat that is carried out results in an *attack*.

Vulnerability

A *vulnerability* is a weakness that can be exploited either because it is protected by insufficient security controls, or because existing security controls are overcome by an attack. IT resource vulnerabilities can have a range of causes, including configuration deficiencies, security policy weaknesses, user errors, hardware or firmware flaws, software bugs, and poor security architecture.

Risk

Risk is the possibility of loss or harm arising from performing an activity. Risk is typically measured according to its threat level and the number of possible or known vulnerabilities. Two metrics that can be used to determine risk for an IT resource are:

- the probability of a threat occurring to exploit vulnerabilities in the IT resource

- the expectation of loss upon the IT resource being compromised

Details regarding risk management are covered later in this chapter.

Security Controls

Security controls are countermeasures used to prevent or respond to security threats and to reduce or avoid risk. Details on how to use security countermeasures are typically outlined in the security policy, which contains a set of rules and practices specifying how to implement a system, service, or security plan for maximum protection of sensitive and critical IT resources.

Security Mechanisms

Countermeasures are typically described in terms of security mechanisms, which are components comprising a defensive framework that protects IT resources, information, and services.

Security Policies

A security policy establishes a set of security rules and regulations. Often, security policies will further define how these rules and regulations are implemented and enforced. For example, the positioning and usage of security controls and mechanisms can be determined by security policies.

SUMMARY OF KEY POINTS

- Confidentiality, integrity, authenticity, and availability are characteristics that can be associated with measuring security.
- Threats, vulnerabilities, and risks are associated with measuring and assessing insecurity, or the lack of security.
- Security controls, mechanisms, and policies are associated with establishing countermeasures and safeguards in support of improving security.

6.2 Threat Agents

A *threat agent* is an entity that poses a threat because it is capable of carrying out an attack. Cloud security threats can originate either internally or externally, from humans or software programs. Corresponding threat agents are described in the upcoming sections. Figure 6.3 illustrates the role a threat agent assumes in relation to vulnerabilities, threats, and risks, and the safeguards established by security policies and security mechanisms.

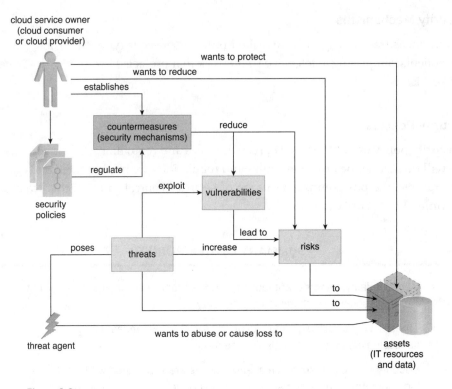

Figure 6.3

How security policies and security mechanisms are used to counter threats, vulnerabilities, and risks caused by threat agents.

Anonymous Attacker

An *anonymous attacker* is a non-trusted cloud service consumer without permissions in the cloud (Figure 6.4). It typically exists as an external software program that launches network-level attacks through public networks. When anonymous attackers have limited information on security policies and defenses, it can inhibit their ability to formulate effective attacks. Therefore, anonymous attackers often resort to committing acts like bypassing user accounts or stealing user credentials, while using methods that either ensure anonymity or require substantial resources for prosecution.

Figure 6.4

The notation used for an anonymous attacker.

Malicious Service Agent

A *malicious service agent* is able to intercept and forward the network traffic that flows within a cloud (Figure 6.5). It typically exists as a service agent (or a program pretending to be a service agent) with compromised or malicious logic. It may also exist as an external program able to remotely intercept and potentially corrupt message contents.

Figure 6.5
The notation used for a malicious service agent.

Trusted Attacker

A *trusted attacker* shares IT resources in the same cloud environment as the cloud consumer and attempts to exploit legitimate credentials to target cloud providers and the cloud tenants with whom they share IT resources (Figure 6.6). Unlike anonymous attackers (which are non-trusted), trusted attackers usually launch their attacks from within a cloud's trust boundaries by abusing legitimate credentials or via the appropriation of sensitive and confidential information.

Figure 6.6
The notation that is used for a trusted attacker.

Trusted attackers (also known as *malicious tenants*) can use cloud-based IT resources for a wide range of exploitations, including the hacking of weak authentication processes, the breaking of encryption, the spamming of e-mail accounts, or to launch common attacks, such as denial of service campaigns.

Malicious Insider

Malicious insiders are human threat agents acting on behalf of or in relation to the cloud provider. They are typically current or former employees or third parties with access to the cloud provider's premises. This type of threat agent carries tremendous damage potential, as the malicious insider may have administrative privileges for accessing cloud consumer IT resources.

NOTE

A notation used to represent a general form of human-driven attack is the workstation combined with a lightning bolt (Figure 6.7). This generic symbol does not imply a specific threat agent, only that an attack was initiated via a workstation.

Figure 6.7
The notation used for an attack originating from a workstation. The human symbol is optional.

SUMMARY OF KEY POINTS

- An anonymous attacker is a non-trusted threat agent that usually attempts attacks from outside of a cloud's boundary.

- A malicious service agent intercepts network communication in an attempt to maliciously use or augment the data.

- A trusted attacker exists as an authorized cloud service consumer with legitimate credentials that it uses to exploit access to cloud-based IT resources.

- A malicious insider is a human that attempts to abuse access privileges to cloud premises.

6.3 Cloud Security Threats

This section introduces several common threats and vulnerabilities in cloud-based environments and describes the roles of the aforementioned threat agents. Security mechanisms that are used to counter these threats are covered in Chapter 10.

Traffic Eavesdropping

Traffic eavesdropping occurs when data being transferred to or within a cloud (usually from the cloud consumer to the cloud provider) is passively intercepted by a malicious service agent for illegitimate information gathering purposes (Figure 6.8). The aim of this attack is to directly compromise the confidentiality of the data and, possibly, the confidentiality of the relationship between the cloud consumer and cloud provider. Because of the passive nature of the attack, it can more easily go undetected for extended periods of time.

Malicious Intermediary

The *malicious intermediary* threat arises when messages are intercepted and altered by a malicious service agent, thereby potentially compromising the message's confidentiality and/or integrity. It may also insert harmful data into the message before forwarding it to its destination. Figure 6.9 illustrates a common example of the malicious intermediary attack.

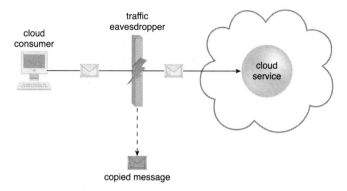

Figure 6.8

An externally positioned malicious service agent carries out a traffic
eavesdropping attack by intercepting a message sent by the cloud service
consumer to the cloud service. The service agent makes an unauthorized copy
of the message before it is sent along its original path to the cloud service.

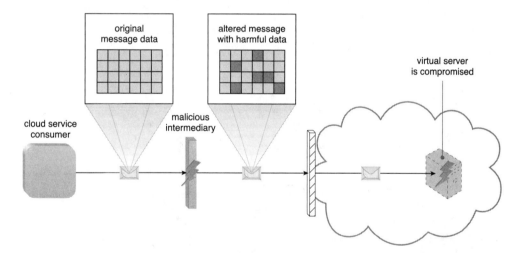

Figure 6.9

The malicious service agent intercepts and modifies a message sent by a cloud service consumer to a cloud service
(not shown) being hosted on a virtual server. Because harmful data is packaged into the message, the virtual server is
compromised.

NOTE

While not as common, the malicious intermediary attack can also be carried out by a malicious cloud service consumer program.

Denial of Service

The objective of the denial of service (DoS) attack is to overload IT resources to the point where they cannot function properly. This form of attack is commonly launched in one of the following ways:

- The workload on cloud services is artificially increased with imitation messages or repeated communication requests.

- The network is overloaded with traffic to reduce its responsiveness and cripple its performance.

- Multiple cloud service requests are sent, each of which is designed to consume excessive memory and processing resources.

Successful DoS attacks produce server degradation and/or failure, as illustrated in Figure 6.10.

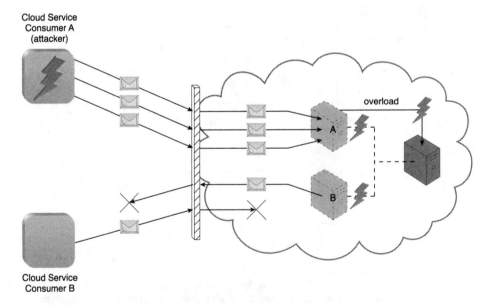

Figure 6.10
Cloud Service Consumer A sends multiple messages to a cloud service (not shown) hosted on Virtual Server A. This overloads the capacity of the underlying physical server, which causes outages with Virtual Servers A and B. As a result, legitimate cloud service consumers, such as Cloud Service Consumer B, become unable to communicate with any cloud services hosted on Virtual Servers A and B.

Insufficient Authorization

The insufficient authorization attack occurs when access is granted to an attacker erroneously or too broadly, resulting in the attacker getting access to IT resources that are normally protected. This is often a result of the attacker gaining direct access to IT resources that were implemented under the assumption that they would only be accessed by trusted consumer programs (Figure 6.11).

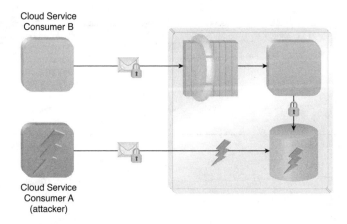

Figure 6.11

Cloud Service Consumer A gains access to a database that was implemented under the assumption that it would only be accessed through a Web service with a published service contract (as per Cloud Service Consumer B).

A variation of this attack, known as *weak authentication*, can result when weak passwords or shared accounts are used to protect IT resources. Within cloud environments, these types of attacks can lead to significant impacts depending on the range of IT resources and the range of access to those IT resources the attacker gains (Figure 6.12).

Virtualization Attack

Virtualization provides multiple cloud consumers with access to IT resources that share underlying hardware but are logically isolated from each other. Because cloud providers grant cloud consumers administrative access to virtualized IT resources (such as virtual servers), there is an inherent risk that cloud consumers could abuse this access to attack the underlying physical IT resources.

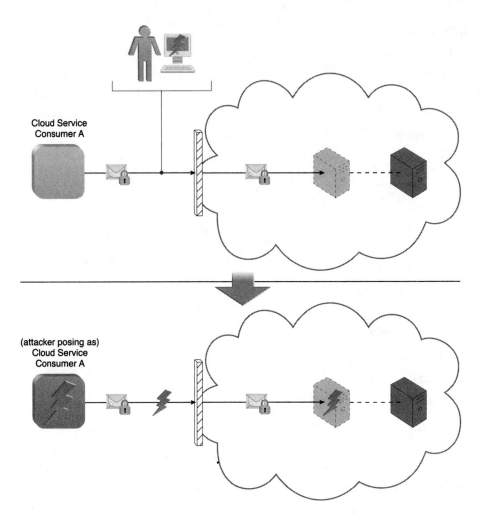

Figure 6.12

An attacker has cracked a weak password used by Cloud Service Consumer A. As a result, a malicious
cloud service consumer (owned by the attacker) is designed to pose as Cloud Service Consumer A in order to
gain access to the cloud-based virtual server.

A *virtualization attack* exploits vulnerabilities in the virtualization platform to jeopardize its confidentiality, integrity, and/or availability. This threat is illustrated in Figure 6.13, where a trusted attacker successfully accesses a virtual server to compromise its underlying physical server. With public clouds, where a single physical IT resource may be providing virtualized IT resources to multiple cloud consumers, such an attack can have significant repercussions.

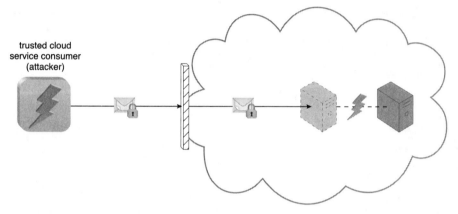

Figure 6.13

An authorized cloud service consumer carries out a virtualization attack by abusing its administrative access to a virtual server to exploit the underlying hardware.

Overlapping Trust Boundaries

If physical IT resources within a cloud are shared by different cloud service consumers, these cloud service consumers have overlapping trust boundaries. Malicious cloud service consumers can target shared IT resources with the intention of compromising cloud consumers or other IT resources that share the same trust boundary. The consequence is that some or all of the other cloud service consumers could be impacted by the attack and/or the attacker could use virtual IT resources against others that happen to also share the same trust boundary.

Figure 6.14 illustrates an example in which two cloud service consumers share virtual servers hosted by the same physical server and, resultantly, their respective trust boundaries overlap.

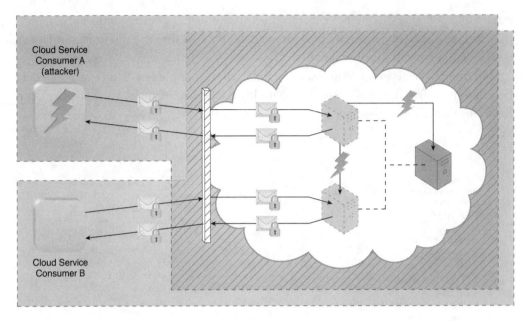

Figure 6.14

Cloud Service Consumer A is trusted by the cloud and therefore gains access to a virtual server, which it then attacks with the intention of attacking the underlying physical server and the virtual server used by Cloud Service Consumer B.

SUMMARY OF KEY POINTS

- Traffic eavesdropping and malicious intermediary attacks are usually carried out by malicious service agents that intercept network traffic.

- A denial of service attack occurs when a targeted IT resource is overloaded with requests in an attempt to cripple or render it unavailable. The insufficient authorization attack occurs when access is granted to an attacker erroneously or too broadly, or when weak passwords are used.

- A virtualization attack exploits vulnerabilities within virtualized environments to gain unauthorized access to underlying physical hardware. Overlapping trust boundaries represent a threat whereby attackers can exploit cloud-based IT resources shared by multiple cloud consumers.

6.4 Additional Considerations

This section provides a diverse checklist of issues and guidelines that relate to cloud security. The listed considerations are in no particular order.

Flawed Implementations

The substandard design, implementation, or configuration of cloud service deployments can have undesirable consequences, beyond runtime exceptions and failures. If the cloud provider's software and/or hardware have inherent security flaws or operational weaknesses, attackers can exploit these vulnerabilities to impair the integrity, confidentiality, and/or availability of cloud provider IT resources and cloud consumer IT resources hosted by the cloud provider.

Figure 6.15 depicts a poorly implemented cloud service that results in a server shutdown. Although in this scenario the flaw is exposed accidentally by a legitimate cloud service consumer, it could have easily been discovered and exploited by an attacker.

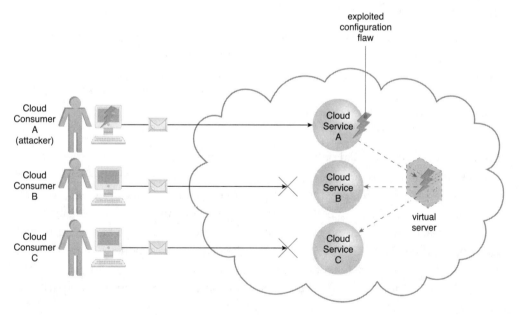

Figure 6.15

Cloud Service Consumer A's message triggers a configuration flaw in Cloud Service A, which in turn causes the virtual server that is also hosting Cloud Services B and C to crash.

Security Policy Disparity

When a cloud consumer places IT resources with a public cloud provider, it may need to accept that its traditional information security approach may not be identical or even similar to that of the cloud provider. This incompatibility needs to be assessed to ensure that any data or other IT assets being relocated to a public cloud are adequately protected. Even when leasing raw infrastructure-based IT resources, the cloud consumer may not be granted sufficient administrative control or influence over security policies that apply to the IT resources leased from the cloud provider. This is primarily because those IT resources are still legally owned by the cloud provider and continue to fall under its responsibility.

Furthermore, with some public clouds, additional third parties, such as security brokers and certificate authorities, may introduce their own distinct set of security policies and practices, further complicating any attempts to standardize the protection of cloud consumer assets.

Contracts

Cloud consumers need to carefully examine contracts and SLAs put forth by cloud providers to ensure that security policies, and other relevant guarantees, are satisfactory when it comes to asset security. There needs to be clear language that indicates the amount of liability assumed by the cloud provider and/or the level of indemnity the cloud provider may ask for. The greater the assumed liability by the cloud provider, the lower the risk to the cloud consumer.

Another aspect to contractual obligations is where the lines are drawn between cloud consumer and cloud provider assets. A cloud consumer that deploys its own solution upon infrastructure supplied by the cloud provider will produce a technology architecture comprised of artifacts owned by both the cloud consumer and cloud provider. If a security breach (or other type of runtime failure) occurs, how is blame determined? Furthermore, if the cloud consumer can apply its own security policies to its solution, but the cloud provider insists that its supporting infrastructure be governed by different (and perhaps incompatible) security policies, how can the resulting disparity be overcome?

Sometimes the best solution is to look for a different cloud provider with more compatible contractual terms.

Risk Management

When assessing the potential impacts and challenges pertaining to cloud adoption, cloud consumers are encouraged to perform a formal risk assessment as part of a risk management strategy. A cyclically executed process used to enhance strategic and tactical security, risk management is comprised of a set of coordinated activities for overseeing and controlling risks. The main activities are generally defined as risk assessment, risk treatment, and risk control (Figure 6.16).

- *Risk Assessment* – In the risk assessment stage, the cloud environment is analyzed to identify potential vulnerabilities and shortcomings that threats can exploit. The cloud provider can be asked to produce statistics and other information about past attacks (successful and unsuccessful) carried out in its cloud. The identified risks are quantified and qualified according to the probability of occurrence and the degree of impact in relation to how the cloud consumer plans to utilize cloud-based IT resources.

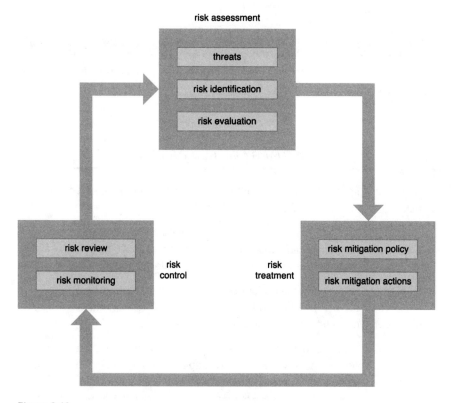

Figure 6.16

The on-going risk management process, which can be initiated from any of the three stages.

- *Risk Treatment* – Mitigation policies and plans are designed during the risk treat-ment stage with the intent of successfully treating the risks that were discovered during risk assessment. Some risks can be eliminated, others can be mitigated, while others can be dealt with via outsourcing or even incorporated into the insur-ance and/or operating loss budgets. The cloud provider itself may agree to assume responsibility as part of its contractual obligations.

- *Risk Control* – The risk control stage is related to risk monitoring, a three-step process that is comprised of surveying related events, reviewing these events to determine the effectiveness of previous assessments and treatments, and identi-fying any policy adjustment needs. Depending on the nature of the monitoring required, this stage may be carried out or shared by the cloud provider.

The threat agents and cloud security threats covered in this chapter (as well as others that may surface) can be identified and documented as part of the risk assessment stage. The cloud security mechanisms covered in Chapter 10 can be documented and refer-enced as part of the corresponding risk treatment.

NOTE

Appendix E provides an overview of a formal risk management framework for cloud computing from NIST.

SUMMARY OF KEY POINTS

- Cloud consumers need to be aware that they may be introducing security risks by deploying flawed cloud-based solutions.

- An understanding of how a cloud provider defines and imposes proprietary, and possibly incompatible, cloud security policies is a critical part of forming assessment criteria when choosing a cloud provider vendor.

- Liability, indemnity, and blame for potential security breaches need to be clearly defined and mutually understood in the legal agreements signed by cloud consumers and cloud providers.

- It is important for cloud consumers, subsequent to gaining an understand-ing of the potential security-related issues specific to a given cloud environ-ment, to perform a corresponding assessment of the identified risks.

6.5 CASE STUDY EXAMPLE

Based on an assessment of its internal applications, ATN analysts identify a set of risks. One such risk is associated with the myTrendek application that was adopted from OTC, a company ATN recently acquired. This application includes a feature that analyzes telephone and Internet usage, and enables a multi-user mode that grants varying access rights. Administrators, supervisors, auditors, and regular users can therefore be assigned different privileges. The application's user-base encompasses internal users and external users, such as business partners and contractors.

The myTrendek application poses a number of security challenges pertaining to usage by internal staff:

- authentication does not require or enforce complex passwords

- communication with the application is not encrypted

- European regulations (ETelReg) require that certain types of data collected by the application be deleted after six months

ATN is planning to migrate this application to a cloud via a PaaS environment, but the weak authentication threat and the lack of confidentiality supported by the application make them reconsider. A subsequent risk assessment further reveals that if the application is migrated to a PaaS environment hosted by a cloud that resides outside of Europe, local regulations may be in conflict with ETelReg. Given that the cloud provider is not concerned with ETelReg compliance, this could easily result in monetary penalties being assessed to ATN. Based on the results of the risk assessment, ATN decides not to proceed with its cloud migration plan.

Part II

Cloud Computing Mechanisms

Technology mechanisms represent well-defined IT artifacts that are established within the IT industry and commonly distinct to a certain computing model or platform. The technology-centric nature of cloud computing requires the establishment of a formal set of mechanisms that act as building blocks for the exploration of cloud technology architectures.

The chapters in this part of the book define 20 common cloud computing mechanisms that can be combined in different and alternative variations. This collection of mechanisms is not exhaustive. There are many more possible mechanism definitions that can be added.

These mechanisms are referenced throughout the numerous architectural models covered in *Part III: Cloud Computing Architecture*.

Chapter 7

Cloud Infrastructure Mechanisms

Cloud infrastructure mechanisms are foundational building blocks of cloud environments that establish primary artifacts to form the basis of fundamental cloud technology architecture.

The following cloud infrastructure mechanisms are described in this chapter:

- Logical Network Perimeter
- Virtual Server
- Cloud Storage Device
- Cloud Usage Monitor
- Resource Replication
- Ready-Made Environment

Not all of these mechanisms are necessarily broad-reaching, nor does each establish an individual architectural layer. Instead, they should be viewed as core components that are common to cloud platforms.

7.1 Logical Network Perimeter

Defined as the isolation of a network environment from the rest of a communications network, the *logical network perimeter* establishes a virtual network boundary that can encompass and isolate a group of related cloud-based IT resources that may be physically distributed (Figure 7.1).

This mechanism can be implemented to:

- isolate IT resources in a cloud from non-authorized users
- isolate IT resources in a cloud from non-users
- isolate IT resources in a cloud from cloud consumers
- control the bandwidth that is available to isolated IT resources

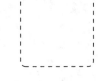

Figure 7.1

The dashed line notation used to indicate the boundary of a logical network perimeter.

Logical network perimeters are typically established via network devices that supply and control the connectivity of a data center and are commonly deployed as virtualized IT environments that include:

- *Virtual Firewall* – An IT resource that actively filters network traffic to and from the isolated network while controlling its interactions with the Internet.

- *Virtual Network* – Usually acquired through VLANs, this IT resource isolates the network environment within the data center infrastructure.

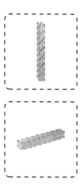

Figure 7.2 introduces the notation used to denote these two IT resources. Figure 7.3 depicts a scenario in which one logical network perimeter contains a cloud consumer's on-premise environment, while another contains a cloud provider's cloud-based environment. These perimeters are connected through a VPN that protects communications, since the VPN is typically implemented by point-to-point encryption of the data packets sent between the communicating endpoints.

Figure 7.2

The symbols used to represent a virtual firewall (top) and a virtual network (bottom).

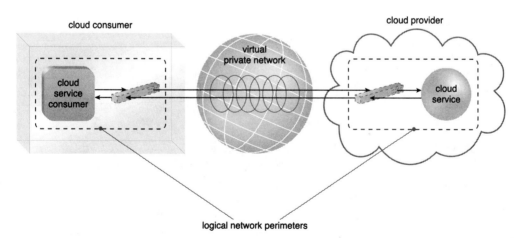

Figure 7.3

Two logical network perimeters surround the cloud consumer and cloud provider environments.

CASE STUDY EXAMPLE

DTGOV has virtualized its network infrastructure to produce a logical network layout favoring network segmentation and isolation. Figure 7.4 depicts the logical network perimeter implemented at each DTGOV data center, as follows:

- The routers that connect to the Internet and extranet are networked to external firewalls, which provide network control and protection to the furthest external network boundaries using virtual networks that logically abstract the external network and extranet perimeters. Devices connected to these network perimeters are loosely isolated and protected from external users. No cloud consumer IT resources are available within these perimeters.

- A logical network perimeter classified as a demilitarized zone (DMZ) is established between the external firewalls and its own firewalls. The DMZ is abstracted as a virtual network hosting the proxy servers (not shown in Figure 7.3) that intermediate access to commonly used network services (DNS, e-mail, Web portal), as well as Web servers with external management functions.

- The network traffic leaving the proxy servers passes through a set of management firewalls that isolate the management network perimeter, which hosts the servers providing the bulk of the management services that cloud consumers can externally access. These services are provided in direct support of self-service and on-demand allocation of cloud-based IT resources.

- All of the traffic to cloud-based IT resources flows through the DMZ to the cloud service firewalls that isolate every cloud consumer's perimeter network, which is abstracted by a virtual network that is also isolated from other networks.

- Both the management perimeter and isolated virtual networks are connected to the intra-data center firewalls, which regulate the network traffic to and from the other DTGOV data centers that are also connected to intra-data center routers at the intra-data center network perimeter.

The virtual firewalls are allocated to and controlled by a single cloud consumer in order to regulate its virtual IT resource traffic. These IT resources are connected through a virtual network that is isolated from other cloud consumers. The virtual firewall and the isolated virtual network jointly form the cloud consumer's logical network perimeter.

Figure 7.4

A logical network layout is established through a set of logical network perimeters using various firewalls and virtual networks.

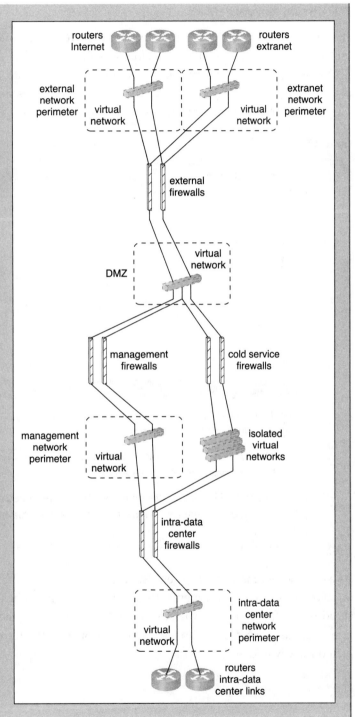

7.2 Virtual Server

A *virtual server* is a form of virtualization software that emulates a physical server. Virtual servers are used by cloud providers to share the same physical server with multiple cloud consumers by providing cloud consumers with individual virtual server instances. Figure 7.5 shows three virtual servers being hosted by two physical servers. The number of instances a given physical server can share is limited by its capacity.

Figure 7.5

The first physical server hosts two virtual servers, while the second physical server hosts one virtual server.

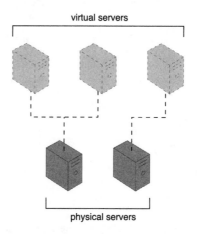

virtual servers

physical servers

NOTE
• The terms virtual server and virtual machine (VM) are used synonymously throughout this book.
• The hypervisor mechanism referenced in this chapter is described in the *Hypervisor* section in Chapter 8.
• The virtual infrastructure manager (VIM) referenced in this chapter is described in Chapter 9 as part of the *Resource Management System* section.

As a commodity mechanism, the virtual server represents the most foundational building block of cloud environments. Each virtual server can host numerous IT resources, cloud-based solutions, and various other cloud computing mechanisms. The instantiation of virtual servers from image files is a resource allocation process that can be completed rapidly and on-demand.

Cloud consumers that install or lease virtual servers can customize their environments independently from other cloud consumers that may be using virtual servers hosted by the same underlying physical server. Figure 7.6 depicts a virtual server that hosts a cloud service being accessed by Cloud Service Consumer B, while Cloud Service Consumer A accesses the virtual server directly to perform an administration task.

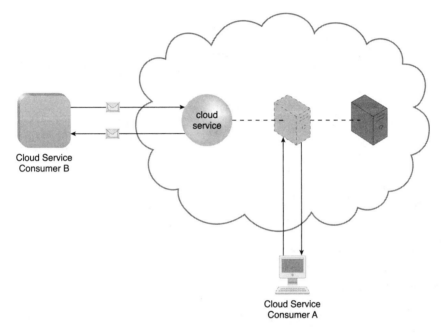

Figure 7.6

A virtual server hosts an active cloud service and is further accessed by a cloud consumer for administrative purposes.

CASE STUDY EXAMPLE

DTGOV's IaaS environment contains hosted virtual servers that were instantiated on physical servers running the same hypervisor software that controls the virtual servers. Their VIM is used to coordinate the physical servers in relation to the creation of virtual server instances. This approach is used at each data center to apply a uniform implementation of the virtualization layer.

Figure 7.7 depicts several virtual servers running over physical servers, all of which are jointly controlled by a central VIM.

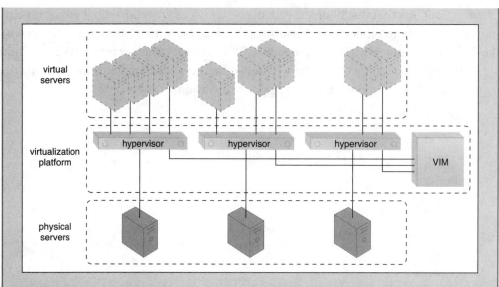

Figure 7.7
Virtual servers are created via the physical servers' hypervisors and a central VIM.

In order to enable the on-demand creation of virtual servers, DTGOV provides cloud consumers with a set of template virtual servers that are made available through pre-made VM images.

These VM images are files that represent the virtual disk images used by the hypervisor to boot the virtual server. DTGOV enables the template virtual servers to have various initial configuration options that differ, based on operating system, drivers, and management tools being used. Some template virtual servers also have additional, pre-installed application server software.

The following virtual server packages are offered to DTGOV's cloud consumers. Each package has different pre-defined performance configurations and limitations:

- *Small Virtual Server Instance* – 1 virtual processor core, 4 GB of virtual RAM, 20 GB of storage space in the root file system

- *Medium Virtual Server Instance* – 2 virtual processor cores, 8 GB of virtual RAM, 20 GB of storage space in the root file system

- *Large Virtual Server Instance* – 8 virtual processor cores, 16 GB of virtual RAM, 20 GB of storage space in the root file system

- *Memory Large Virtual Server Instance* – 8 virtual processor cores, 64 GB of virtual RAM, 20 GB of storage space in the root file system

- *Processor Large Virtual Server Instance* – 32 virtual processor cores, 16 GB of virtual RAM, 20 GB of storage space in the root file system

- *Ultra-Large Virtual Server Instance* – 128 virtual processor cores, 512 GB of virtual RAM, 40 GB of storage space in the root file system

Additional storage capacity can be added to a virtual server by attaching a virtual disk from a cloud storage device. All of the template virtual machine images are stored on a common cloud storage device that is accessible only through the cloud consumers' management tools that are used to control the deployed IT resources. Once a new virtual server needs to be instantiated, the cloud consumer can choose the most suitable virtual server template from the list of available configurations. A copy of the virtual machine image is made and allocated to the cloud consumer, who can then assume the administrative responsibilities.

The allocated VM image is updated whenever the cloud consumer customizes the virtual server. After the cloud consumer initiates the virtual server, the allocated VM image and its associated performance profile is passed to the VIM, which creates the virtual server instance from the appropriate physical server.

DTGOV uses the process described in Figure 7.8 to support the creation and management of virtual servers that have different initial software configurations and performance characteristics.

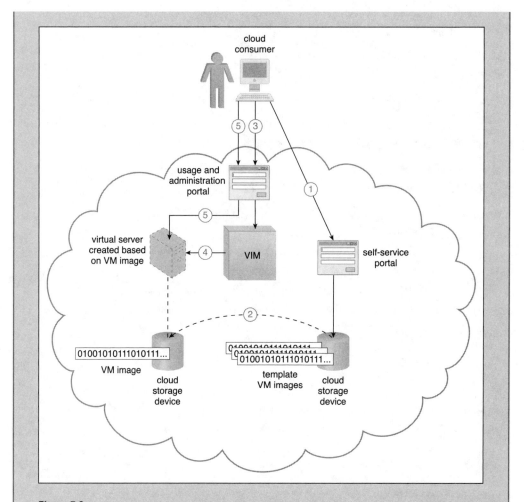

Figure 7.8

The cloud consumer uses the self-service portal to select a template virtual server for creation (1). A copy of the corresponding VM image is created in a cloud consumer-controlled cloud storage device (2). The cloud consumer initiates the virtual server using the usage and administration portal (3), which interacts with the VIM to create the virtual server instance via the underlying hardware (4). The cloud consumer is able to use and customize the virtual server via other features on the usage and administration portal (5). (Note that the self-service portal and usage and administration portal are explained in Chapter 9.)

7.3 Cloud Storage Device

The *cloud storage device* mechanism represents storage devices that are designed specifically for cloud-based provisioning. Instances of these devices can be virtualized, similar to how physical servers can spawn virtual server images. Cloud storage devices are commonly able to provide fixed-increment capacity allocation in support of the pay-per-use mechanism. Cloud storage devices can be exposed for remote access via cloud storage services.

NOTE

This is a parent mechanism that represents cloud storage devices in general. There are numerous specialized cloud storage devices, several of which are described in the architectural models covered in Part III of this book.

A primary concern related to cloud storage is the security, integrity, and confidentiality of data, which becomes more prone to being compromised when entrusted to external cloud providers and other third parties. There can also be legal and regulatory implications that result from relocating data across geographical or national boundaries. Another issue applies specifically to the performance of large databases. LANs provide locally stored data with network reliability and latency levels that are superior to those of WANs.

Cloud Storage Levels

Cloud storage device mechanisms provide common logical units of data storage, such as:

- *Files* – Collections of data are grouped into files that are located in folders.
- *Blocks* – The lowest level of storage and the closest to the hardware, a block is the smallest unit of data that is still individually accessible.
- *Datasets* – Sets of data are organized into a table-based, delimited, or record format.
- *Objects* – Data and its associated metadata are organized as Web-based resources.

Each of these data storage levels is commonly associated with a certain type of technical interface which corresponds to a particular type of cloud storage device and cloud storage service used to expose its API (Figure 7.9).

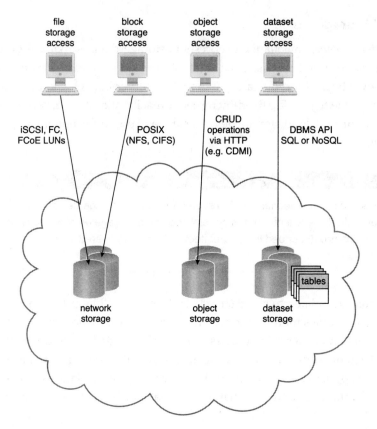

Figure 7.9

Different cloud service consumers utilize different technologies to interface with virtualized cloud storage devices. (Adapted from the CDMI Cloud Storage Reference Model.)

Network Storage Interfaces

Legacy network storage most commonly falls under the category of network storage interfaces. It includes storage devices in compliance with industry standard protocols, such as SCSI for storage blocks and the server message block (SMB), common Internet file system (CIFS), and network file system (NFS) for file and network storage. File storage entails storing individual data in separate files that can be different sizes and formats and organized into folders and subfolders. Original files are often replaced by the new files that are created when data has been modified.

When a cloud storage device mechanism is based on this type of interface, its data searching and extraction performance will tend to be suboptimal. Storage processing levels and thresholds for file allocation are usually determined by the file system itself.

Block storage requires data to be in a fixed format (known as a *data block*), which is the smallest unit that can be stored and accessed and the storage format closest to hardware. Using either the logical unit number (LUN) or virtual volume block-level storage will typically have better performance than file-level storage.

Object Storage Interfaces

Various types of data can be referenced and stored as Web resources. This is referred to as object storage, which is based on technologies that can support a range of data and media types. Cloud Storage Device mechanisms that implement this interface can typically be accessed via REST or Web service-based cloud services using HTTP as the prime protocol. The Storage Networking Industry Association's Cloud Data Management Interface (SNIA's CDMI) supports the use of object storage interfaces.

Database Storage Interfaces

Cloud storage device mechanisms based on database storage interfaces typically support a query language in addition to basic storage operations. Storage management is carried out using a standard API or an administrative user-interface.

This classification of storage interface is divided into two main categories according to storage structure, as follows.

Relational Data Storage

Traditionally, many on-premise IT environments store data using relational databases or relational database management systems (RDBMSs). Relational databases (or relational storage devices) rely on tables to organize similar data into rows and columns. Tables can have relationships with each other to give the data increased structure, to protect data integrity, and to avoid data redundancy (which is referred to as data normalization). Working with relational storage commonly involves the use of the industry standard Structured Query Language (SQL).

A cloud storage device mechanism implemented using relational data storage could be based on any number of commercially available database products, such as IBM DB2, Oracle Database, Microsoft SQL Server, and MySQL.

Challenges with cloud-based relational databases commonly pertain to scaling and performance. Scaling a relational cloud storage device vertically can be more complex and cost-ineffective than horizontal scaling. Databases with complex relationships and/ or containing large volumes of data can be afflicted with higher processing overhead and latency, especially when accessed remotely via cloud services.

Non-Relational Data Storage

Non-relational storage (also commonly referred to as *NoSQL* storage) moves away from the traditional relational database model in that it establishes a "looser" structure for stored data with less emphasis on defining relationships and realizing data normalization. The primary motivation for using non-relational storage is to avoid the potential complexity and processing overhead that can be imposed by relational databases. Also, non-relational storage can be more horizontally scalable than relational storage.

The trade-off with non-relational storage is that the data loses much of the native form and validation due to limited or primitive schemas or data models. Furthermore, non-relational repositories don't tend to support relational database functions, such as transactions or joins.

Normalized data exported into a non-relational storage repository will usually become denormalized, meaning that the size of the data will typically grow. An extent of normalization can be preserved, but usually not for complex relationships. Cloud providers often offer non-relational storage that provides scalability and availability of stored data over multiple server environments. However, many non-relational storage mechanisms are proprietary and therefore can severely limit data portability.

CASE STUDY EXAMPLE

DTGOV provides cloud consumers access to a cloud storage device based on an object storage interface. The cloud service that exposes this API offers basic functions on stored objects, such as search, create, delete, and update. The search function uses a hierarchical object arrangement that resembles a file system. DTGOV further offers a cloud service that is used exclusively with virtual servers and enables the creation of cloud storage devices via a block storage network interface. Both cloud services use APIs that are compliant with SNIA's CDMI v1.0.

The object-based cloud storage device has an underlying storage system with variable storage capacity, which is directly controlled by a software component that also exposes the interface. This software enables the creation of isolated cloud storage devices that are allocated to cloud consumers. The storage system uses a security credential management system to administer user-based access control to the device's data objects (Figure 7.10).

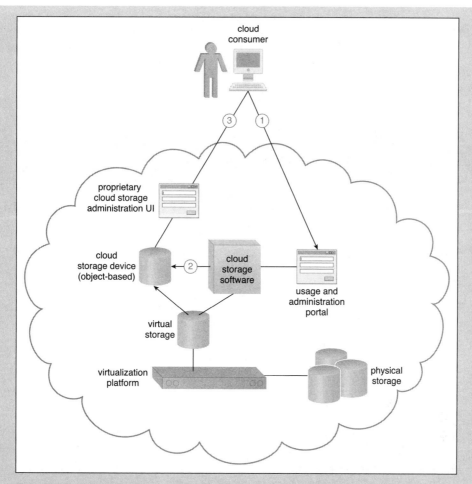

Figure 7.10

The cloud consumer interacts with the usage and administration portal to create a cloud storage device and define access control policies (1). The usage and administration portal interact with the cloud storage software to create the cloud storage device instance and apply the required access policy to its data objects (2). Each data object is assigned to a cloud storage device and all of the data objects are stored in the same virtual storage volume. The cloud consumer uses the proprietary cloud storage device UI to interact directly with the data objects (3). (Note that the usage and administration portal is explained in Chapter 9.)

Access control is granted on a per-object basis and uses separate access policies for creating, reading from, and writing to each data object. Public access permissions are allowed, although they are read-only. Access groups are formed by nominated users that must be previously registered via the credential management system. Data objects can be accessed from both Web applications and Web service interfaces, which are implemented by the cloud storage software.

The creation of the cloud consumers' block-based cloud storage devices is managed by the virtualization platform, which instantiates the LUN's implementation of the virtual storage (Figure 7.11). The cloud storage device (or the LUN) must be assigned by the VIM to an existing virtual server before it can be used. The capacity of block-based cloud storage devices is expressed by one GB increments. It can be created as fixed storage that cloud consumers can modify administratively or as variable size storage that has an initial 5 GB capacity that automatically increases and decreases by 5 GB increments according to usage demands.

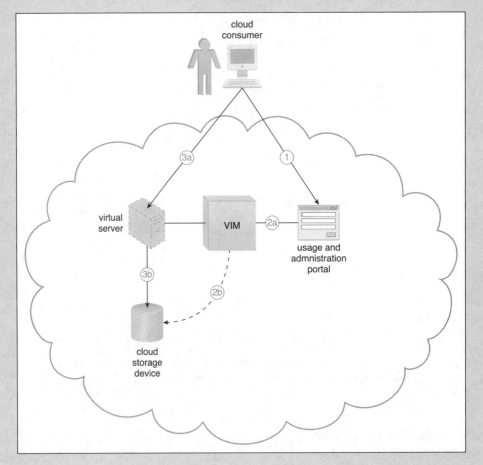

Figure 7.11

The cloud consumer uses the usage and administration portal to create and assign a cloud storage device to an existing virtual server (1). The usage and administration portal interacts with the VIM software (2a), which creates and configures the appropriate LUN (2b). Each cloud storage device uses a separate LUN controlled by the virtualization platform. The cloud consumer remotely logs into the virtual server directly (3a) to access the cloud storage device (3b).

7.4 Cloud Usage Monitor

The *cloud usage monitor* mechanism is a lightweight and autonomous software program responsible for collecting and processing IT resource usage data.

> **NOTE**
>
> This is a parent mechanism that represents a broad range of cloud usage monitors, several of which are established as specialized mechanisms in Chapter 8 and several more of which are described in the cloud architectural models covered in Part III of this book.

Depending on the type of usage metrics they are designed to collect and the manner in which usage data needs to be collected, cloud usage monitors can exist in different formats. The upcoming sections describe three common agent-based implementation formats. Each can be designed to forward collected usage data to a log database for post-processing and reporting purposes.

Monitoring Agent

A *monitoring agent* is an intermediary, event-driven program that exists as a service agent and resides along existing communication paths to transparently monitor and analyze dataflows (Figure 7.12). This type of cloud usage monitor is commonly used to measure network traffic and message metrics.

Resource Agent

A *resource agent* is a processing module that collects usage data by having event-driven interactions with specialized resource software (Figure 7.13). This module is used to monitor usage metrics based on pre-defined, observable events at the resource software level, such as initiating, suspending, resuming, and vertical scaling.

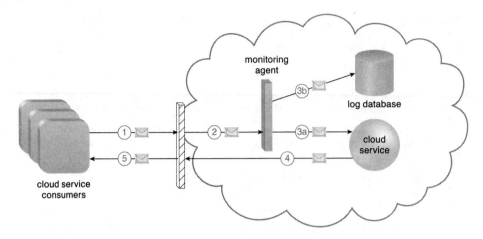

Figure 7.12

A cloud service consumer sends a request message to a cloud service (1). The monitoring agent intercepts the message to collect relevant usage data (2) before allowing it to continue to the cloud service (3a). The monitoring agent stores the collected usage data in a log database (3b). The cloud service replies with a response message (4) that is sent back to the cloud service consumer without being intercepted by the monitoring agent (5).

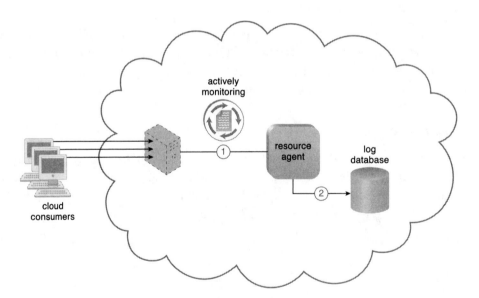

Figure 7.13

The resource agent is actively monitoring a virtual server and detects an increase in usage (1). The resource agent receives a notification from the underlying resource management program that the virtual server is being scaled up and stores the collected usage data in a log database, as per its monitoring metrics (2).

Polling Agent

A *polling agent* is a processing module that collects cloud service usage data by polling IT resources. This type of cloud service monitor is commonly used to periodically monitor IT resource status, such as uptime and downtime (Figure 7.14).

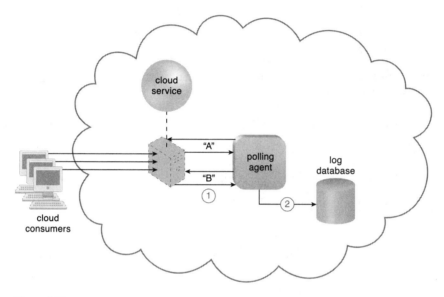

Figure 7.14

A polling agent monitors the status of a cloud service hosted by a virtual server by sending periodic polling request messages and receiving polling response messages that report usage status "A" after a number of polling cycles, until it receives a usage status of "B" (1), upon which the polling agent records the new usage status in the log database (2).

CASE STUDY EXAMPLE

One of the challenges encountered during DTGOV's cloud adoption initiative has been ensuring that their collected usage data is accurate. The resource allocation methods of previous IT outsourcing models had resulted in their clients being billed chargeback fees based on the number of physical servers that was listed in annual leasing contracts, regardless of actual usage.

DTGOV now needs to define a model that allows virtual servers of varying performance levels to be leased and billed hourly. Usage data needs to be at an extremely granular level in order to achieve the necessary degree of accuracy. DTGOV implements a resource agent that relies on the resource usage events generated by the VIM platform to calculate the virtual server usage data.

The resource agent is designed with logic and metrics that are based on the following rules:

1. Each resource usage event that is generated by the VIM software can contain the following data:

   - Event Type (EV_TYPE) – Generated by the VIM platform, there are five types of events:

     VM Starting (creation at the hypervisor)

     VM Started (completion of the boot procedure)

     VM Stopping (shutting down)

     VM Stopped (termination at the hypervisor)

     VM Scaled (change of performance parameters)

   - VM Type (VM_TYPE) – This represents a type of virtual server, as dictated by its performance parameters. A predefined list of possible virtual server configurations provides the parameters that are described by the metadata whenever a VM starts or scales.

   - Unique VM Identifier (VM_ID) – This identifier is provided by the VIM platform.

   - Unique Cloud Consumer Identifier (CS_ID) – Another identifier provided by the VIM platform to represent the cloud consumer.

   - Event Timestamp (EV_T) – An identification of an event occurrence that is expressed in date-time format, with the time zone of the data center and referenced to UTC as defined in RFC 3339 (as per the ISO 8601 profile).

2. Usage measurements are recorded for every virtual server that a cloud consumer creates.

3. Usage measurements are recorded for a measurement period whose length is defined by two timestamps called t_{start} and t_{end}. The start of the measurement period defaults to the beginning of the calendar month (t_{start} = 2012-12-01T00:00:00-08:00) and finishes at the end of the calendar month (t_{end} = 2012-12-31T23:59:59-08:00). Customized measurement periods are also supported.

4. Usage measurements are recorded at each minute of usage. The virtual server usage measurement period starts when the virtual server is created at the hypervisor and stops at its termination.

5. Virtual servers can be started, scaled, and stopped multiple times during the measurement period. The time interval between each occurrence i (i = 1, 2, 3, …) of these pairs of successive events that are declared for a virtual server is called a usage cycle that is known as T_{cycle_i}:

   • VM_Starting, VM_Stopping – VM size is unchanged at the end of the cycle

   • VM_Starting, VM_Scaled – VM size has changed at the end of the cycle

   • VM_Scaled, VM_Scaled – VM size has changed while scaling, at the end of the cycle

   • VM_Scaled, VM_Stopping – VM size has changed at the end of the cycle

6. The total usage, U_{total}, for each virtual server during the measurement period is calculated using the following resource usage event log database equations:

   • For each VM_TYPE and VM_ID in the log database: $U_{total\_VM\_type\_j} = \sum_{t_{start}}^{t_{end}} T_{cycle_i}$

   • As per the total usage time that is measured for each VM_TYPE, the vector of usage for each VM_ID is U_{total}: U_{total} = {type 1, $U_{total\_VM\_type\_1}$, type 2, $U_{total\_VM\_type\_2}$, …}

Figure 7.15 depicts the resource agent interacting with the VIM's event-driven API.

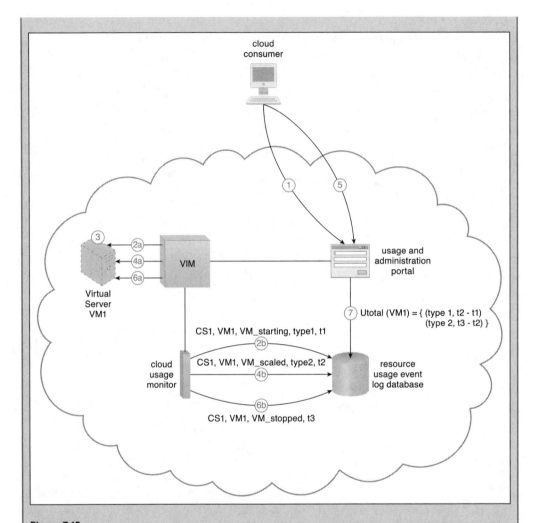

Figure 7.15

The cloud consumer (CS_ID = CS1) requests the creation of a virtual server (VM_ID = VM1) of configuration size *type 1* (VM_TYPE = type1) (1). The VIM creates the virtual server (2a). The VIM's event-driven API generates a resource usage event with timestamp = *t1*, which the cloud usage monitor software agent captures and records in the resource usage event log database (2b). Virtual server usage increases and reaches the auto-scaling threshold (3). The VIM scales up Virtual Server VM1 (4a) from configuration *type 1* to *type 2* (VM_TYPE = type2). The VIM's event-driven API generates a resource usage event with timestamp = *t2*, which is captured and recorded at the resource usage event log database by the cloud usage monitor software agent (4b). The cloud consumer shuts down the virtual server (5). The VIM stops Virtual Server VM1 (6a) and its event-driven API generates a resource usage event with timestamp = *t3*, which the cloud usage monitor software agent captures and records at the log database (6b). The usage and administration portal accesses the log database and calculates the total usage (Utotal) for Virtual Server Utotal VM1 (7).

7.5 Resource Replication

Defined as the creation of multiple instances of the same IT resource, replication is typically performed when an IT resource's availability and performance need to be enhanced. Virtualization technology is used to implement the *resource replication* mechanism to replicate cloud-based IT resources (Figure 7.16).

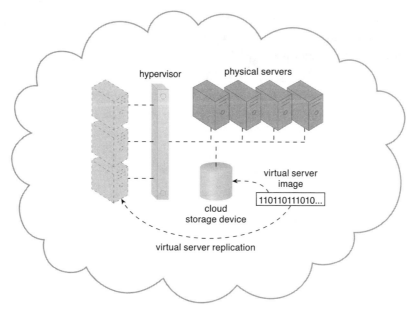

Figure 7.16
The hypervisor replicates several instances of a virtual server, using a stored virtual server image.

NOTE
This is a parent mechanism that represents different types of software programs capable of replicating IT resources. The most common example is the hypervisor mechanism described in Chapter 8. For example, the virtualization platform's hypervisor can access a virtual server image to create several instances, or to deploy and replicate ready-made environments and entire applications. Other common types of replicated IT resources include cloud service implementations and various forms of data and cloud storage device replication.

CASE STUDY EXAMPLE

DTGOV establishes a set of high-availability virtual servers that can be automatically relocated to physical servers running in different data centers in response to severe failure conditions. This is illustrated in the scenario depicted in Figures 7.17 to 7.19, where a virtual server that resides on a physical server running at one data center experiences a failure condition. VIMs from different data centers coordinate to overcome the unavailability by reallocating the virtual server to a different physical server running in another data center.

Figure 7.17

A high-availability virtual server is running in Data Center A. VIM instances in Data Centers A and B are executing a coordination function that allows detection of failure conditions. Stored VM images are replicated between data centers as a result of the high-availability architecture.

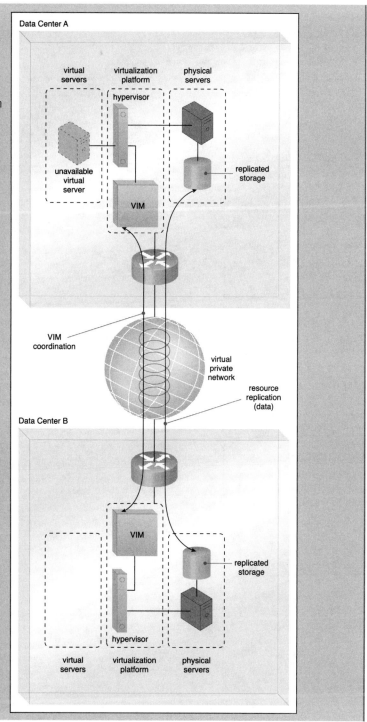

Figure 7.18

The virtual server becomes unavailable in Data Center A. The VIM in Data Center B detects the failure condition and starts to reallocate the high-availability server from Data Center A to Data Center B.

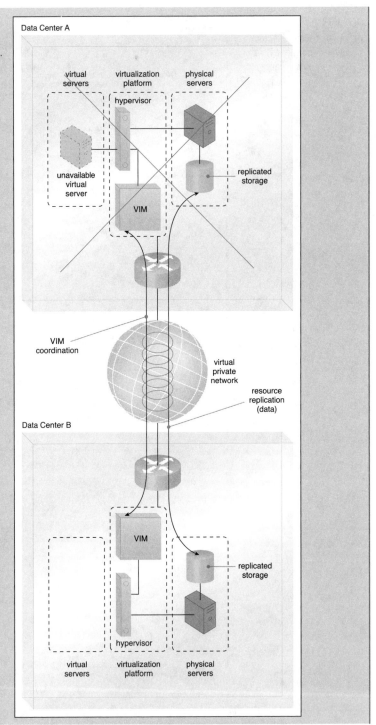

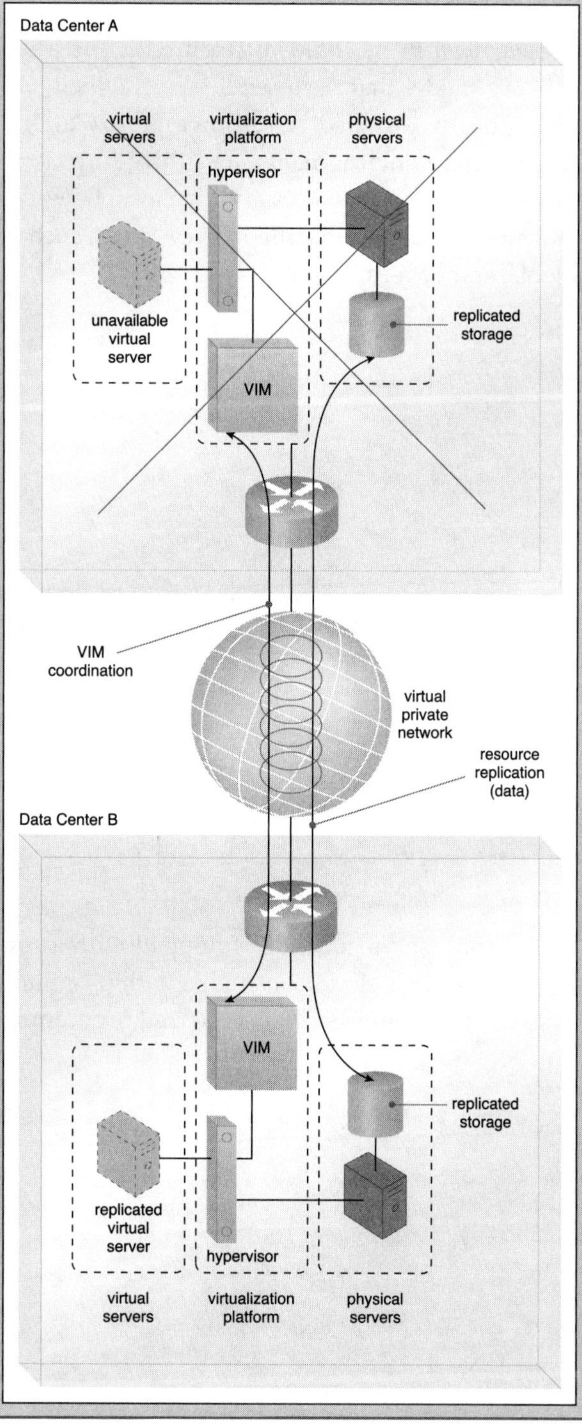

Figure 7.19

A new instance of the virtual server is created and made available in Data Center B.

7.6 Ready-Made Environment

The *ready-made environment* mechanism (Figure 7.20) is a defining component of the PaaS cloud delivery model that represents a pre-defined, cloud-based platform comprised of a set of already installed IT resources, ready to be used and customized by a cloud consumer. These environments are utilized by cloud consumers to remotely develop and deploy their own services and applications within a cloud. Typical ready-made environments include pre-installed IT resources, such as databases, middleware, development tools, and governance tools.

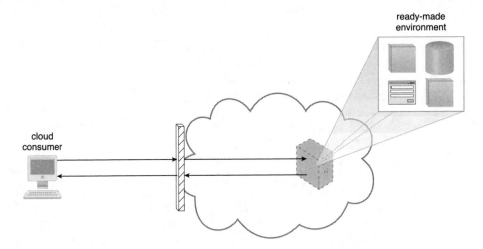

Figure 7.20
A cloud consumer accesses a ready-made environment hosted on a virtual server.

A ready-made environment is generally equipped with a complete software development kit (SDK) that provides cloud consumers with programmatic access to the development technologies that comprise their preferred programming stacks.

Middleware is available for multitenant platforms to support the development and deployment of Web applications. Some cloud providers offer runtime execution environments for cloud services that are based on different runtime performance and billing parameters. For example, a front-end instance of a cloud service can be configured to respond to time-sensitive requests more effectively than a back-end instance. The former variation will be billed at a different rate than the latter.

As further demonstrated in the upcoming case study example, a solution can be partitioned into groups of logic that can be designated for both frontend and backend instance invocation so as to optimize runtime execution and billing.

CASE STUDY EXAMPLE

ATN developed and deployed several non-critical business applications using a leased PaaS environment. One was a Java-based Part Number Catalog Web application used for the switches and routers they manufacture. This application is used by different factories, but it does not manipulate transaction data, which is instead processed by a separate stock control system.

The application logic was split into front-end and back-end processing logic. The front-end logic was used to process simple queries and updates to the catalog. The back-end part contains the logic required to render the complete catalog and correlate similar components and legacy part numbers.

Figure 7.21 illustrates the development and deployment environment for ATN's Part Number Catalog application. Note how the cloud consumer assumes both the developer and end-user roles.

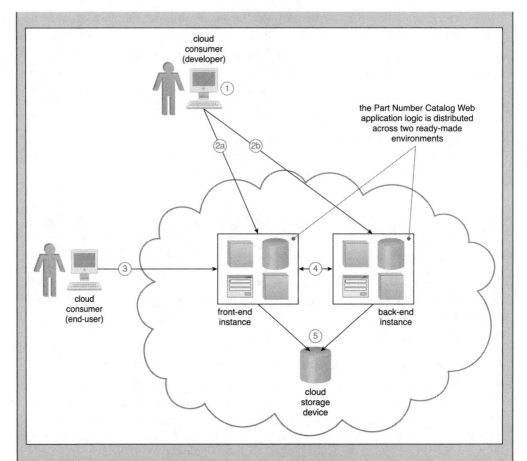

Figure 7.21

The developer uses the provided SDK to develop the Part Number Catalog Web application (1). The application software is deployed on a Web platform that was established by two ready-made environments called the front-end instance (2a) and the back-end instance (2b). The application is made available for usage and one end-user accesses its front-end instance (3). The software running in the front-end instance invokes a long-running task at the back-end instance that corresponds to the processing required by the end-user (4). The application software deployed at both the front-end and back-end instances is backed by a cloud storage device that provides persistent storage of the application data (5).

Chapter 8

Specialized Cloud Mechanisms

A typical cloud technology architecture contains numerous moving parts to address distinct usage requirements of IT resources and solutions. Each mechanism covered in this chapter fulfills a specific runtime function in support of one or more cloud characteristics.

The following specialized cloud mechanisms are described in this chapter:

- Automated Scaling Listener

- Load Balancer

- SLA Monitor

- Pay-Per-Use Monitor

- Audit Monitor

- Failover System

- Hypervisor

- Resource Cluster

- Multi-Device Broker

- State Management Database

All of these mechanisms can be considered extensions to cloud infrastructure, and can be combined in numerous ways as part of distinct and custom technology architectures, many examples of which are provided in Part III of this book.

8.1 Automated Scaling Listener

The *automated scaling listener* mechanism is a service agent that monitors and tracks communications between cloud service consumers and cloud services for dynamic scaling purposes. Automated scaling listeners are deployed within the cloud, typically near the firewall, from where they automatically track workload status information. Workloads can be determined by the volume of cloud consumer-generated requests or via back-end processing demands triggered by certain types of requests. For example, a small amount of incoming data can result in a large amount of processing.

Automated scaling listeners can provide different types of responses to workload fluctuation conditions, such as:

- Automatically scaling IT resources out or in based on parameters previously
  defined by the cloud consumer (commonly referred to as *auto-scaling*).

- Automatic notification of the cloud consumer when workloads exceed current
  thresholds or fall below allocated resources (Figure 8.1). This way, the cloud consumer can choose to adjust its current IT resource allocation.

Different cloud provider vendors have different names for service agents that act as
automated scaling listeners.

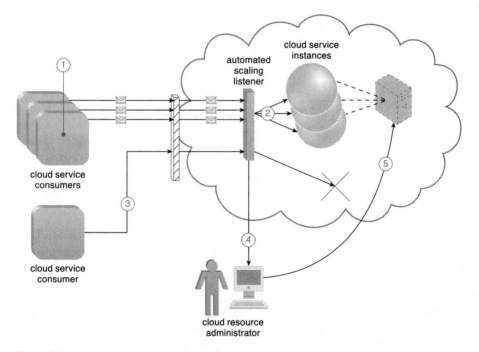

Figure 8.1

Three cloud service consumers attempt to access one cloud service simultaneously (1). The automated scaling
listener scales out and initiates the creation of three redundant instances of the service (2). A fourth cloud
service consumer attempts to use the cloud service (3). Programmed to allow up to only three instances of the
cloud service, the automated scaling listener rejects the fourth attempt and notifies the cloud consumer that the
requested workload limit has been exceeded (4). The cloud consumer's cloud resource administrator accesses the
remote administration environment to adjust the provisioning setup and increase the redundant instance limit (5).

CASE STUDY EXAMPLE

NOTE

This case study example makes reference to the live VM migration component, which is introduced in the *Hypervisor Clustering Architecture* section in Chapter 12, and further described and demonstrated in subsequent architecture scenarios.

DTGOV's physical servers vertically scale virtual server instances, starting with the smallest virtual machine configuration (1 virtual processor core, 4 GB of virtual RAM) to the largest (128 virtual processor cores, 512 GB of virtual RAM). The virtualization platform is configured to automatically scale a virtual server at runtime, as follows:

- *Scaling-Down* – The virtual server continues residing on the same physical host server while being scaled down to a lower performance configuration.

- *Scaling-Up* – The virtual server's capacity is doubled on its original physical host server. The VIM may also live migrate the virtual server to another physical server if the original host server is overcommitted. Migration is automatically performed at runtime and does not require the virtual server to shut down.

Auto-scaling settings controlled by cloud consumers determine the runtime behavior of automated scaling listener agents, which run on the hypervisor that monitors the resource usage of the virtual servers. For example, one cloud consumer has it set up so that whenever resource usage exceeds 80% of a virtual server's capacity for 60 consecutive seconds, the automated scaling listener triggers the scaling-up process by sending the VIM platform a scale-up command. Conversely, the automated scaling listener also commands the VIM to scale down whenever resource usage dips 15% below capacity for 60 consecutive seconds (Figure 8.2).

Figure 8.3 illustrates the live migration of a virtual machine, as performed by the VIM.

The scaling down of the virtual server by the VIM is depicted in Figure 8.4.

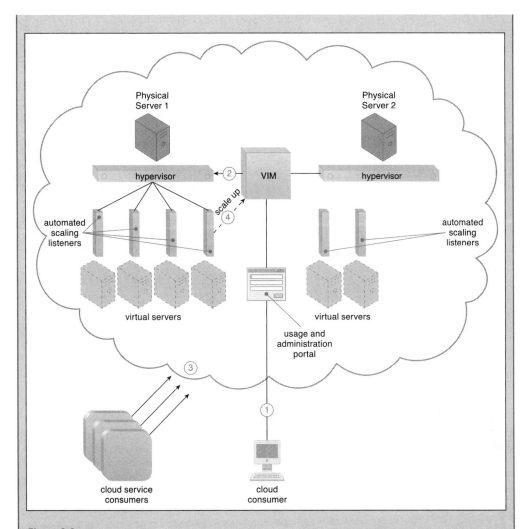

Figure 8.2

A cloud consumer creates and starts a virtual server with 8 virtual processor cores and 16 GB of virtual RAM (1). The VIM creates the virtual server at the cloud service consumer's request and allocates it to Physical Server 1 to join 3 other active virtual servers (2). Cloud consumer demand causes the virtual server usage to increase by over 80% of the CPU capacity for 60 consecutive seconds (3). The automated scaling listener running at the hypervisor detects the need to scale up and commands the VIM accordingly (4).

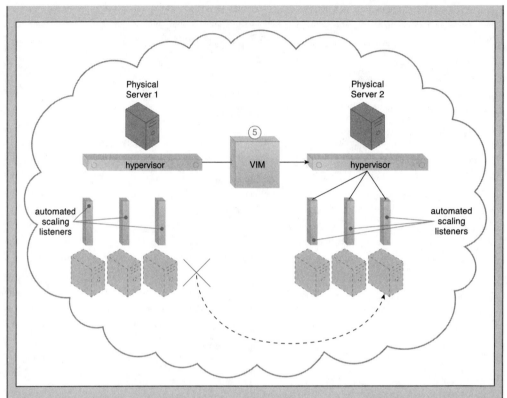

Figure 8.3

The VIM determines that scaling up the virtual server on Physical Server 1 is not possible and proceeds to live migrate it to Physical Server 2.

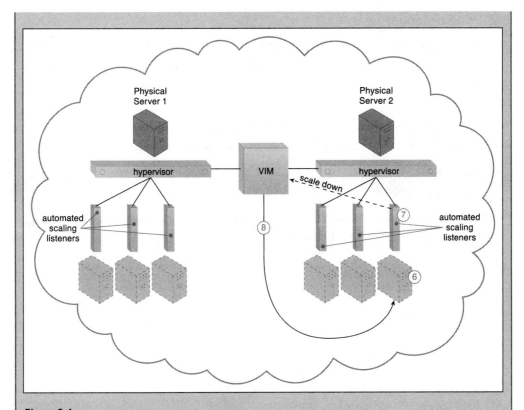

Figure 8.4

The virtual server's CPU/RAM usage remains below 15% capacity for 60 consecutive seconds (6). The automated scaling listener detects the need to scale down and commands the VIM (7), which scales down the virtual server (8) while it remains active on Physical Server 2.

8.2 Load Balancer

A common approach to horizontal scaling is to balance a workload across two or more IT resources to increase performance and capacity beyond what a single IT resource can provide. The *load balancer* mechanism is a runtime agent with logic fundamentally based on this premise.

Beyond simple division of labor algorithms (Figure 8.5), load balancers can perform a range of specialized runtime workload distribution functions that include:

- *Asymmetric Distribution* – larger workloads are issued to IT resources with higher processing capacities

- *Workload Prioritization* – workloads are scheduled, queued, discarded, and distributed workloads according to their priority levels

- *Content-Aware Distribution* – requests are distributed to different IT resources as dictated by the request content

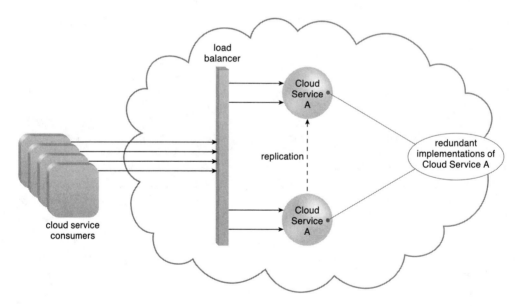

Figure 8.5

A load balancer implemented as a service agent transparently distributes incoming workload request messages across two redundant cloud service implementations, which in turn maximizes performance for the cloud service consumers.

A load balancer is programmed or configured with a set of performance and QoS rules and parameters with the general objectives of optimizing IT resource usage, avoiding overloads, and maximizing throughput.

The load balancer mechanisms can exist as a:

- multi-layer network switch

- dedicated hardware appliance

- dedicated software-based system (common in server operating systems)

- service agent (usually controlled by cloud management software)

The load balancer is typically located on the communication path between the IT resources generating the workload and the IT resources performing the workload processing. This mechanism can be designed as a transparent agent that remains hidden from the cloud service consumers, or as a proxy component that abstracts the IT resources performing their workload.

CASE STUDY EXAMPLE

The ATN Part Number Catalog cloud service does not manipulate transaction data even though it is used by multiple factories in different regions. It has peak usage periods during the first few days of every month that coincide with the preparatory processing of heavy stock control routines at the factories. ATN followed their cloud provider's recommendations and upgraded the cloud service to be highly scalable in order to support the anticipated workload fluctuations.

After developing the necessary upgrades, ATN decides to test the scalability by using a robot automation testing tool that simulates heavy workloads. The tests need to determine whether the application can seamlessly scale to serve peak workloads that are 1,000 times greater than their average workloads. The robots proceed to simulate workloads that last 10 minutes.

The application's resulting auto-scaling functionality is demonstrated in Figure 8.6.

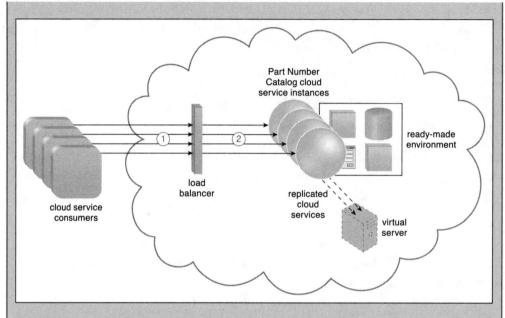

Figure 8.6

New instances of the cloud services are automatically created to meet increasing usage requests. The load balancer uses round-robin scheduling to ensure that the traffic is distributed evenly among the active cloud services.

8.3 SLA Monitor

The SLA monitor mechanism is used to specifically observe the runtime performance of cloud services to ensure that they are fulfilling the contractual QoS requirements that are published in SLAs (Figure 8.7). The data collected by the SLA monitor is processed by an SLA management system to be aggregated into SLA reporting metrics. The system can proactively repair or failover cloud services when exception conditions occur, such as when the SLA monitor reports a cloud service as "down."

The SLA management system mechanism is discussed in Chapter 9.

Figure 8.7

The SLA monitor polls the cloud service by sending over polling request messages (M_{REQ1} to M_{REQN}). The monitor receives polling response messages (M_{REP1} to M_{REPN}) that report that the service was "up" at each polling cycle (1a). The SLA monitor stores the "up" time—time period of all polling cycles 1 to N—in the log database (1b).

The SLA monitor polls the cloud service that sends polling request messages (M_{REQN+1} to M_{REQN+M}). Polling response messages are not received (2a). The response messages continue to time out, so the SLA monitor stores the "down" time—time period of all polling cycles N+1 to N+M—in the log database (2b).

The SLA monitor sends a polling request message ($M_{REQN+M+1}$) and receives the polling response message ($M_{REPN+M+1}$) (3a). The SLA monitor stores the "up" time in the log database (3b).

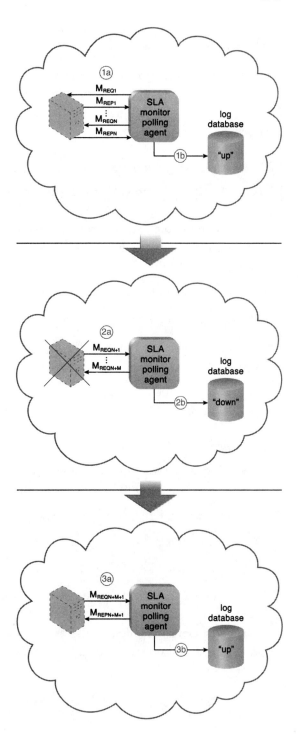

CASE STUDY EXAMPLE

The standard SLA for virtual servers in DTGOV's leasing agreements defines a minimum IT resource availability of 99.95%, which is tracked using two SLA monitors: one based on a polling agent and the other based on a regular monitoring agent implementation.

SLA Monitor Polling Agent

DTGOV's polling SLA monitor runs in the external perimeter network to detect physical server timeouts. It is able to identify data center network, hardware, and software failures (with minute-granularity) that result in physical server non-responsiveness. Three consecutive timeouts of 20-second polling periods are required to declare IT resource unavailability.

Three types of events are generated:

- *PS_Timeout* – the physical server polling has timed out

- *PS_Unreachable* – the physical server polling has consecutively timed out three times

- *PS_Reachable* – the previously unavailable physical server becomes responsive to polling again

SLA Monitoring Agent

The VIM's event-driven API implements the SLA monitor as a monitoring agent to generate the following three events:

- *VM_Unreachable* – the VIM cannot reach the VM

- *VM Failure* – the VM has failed and is unavailable

- *VM_Reachable* – the VM is reachable

The events generated by the polling agent have timestamps that are logged into an SLA event log database and used by the SLA management system to calculate IT resource availability. Complex rules are used to correlate events from different polling SLA monitors and the affected virtual servers, and to discard any false positives for periods of unavailability.

Figures 8.8 and 8.9 show the steps taken by SLA monitors during a data center network failure and recovery.

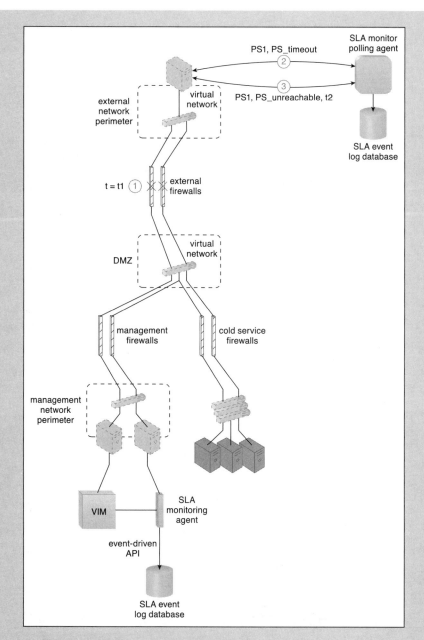

Figure 8.8

At timestamp = t1, a firewall cluster has failed and all of the IT resources in the data center become
unavailable (1). The SLA monitor polling agent stops receiving responses from physical servers and
starts to issue PS_timeout events (2). The SLA monitor polling agent starts issuing PS_unreachable
events after three successive PS_timeout events. The timestamp is now t2 (3).

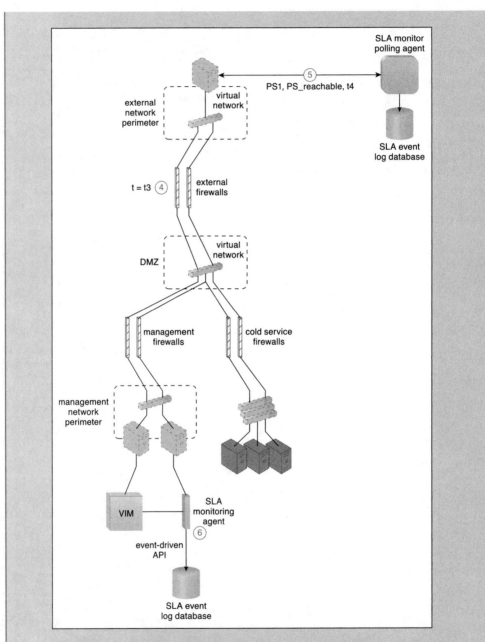

Figure 8.9

The IT resource becomes operational at timestamp = t3 (4). The SLA monitor polling agent receives responses from the physical servers and issues PS_reachable events. The timestamp is now t4 (5). The SLA monitoring agent did not detect any unavailability since the communication between the VIM platform and physical servers was not affected by the failure (6).

The SLA management system uses the information stored in the log database to calculate the period of unavailability as t4 – t3, which affected all of the virtual servers in the data center.

Figures 8.10 and 8.11 illustrate the steps that are taken by the SLA monitors during the failure and subsequent recovery of a physical server that is hosting three virtual servers (VM1, VM2, VM3).

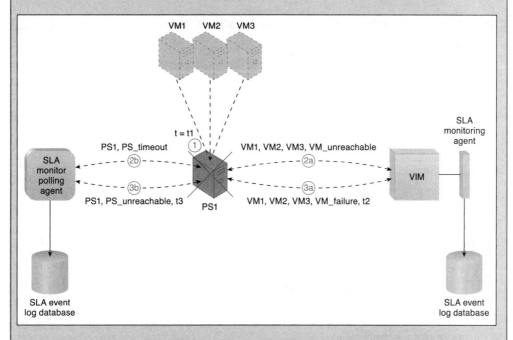

Figure 8.10

At timestamp = t1, the physical host server has failed and becomes unavailable (1). The SLA monitoring agent captures a VM_unreachable event that is generated for each virtual server in the failed host server (2a). The SLA monitor polling agent stops receiving responses from the host server and issues PS_timeout events (2b). At timestamp = t2, the SLA monitoring agent captures a VM_failure event that is generated for each of the failed host server's three virtual servers (3a). The SLA monitor polling agent starts to issue PS_unavailable events after three successive PS_timeout events at timestamp = t3 (3b).

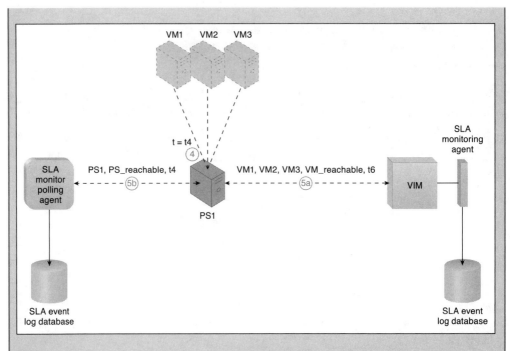

Figure 8.11
The host server becomes operational at timestamp = t4 (4). The SLA monitor polling agent receives responses from the physical server and issues PS_reachable events at timestamp = t5 (5a). At timestamp = t6, the SLA monitoring agent captures a VM_reachable event that is generated for each virtual server (5b). The SLA management system calculates the unavailability period that affected all of the virtual servers as t6 – t2.

8.4 Pay-Per-Use Monitor

The *pay-per-use monitor* mechanism measures cloud-based IT resource usage in accordance with predefined pricing parameters and generates usage logs for fee calculations and billing purposes.

Some typical monitoring variables are:

- request/response message quantity
- transmitted data volume
- bandwidth consumption

The data collected by the pay-per-use monitor is processed by a billing management system that calculates the payment fees. The billing management system mechanism is covered in Chapter 9.

Figure 8.12 shows a pay-per-use monitor implemented as a resource agent used to determine the usage period of a virtual server.

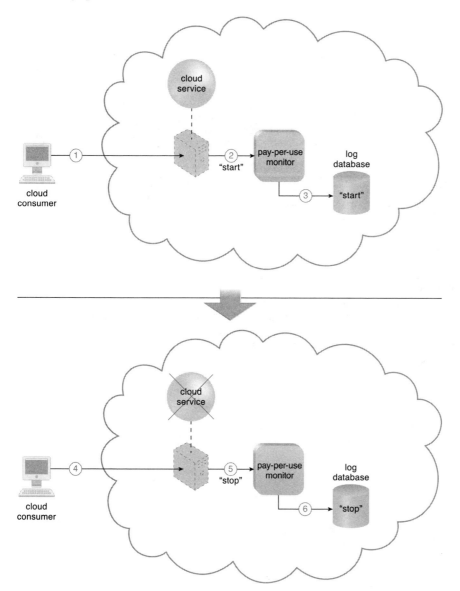

Figure 8.12

A cloud consumer requests the creation of a new instance of a cloud service (1). The IT resource is instantiated and the pay-per-use monitor receives a "start" event notification from the resource software (2). The pay-per-use monitor stores the value timestamp in the log database (3). The cloud consumer later requests that the cloud service instance be stopped (4). The pay-per-use monitor receives a "stop" event notification from the resource software (5) and stores the value timestamp in the log database (6).

Figure 8.13 illustrates a pay-per-use monitor designed as a monitoring agent that transparently intercepts and analyzes runtime communication with a cloud service.

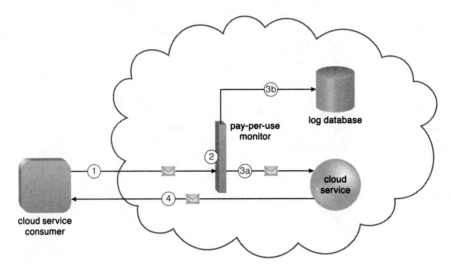

Figure 8.13

A cloud service consumer sends a request message to the cloud service (1). The pay-per-use monitor intercepts the message (2), forwards it to the cloud service (3a), and stores the usage information in accordance with its monitoring metrics (3b). The cloud service forwards the response messages back to the cloud service consumer to provide the requested service (4).

CASE STUDY EXAMPLE

DTGOV decides to invest in a commercial system capable of generating invoices based on events pre-defined as "billable" and customizable pricing models. The installation of the system results in two proprietary databases: the billing event database and the pricing scheme database.

Runtime events are collected via cloud usage monitors that are implemented as extensions to the VIM platform using the VIM's API. The pay-per-use monitor polling agent periodically supplies the billing system with billable events information. A separate monitoring agent provides further supplemental billing-related data, such as:

- *Cloud Consumer Subscription Type* – This information is used to identify the type of pricing model for usage fee calculations, including pre-paid subscription with usage quota, post-paid subscription with maximum usage quota, and post-paid subscription with unlimited usage.

- *Resource Usage Category* – The billing management system uses this information to identify the range of usage fees that are applicable to each usage event. Examples include normal usage, reserved IT resource usage, and premium (managed) service usage.

- *Resource Usage Quota Consumption* – When usage contracts define IT resource usage quotas, usage event conditions are typically supplemented with quota consumption and updated quota limits.

Figure 8.14 illustrates the steps that are taken by DTGOV's pay-per-use monitor during a typical usage event.

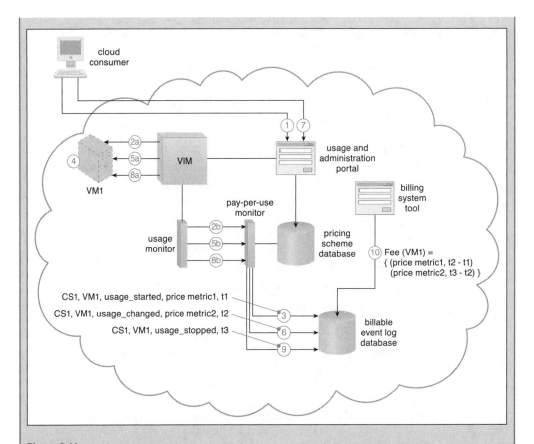

Figure 8.14

The cloud consumer (CS_ID = CS1) creates and starts a virtual server (VM_ID = VM1) of configuration size *type 1*
(VM_TYPE = type1) (1). The VIM creates the virtual server instance as requested (2a). The VIM's event-driven API
generates a resource usage event with timestamp = *t1*, which is captured and forwarded to the pay-per-use monitor
by the cloud usage monitor (2b). The pay-per-use monitor interacts with the pricing scheme database to identify the
chargeback and usage metrics that apply to the resource usage. A "started usage" billable event is generated and stored
in the billable event log database (3). The virtual server's usage increases and reaches the auto-scaling threshold (4).
The VIM scales up Virtual Server VM1 (5a) from configuration *type 1* to *type 2* (VM_TYPE = type2). The VIM's event-
driven API generates a resource usage event with timestamp = *t2*, which is captured and forwarded to the pay-per-use
monitor by the cloud usage monitor (5b). The pay-per-use monitor interacts with the pricing scheme database to identify
the chargeback and usage metrics that apply to the updated IT resource usage. A "changed usage" billable event is
generated and stored in the billable event log database (6). The cloud consumer shuts down the virtual server (7) and the
VIM stops Virtual Server VM1 (8a). The VIM's event-driven API generates a resource usage event with timestamp = *t3*,
which is captured and forwarded to the pay-per-use monitor by the cloud usage monitor (8b). The pay-per-use monitor
interacts with the pricing scheme database to identify the chargeback and usage metrics that apply to the updated IT
resource usage. A "finished usage" billable event is generated and stored in the billable event log database (9). The
billing system tool can now be used by the cloud provider to access the log database and calculate the total usage fee for
the virtual server as (Fee(VM1)) (10).

8.5 Audit Monitor

The *audit monitor* mechanism is used to collect audit tracking data for networks and IT resources in support of (or dictated by) regulatory and contractual obligations. Figure 8.15 depicts an audit monitor implemented as a monitoring agent that intercepts "login" requests and stores the requestor's security credentials, as well as both failed and successful login attempts, in a log database for future audit reporting purposes.

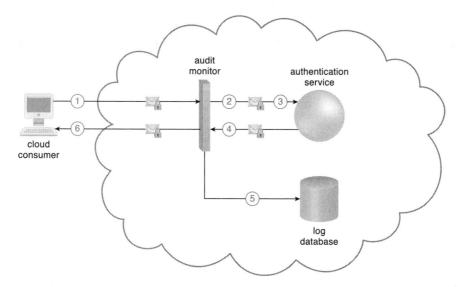

Figure 8.15

A cloud service consumer requests access to a cloud service by sending a login request message with security credentials (1). The audit monitor intercepts the message (2) and forwards it to the authentication service (3). The authentication service processes the security credentials. A response message is generated for the cloud service consumer, in addition to the results from the login attempt (4). The audit monitor intercepts the response message and stores the entire collected login event details in the log database, as per the organization's audit policy requirements (5). Access has been granted, and a response is sent back to the cloud service consumer (6).

CASE STUDY EXAMPLE

A key feature of Innovartus' role-playing solution is its unique user-interface. However, the advanced technologies used for its design have imposed licensing restrictions that legally prevent Innovartus from charging users in certain geographical regions for usage of the solution. Innovartus' legal department is working on getting these issues resolved. But in the meantime, it has provided the IT department with a list of countries in which the application can either not be accessed by users or in which user access needs to be free of charge.

In order to collect information about the origin of clients accessing the application, Innovartus asks its cloud provider to establish an audit monitoring system. The cloud provider deploys an audit monitoring agent to intercept each inbound message, analyze its corresponding HTTP header, and collect details about the origin of the end-user. As per Innovartus' request, the cloud provider further adds a log database to collect the regional data of each end-user request for future reporting purposes. Innovartus further upgrades its application so that end-users from select countries are able to access the application at no charge (Figure 8.16).

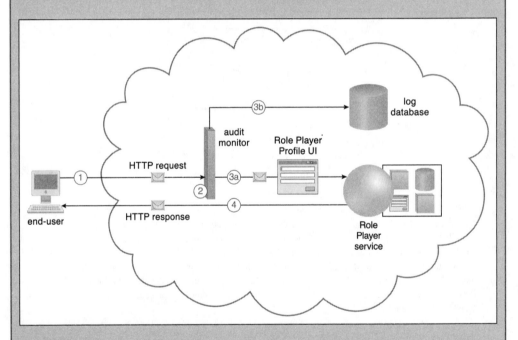

Figure 8.16

An end-user attempts access to the Role Player cloud service (1). An audit monitor transparently intercepts the HTTP request message and analyzes the message header to determine the geographical origin of the end-user (2). The audit monitoring agent determines that the end-user is from a region that Innovartus is not authorized to charge a fee for access to the application. The agent forwards the message to the cloud service (3a) and generates the audit track information for storage in the log database (3b). The cloud service receives the HTTP message and grants the end-user access at no charge (4).

8.6 Failover System

The *failover system* mechanism is used to increase the reliability and availability of IT resources by using established clustering technology to provide redundant implementations. A failover system is configured to automatically switch over to a redundant or standby IT resource instance whenever the currently active IT resource becomes unavailable.

Failover systems are commonly used for mission-critical programs and reusable services that can introduce a single point of failure for multiple applications. A failover system can span more than one geographical region so that each location hosts one or more redundant implementations of the same IT resource.

The resource replication mechanism is sometimes utilized by the failover system to provide redundant IT resource instances, which are actively monitored for the detection of errors and unavailability conditions.

Failover systems come in two basic configurations:

Active-Active

In an active-active configuration, redundant implementations of the IT resource actively serve the workload synchronously (Figure 18.17). Load balancing among active instances is required. When a failure is detected, the failed instance is removed from the load balancing scheduler (Figure 18.18). Whichever IT resource remains operational when a failure is detected takes over the processing (Figure 18.19).

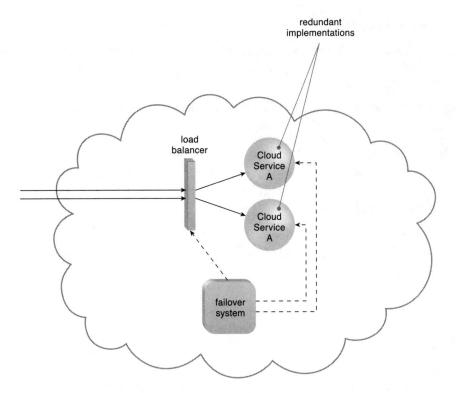

Figure 8.17
The failover system monitors the operational status of Cloud Service A.

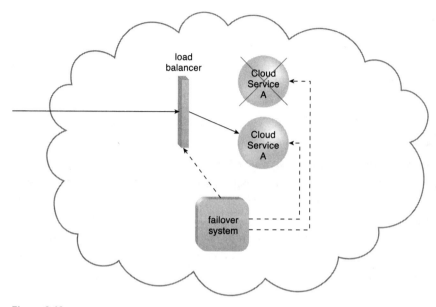

Figure 8.18

When a failure is detected in one Cloud Service A implementation, the failover system commands the load balancer to switch over the workload to the redundant Cloud Service A implementation.

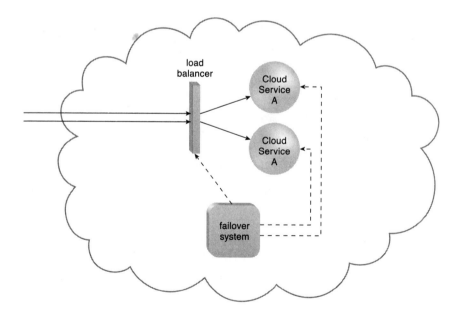

Figure 8.19

The failed Cloud Service A implementation is recovered or replicated into an operational cloud service. The failover system now commands the load balancer to distribute the workload again.

Active-Passive

In an active-passive configuration, a standby or inactive implementation is activated to take over the processing from the IT resource that becomes unavailable, and the corresponding workload is redirected to the instance taking over the operation (Figures 8.20 to 8.22).

Some failover systems are designed to redirect workloads to active IT resources that rely on specialized load balancers that detect failure conditions and exclude failed IT resource instances from the workload distribution. This type of failover system is suitable for IT resources that do not require execution state management and provide stateless processing capabilities. In technology architectures that are typically based on clustering and virtualization technologies, the redundant or standby IT resource implementations are also required to share their state and execution context. A complex task that was executed on a failed IT resource can remain operational in one of its redundant implementations.

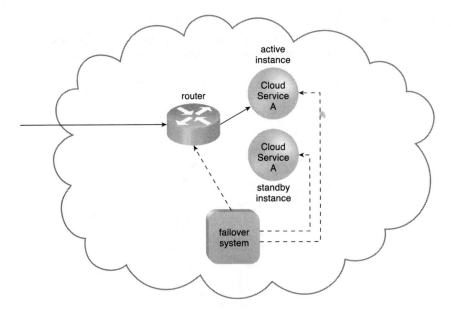

Figure 8.20

The failover system monitors the operational status of Cloud Service A. The Cloud Service A implementation acting as the active instance is receiving cloud service consumer requests.

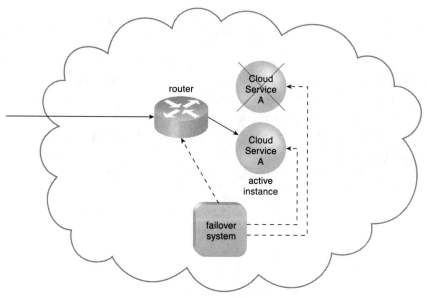

Figure 8.21

The Cloud Service A implementation acting as the active instance encounters a failure that is detected
by the failover system, which subsequently activates the inactive Cloud Service A implementation and
redirects the workload toward it. The newly invoked Cloud Service A implementation now assumes the
role of active instance.

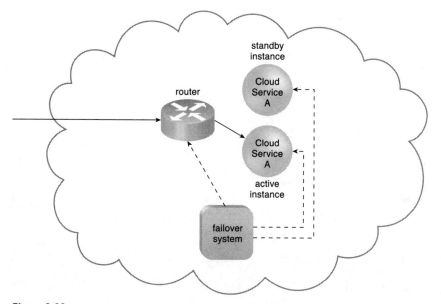

Figure 8.22

The failed Cloud Service A implementation is recovered or replicated an operational cloud service, and is
now positioned as the standby instance, while the previously invoked Cloud Service A continues to serve
as the active instance.

DTGOV creates a resilient virtual server to support the allocation of virtual server instances that are hosting critical applications, which are being replicated in multiple data centers. The replicated resilient virtual server has an associated active-passive failover system. Its network traffic flow can be switched between the IT resource instances that are residing at different data centers, if the active instance were to fail (Figure 8.23).

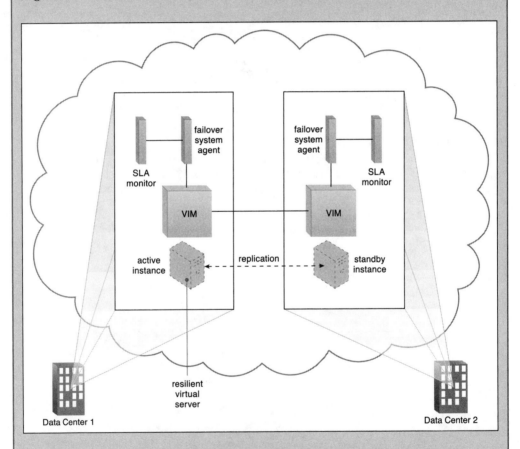

Figure 8.23

A resilient virtual server is established by replicating the virtual server instance across two different data centers, as performed by the VIM that is running at both data centers. The active instance receives the network traffic and is vertically scaling in response, while the standby instance has no workload and runs at the minimum configuration.

Figure 8.24 illustrates SLA monitors detecting failure in an active instance of a virtual server.

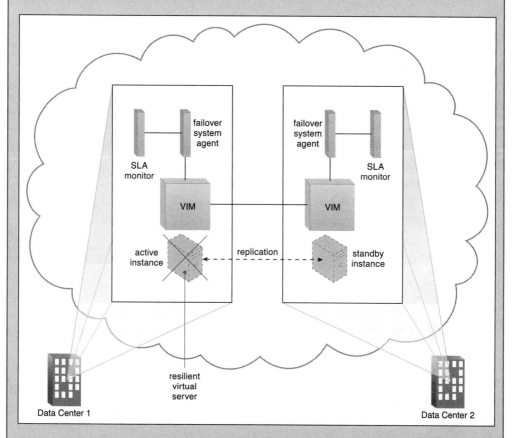

Figure 8.24
SLA monitors detect when the active virtual server instance becomes unavailable.

Figure 8.25 shows traffic being switched over to the standby instance, which has now become active.

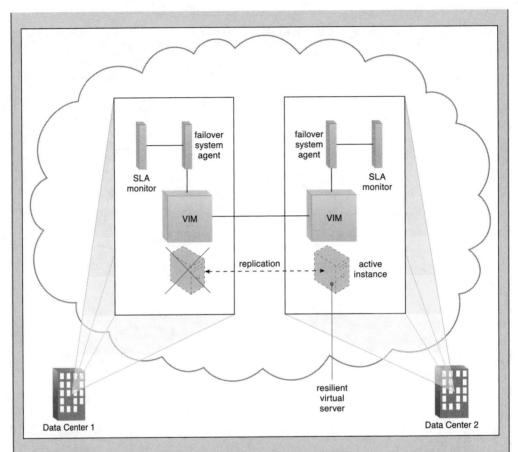

Figure 8.25

The failover system is implemented as an event-driven software agent that intercepts the message notifications the SLA monitors send regarding server unavailability. In response, the failover system interacts with the VIM and network management tools to redirect all of the network traffic to the now-active standby instance.

In Figure 8.26, the failed virtual server becomes operational and turns into the standby instance.

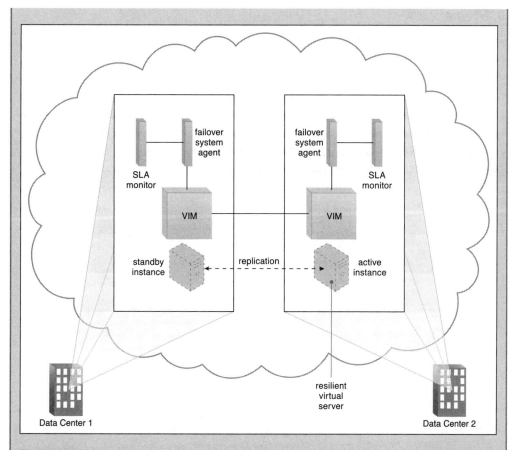

Figure 8.26

The failed virtual server instance is revived and scaled down to the minimum standby instance configuration after it resumes normal operation.

8.7 Hypervisor

The *hypervisor* mechanism is a fundamental part of virtualization infrastructure that is primarily used to generate virtual server instances of a physical server. A hypervisor is generally limited to one physical server and can therefore only create virtual images of that server (Figure 8.27). Similarly, a hypervisor can only assign virtual servers it generates to resource pools that reside on the same underlying physical server. A hypervisor has limited virtual server management features, such as increasing the virtual server's capacity or shutting it down. The VIM provides a range of features for administering multiple hypervisors across physical servers.

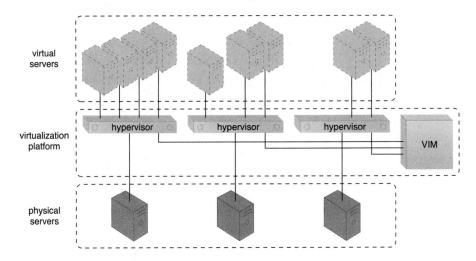

Figure 8.27

Virtual servers are created via individual hypervisor on individual physical servers. All three hypervisors are jointly controlled by the same VIM.

Hypervisor software can be installed directly in bare-metal servers and provides features for controlling, sharing and scheduling the usage of hardware resources, such as processor power, memory, and I/O. These can appear to each virtual server's operating system as dedicated resources.

CASE STUDY EXAMPLE

DTGOV has established a virtualization platform in which the same hypervisor software product is running on all physical servers. The VIM coordinates the hardware resources in each data center so that virtual server instances can be created from the most expedient underlying physical server.

As a result, cloud consumers are able to lease virtual servers with auto-scaling features. In order to offer flexible configurations, the DTGOV virtualization platform provides live VM migration of virtual servers among physical servers inside the same data center. This is illustrated in Figures 8.23 and 8.24, where a virtual server live-migrates from one busy physical server to another that is idle, allowing it to scale up in response to an increase in its workload.

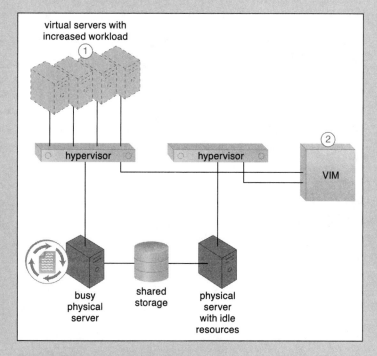

Figure 8.28

A virtual server capable of auto-scaling experiences an increase in its workload (1). The VIM decides that the virtual server cannot scale up because its underlying physical server host is being used by other virtual servers (2).

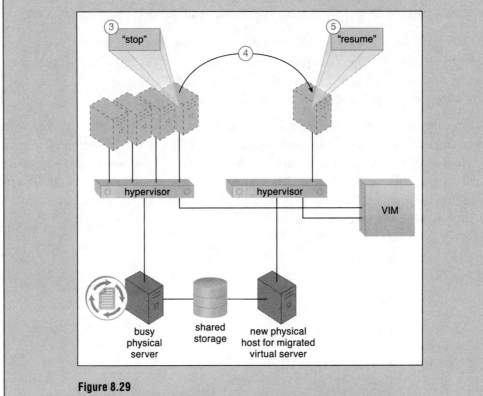

Figure 8.29

The VIM commands the hypervisor on the busy physical server to suspend execution of the virtual server (3). The VIM then commands the instantiation of the virtual server on the idle physical server. State information (such as dirty memory pages and processor registers) is synchronized via a shared cloud storage device (4). The VIM commands the hypervisor at the new physical server to resume the virtual server processing (5).

8.8 Resource Cluster

Cloud-based IT resources that are geographically diverse can be logically combined into groups to improve their allocation and use. The *resource cluster* mechanism (Figure 8.30) is used to group multiple IT resource instances so that they can be operated as a single IT resource. This increases the combined computing capacity, load balancing, and availability of the clustered IT resources.

Figure 8.30
The curved dashed lines are used to indicate that IT resources are clustered.

Resource cluster architectures rely on high-speed dedicated network connections, or cluster nodes, between IT resource instances to communicate about workload distribution, task scheduling, data sharing, and system synchronization. A cluster management platform that is running as distributed middleware in all of the cluster nodes is usually responsible for these activities. This platform implements a coordination function that allows distributed IT resources to appear as one IT resource, and also executes IT resources inside the cluster.

Common resource cluster types include:

- *Server Cluster* – Physical or virtual servers are clustered to increase performance and availability. Hypervisors running on different physical servers can be configured to share virtual server execution state (such as memory pages and processor register state) in order to establish clustered virtual servers. In such configurations, which usually require physical servers to have access to shared storage, virtual servers are able to live-migrate from one to another. In this process, the virtualization platform suspends the execution of a given virtual server at one physical server and resumes it on another physical server. The process is transparent to the virtual server operating system and can be used to increase scalability by live-migrating a virtual server that is running at an overloaded physical server to another physical server that has suitable capacity.

- *Database Cluster* – Designed to improve data availability, this high-availability resource cluster has a synchronization feature that maintains the consistency of data being stored at different storage devices used in the cluster. The redundant capacity is usually based on an active-active or active-passive failover system committed to maintaining the synchronization conditions.

- *Large Dataset Cluster* – Data partitioning and distribution is implemented so that the target datasets can be efficiently partitioned without compromising data integrity or computing accuracy. Each cluster node processes workloads without communicating with other nodes as much as in other cluster types.

Many resource clusters require cluster nodes to have almost identical computing capacity and characteristics in order to simplify the design of and maintain consistency within the resource cluster architecture. The cluster nodes in high-availability cluster architectures need to access and share common storage IT resources. This can require two layers of communication between the nodes—one for accessing the storage device and another to execute IT resource orchestration (Figure 8.31). Some resource clusters are designed with more loosely coupled IT resources that only require the network layer (Figure 8.32).

Figure 8.31

Load balancing and resource replication are implemented through a cluster-enabled hypervisor. A dedicated storage area network is used to connect the clustered storage and the clustered servers, which are able to share common cloud storage devices. This simplifies the storage replication process, which is independently carried out at the storage cluster. (See the *Hypervisor Clustering Architecture* section in Chapter 12 for a more detailed description.)

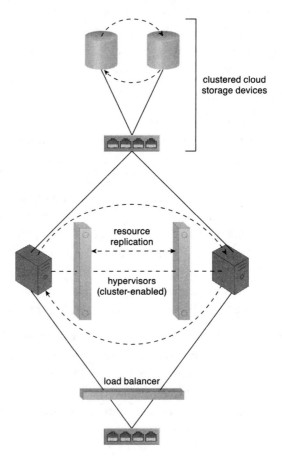

clustered cloud storage devices

resource replication

hypervisors (cluster-enabled)

load balancer

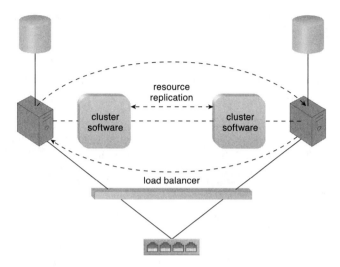

Figure 8.32

A loosely coupled server cluster that incorporates a load balancer. There is
no shared storage. Resource replication is used to replicate cloud storage
devices through the network by the cluster software.

There are two basic types of resource clusters:

- *Load Balanced Cluster* – This resource cluster specializes in distributing workloads
  among cluster nodes to increase IT resource capacity while preserving the central-
  ization of IT resource management. It usually implements a load balancer mechanism that is either embedded within the cluster management platform or set up as
  a separate IT resource.

- *HA Cluster* – A high-availability cluster maintains system availability in the event
  of multiple node failures, and has redundant implementations of most or all of
  the clustered IT resources. It implements a failover system mechanism that monitors failure conditions and automatically redirects the workload away from any
  failed nodes.

The provisioning of clustered IT resources can be considerably more expensive than
the provisioning of individual IT resources that have an equivalent computing capacity.

CASE STUDY EXAMPLE

DTGOV is considering introducing a clustered virtual server to run in a high-availability cluster as part of the virtualization platform (Figure 8.33). The virtual servers can live migrate among the physical servers, which are pooled in a high-availability hardware cluster that is controlled by coordinated cluster-enabled hypervisors. The coordination function keeps replicated snapshots of the running virtual servers to facilitate migration to other physical servers in the event of a failure.

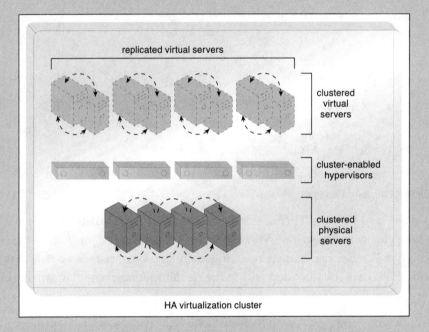

Figure 8.33

An HA virtualization cluster of physical servers is deployed using a cluster-enabled hypervisor, which guarantees that the physical servers are constantly in sync. Every virtual server that is instantiated in the cluster is automatically replicated in at least two physical servers.

Figure 8.34 identifies the virtual servers that are migrated from their failed physical host server to other available physical servers.

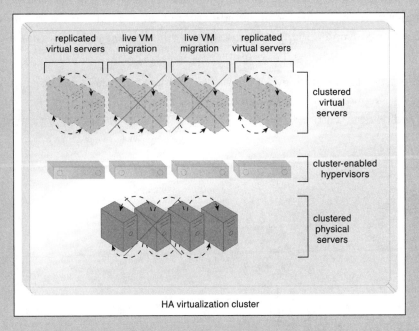

Figure 8.34

All of the virtual servers that are hosted on a physical server experiencing failure are automatically migrated to other physical servers.

8.9 Multi-Device Broker

An individual cloud service may need to be accessed by a range of cloud service consumers differentiated by their hosting hardware devices and/or communication requirements. To overcome incompatibilities between a cloud service and a disparate cloud service consumer, mapping logic needs to be created to transform (or convert) information that is exchanged at runtime.

The *multi-device broker* mechanism is used to facilitate runtime data transformation so as to make a cloud service accessible to a wider range of cloud service consumer programs and devices (Figure 8.35).

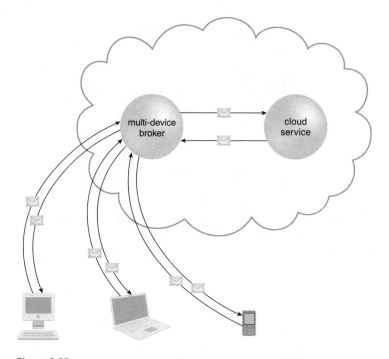

Figure 8.35

A multi-device broker contains the mapping logic necessary to transform data exchanges between a cloud service and different types of cloud service consumer devices. This scenario depicts the multi-device broker as a cloud service with its own API. This mechanism can also be implemented as a service agent that intercepts messages at runtime to perform necessary transformations.

Multi-device brokers commonly exist as gateways or incorporate gateway components, such as:

- *XML Gateway* – transmits and validates XML data

- *Cloud Storage Gateway* – transforms cloud storage protocols and encodes storage devices to facilitate data transfer and storage

- *Mobile Device Gateway* – transforms the communication protocols used by mobile devices into protocols that are compatible with a cloud service

The levels at which transformation logic can be created include:

- transport protocols

- messaging protocols

- storage device protocols

- data schemas/data models

For example, a multi-device broker may contain mapping logic that coverts both transport and messaging protocols for a cloud service consumer accessing a cloud service with a mobile device.

CASE STUDY EXAMPLE

Innovartus has decided to make its role-playing application available to various mobile and smartphone devices. A complication that hindered Innovartus' development team during the mobile enhancement design stage was the difficulty in reproducing identical user experiences across different mobile platforms. To resolve this issue, Innovartus implements a multi-device broker to intercept incoming messages from devices, identify the software platform, and convert the message format into the native, server-side application format (Figure 8.36).

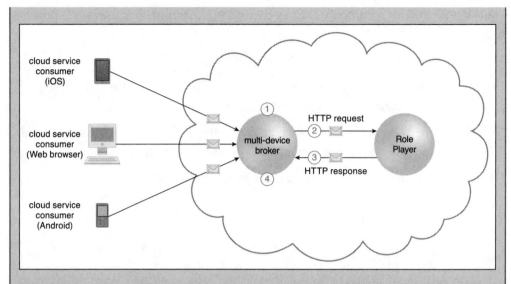

Figure 8.36

The multi-device broker intercepts incoming messages and detects the platform (Web browser, iOS, Android) of the source device (1). The multi-device broker transforms the message into the standard format required by the Innovartus cloud service (2). The cloud service processes the request and responds using the same standard format (3). The multi-device broker transforms the response message into the format required by the source device and delivers the message (4).

8.10 State Management Database

A *state management database* is a storage device that is used to temporarily persist state data for software programs. As an alternative to caching state data in memory, software programs can off-load state data to the database in order to reduce the amount of run-time memory they consume (Figures 8.37 and 8.38). By doing so, the software programs and the surrounding infrastructure are more scalable. State management databases are commonly used by cloud services, especially those involved in long-running runtime activities.

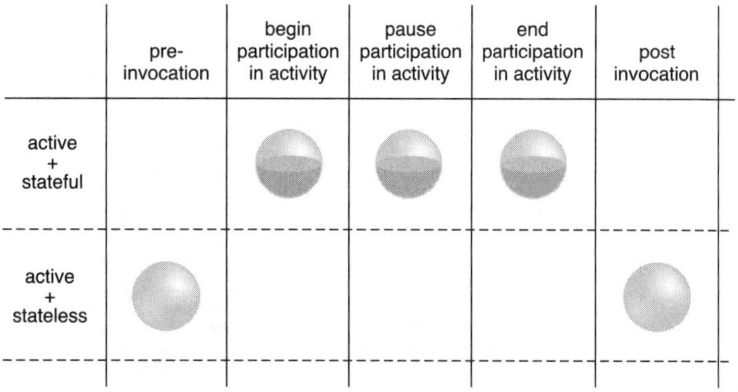

Figure 8.37

During the lifespan of a cloud service instance it may be required to remain stateful and keep state data cached in memory, even when idle.

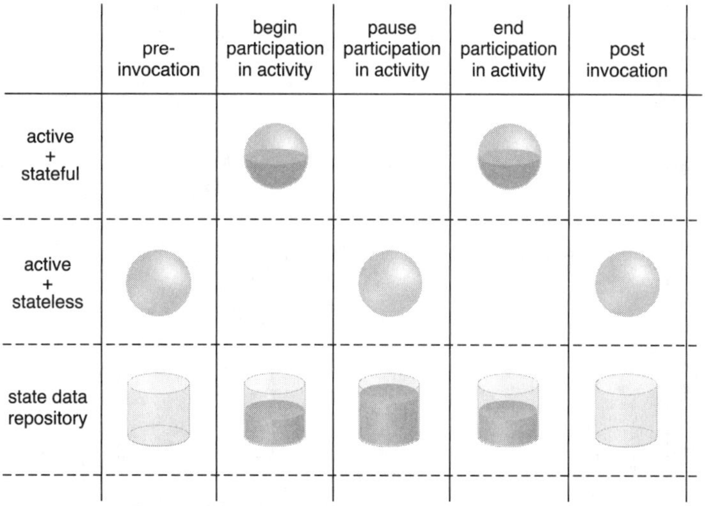

	pre-invocation	begin participation in activity	pause participation in activity	end participation in activity	post invocation
active + stateful		◑	◑	◑	
active + stateless	◯				◯

Figure 8.38

By deferring state data to a state repository, the cloud service is able to transition to a stateless condition (or a partially stateless condition), thereby temporarily freeing system resources.

	pre-invocation	begin participation in activity	pause participation in activity	end participation in activity	post invocation
active + stateful		◑		◑	
active + stateless	◯		◯		◯
state data repository	▱	▰	▰	▰	▱

CASE STUDY EXAMPLE

ATN is expanding its ready-made environment architecture to allow for the deferral of state information for extended periods by utilizing the state management database mechanism. Figure 8.39 demonstrates how a cloud service consumer working with a ready-made environment pauses activity, causing the environment to off-load cached state data.

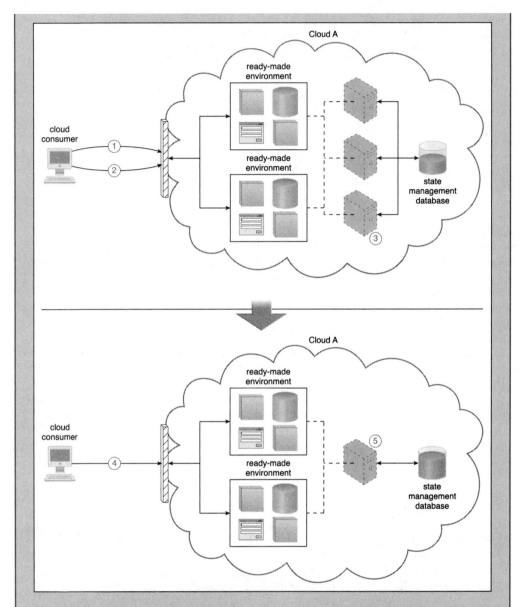

Figure 8.39

The cloud consumer accesses the ready-made environment and requires three virtual servers to perform all activities (1). The cloud consumer pauses activity. All of the state data needs to be preserved for future access to the ready-made environment (2). The underlying infrastructure is automatically scaled in by reducing the number of virtual servers. State data is saved in the state management database and one virtual server remains active to allow for future logins by the cloud consumer (3). At a later point, the cloud consumer logs in and accesses the ready-made environment to continue activity (4). The underlying infrastructure is automatically scaled out by increasing the number of virtual servers and by retrieving the state data from the state management database (5).

Chapter 9

Cloud Management Mechanisms

Cloud-based IT resources need to be set up, configured, maintained, and monitored. The systems covered in this chapter are mechanisms that encompass and enable these types of management tasks. They form key parts of cloud technology architectures by facilitating the control and evolution of the IT resources that form cloud platforms and solutions.

The following management-related mechanisms are described in this chapter:

- Remote Administration System

- Resource Management System

- SLA Management System

- Billing Management System

These systems typically provide integrated APIs and can be offered as individual products, custom applications, or combined into various product suites or multi-function applications.

9.1 Remote Administration System

The *remote administration system* mechanism (Figure 9.1) provides tools and user-interfaces for external cloud resource administrators to configure and administer cloud-based IT resources.

remote administration
system

Figure 9.1

The symbol used in this book for the remote administration system. The displayed user-interface will typically be labeled to indicate a specific type of portal.

A remote administration system can establish a portal for access to administration and management features of various underlying systems, including the resource management, SLA management, and billing management systems described in this chapter (Figure 9.2).

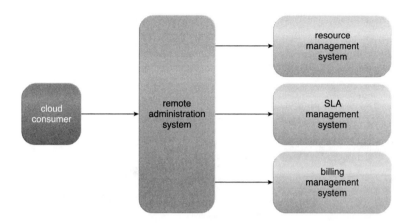

Figure 9.2

The remote administration system abstracts underlying management systems to expose and centralize administration controls to external cloud resource administrators. The system provides a customizable user console, while programmatically interfacing with underlying management systems via their APIs.

The tools and APIs provided by a remote administration system are generally used by the cloud provider to develop and customize online portals that provide cloud consumers with a variety of administrative controls.

The following are the two primary types of portals that are created with the remote administration system:

- *Usage and Administration Portal* – A general purpose portal that centralizes management controls to different cloud-based IT resources and can further provide IT resource usage reports. This portal is part of numerous cloud technology architectures covered in Chapters 11 to 13.

usage and administration portal

- *Self-Service Portal* – This is essentially a shopping portal that allows cloud consumers to search an up-to-date list of cloud services and IT resources that are available from a cloud provider (usually for lease). The cloud consumer submits its chosen items to the cloud provider for provisioning. This portal is primarily associated with the rapid provisioning architecture described in Chapter 12.

self-service portal

Figure 9.3 illustrates a scenario involving a remote administration system and both usage and administration and self-service portals.

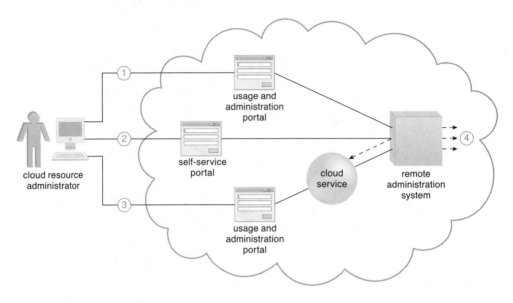

Figure 9.3

A cloud resource administrator uses the usage and administration portal to configure an already leased virtual server (not shown) to prepare it for hosting (1). The cloud resource administrator then uses the self-service portal to select and request the provisioning of a new cloud service (2). The cloud resource administrator then accesses the usage and administration portal again to configure the newly provisioned cloud service that is hosted on the virtual server (3). Throughout these steps, the remote administration system interacts with the necessary management systems to perform the requested actions (4).

Depending on:

- the type of cloud product or cloud delivery model the cloud consumer is leasing or using from the cloud provider,

- the level of access control granted by the cloud provider to the cloud consumer, and

- further depending on which underlying management systems the remote administration system interfaces with,

...tasks that can commonly be performed by cloud consumers via a remote administration console include:

- configuring and setting up cloud services

- provisioning and releasing IT resource for on-demand cloud services

- monitoring cloud service status, usage, and performance

- monitoring QoS and SLA fulfillment

- managing leasing costs and usage fees

- managing user accounts, security credentials, authorization, and access control

- tracking internal and external access to leased services

- planning and assessing IT resource provisioning

- capacity planning

While the user-interface provided by the remote administration system will tend to be proprietary to the cloud provider, there is a preference among cloud consumers to work with remote administration systems that offer standardized APIs. This allows a cloud consumer to invest in the creation of its own front-end with the fore-knowledge that it can reuse this console if it decides to move to another cloud provider that supports the same standardized API. Additionally, the cloud consumer would be able to further leverage standardized APIs if it is interested in leasing and centrally administering IT resources from multiple cloud providers and/or IT resources residing in cloud and on-premise environments.

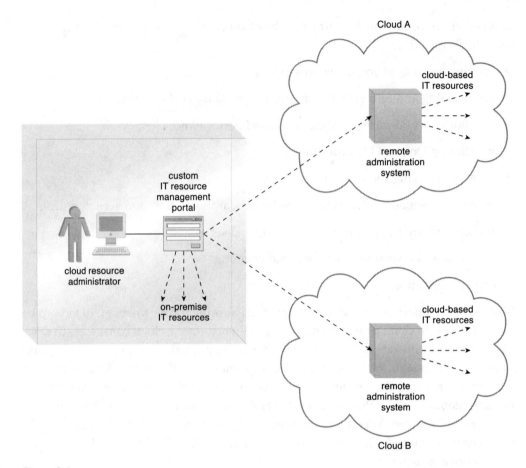

Figure 9.4

Standardized APIs published by remote administration systems from different clouds enable a cloud consumer to develop a custom portal that centralizes a single IT resource management portal for both cloud-based and on-premise IT resources.

CASE STUDY EXAMPLE

DTGOV has been offering its cloud consumers a user-friendly remote administration system for some time, and recently determined that upgrades are required in order to accommodate the growing number of cloud consumers and increasing diversity of requests. DTGOV is planning a development project to extend the remote administration system to fulfill the following requirements:

- Cloud consumers need to be able to self-provision virtual servers and virtual storage devices. The system specifically needs to interoperate with the cloud-enabled VIM platform's proprietary API to enable self-provisioning capabilities.

- A single sign-on mechanism (described in Chapter 10) needs to be incorporated to centrally authorize and control cloud consumer access.

- An API that supports the provisioning, starting, stopping, releasing, up-down scaling, and replicating of commands for virtual servers and cloud storage devices needs to be exposed.

In support of these features, a self-service portal is developed and the feature-set of DTGOV's existing usage and administration portal is extended.

9.2 Resource Management System

The *resource management system* mechanism helps coordinate IT resources in response to management actions performed by both cloud consumers and cloud providers (Figure 9.5). Core to this system is the virtual infrastructure manager (VIM) that coordinates the server hardware so that virtual server instances can be created from the most expedient underlying physical server. A VIM is a commercial product that can be used to manage a range of virtual IT resources across multiple physical servers. For example, a VIM can create and manage multiple instances of a hypervisor across different physical servers or allocate a virtual server on one physical server to another (or to a resource pool).

Figure 9.5

A resource management system encompassing a VIM platform and a virtual machine image repository. The VIM may have additional repositories, including one dedicated to storing operational data.

Tasks that are typically automated and implemented through the resource management system include:

- managing virtual IT resource templates that are used to create pre-built instances, such as virtual server images

- allocating and releasing virtual IT resources into the available physical infrastructure in response to the starting, pausing, resuming, and termination of virtual IT resource instances

- coordinating IT resources in relation to the involvement of other mechanisms, such as resource replication, load balancer, and failover system

- enforcing usage and security policies throughout the lifecycle of cloud service instances

- monitoring operational conditions of IT resources

Resource management system functions can be accessed by cloud resource administrators employed by the cloud provider or cloud consumer. Those working on behalf of a cloud provider will often be able to directly access the resource management system's native console.

Resource management systems typically expose APIs that allow cloud providers to build remote administration system portals that can be customized to selectively offer resource management controls to external cloud resource administrators acting on behalf of cloud consumer organizations via usage and administration portals.

Both forms of access are depicted in Figure 9.6.

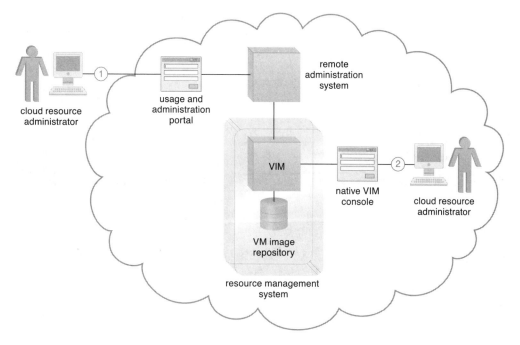

Figure 9.6

The cloud consumer's cloud resource administrator accesses a usage and administration portal externally to administer a leased IT resource (1). The cloud provider's cloud resource administrator uses the native user-interface provided by the VIM to perform internal resource management tasks (2).

CASE STUDY EXAMPLE

The DTGOV resource management system is an extension of a new VIM product it purchased, and provides the following primary features:

- management of virtual IT resources with a flexible allocation of pooled IT resources across different data centers

- management of cloud consumer databases

- isolation of virtual IT resources at logical perimeter networks

- management of a template virtual server image inventory available for immediate instantiation

- automated replication ("snapshotting") of virtual server images for virtual server creation

- automated up-down scaling of virtual servers according to usage thresholds to enable live VM migration among physical servers

- an API for the creation and management of virtual servers and virtual storage devices

- an API for the creation of network access control rules

- an API for the up-down scaling of virtual IT resources

- an API for the migration and replication of virtual IT resources across multiple data centers

- interoperation with a single sign-on mechanism through an LDAP interface

Custom-designed SNMP command scripts are further implemented to interoperate with the network management tools to establish isolated virtual networks across multiple data centers.

9.3 SLA Management System

The *SLA management system* mechanism represents a range of commercially available cloud management products that provide features pertaining to the administration, collection, storage, reporting, and runtime notification of SLA data (Figure 9.7).

Figure 9.7

An SLA management system encompassing an SLA manager and QoS measurements repository.

SLA management
system

An SLA management system deployment will generally include a repository used to store and retrieve collected SLA data based on pre-defined metrics and reporting parameters. It will further rely on one or more SLA monitor mechanisms to collect the SLA data that can then be made available in near-real time to usage and administration portals to provide on-going feedback regarding active cloud services (Figure 9.8). The metrics monitored for individual cloud services are aligned with the SLA guarantees in corresponding cloud provisioning contracts.

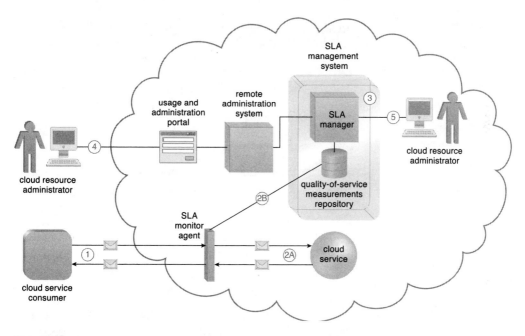

Figure 9.8

A cloud service consumer interacts with a cloud service (1). An SLA monitor intercepts the exchanged messages, evaluates the interaction, and collects relevant runtime data in relation to quality-of-service guarantees defined in the cloud service's SLA (2A). The data collected is stored in a repository (2B) that is part of the SLA management system (3). Queries can be issued and reports can be generated for an external cloud resource administrator via a usage and administration portal (4) or for an internal cloud resource administrator via the SLA management system's native user-interface (5).

CASE STUDY EXAMPLE

DTGOV implements an SLA management system that interoperates with its existing VIM. This integration allows DTGOV cloud resource administrators to monitor the availability of a range of hosted IT resources via SLA monitors.

DTGOV works with the SLA management system's report design features to create the following pre-defined reports that are made available via custom dashboards:

- *Per-Data Center Availability Dashboard* – Publicly accessible through DTGOV's corporate cloud portal, this dashboard shows the overall operational conditions of each group of IT resources at each data center, in realtime.

- *Per-Cloud Consumer Availability Dashboard* – This dashboard displays realtime operational conditions of individual IT resources. Information about each IT resource can only be accessed by the cloud provider and the cloud consumer leasing or owning the IT resource.

- *Per-Cloud Consumer SLA Report* – This report consolidates and summarizes SLA statistics for cloud consumer IT resources, including downtimes and other time-stamped SLA events.

The SLA events generated by the SLA monitors represent the status and performance of physical and virtual IT resources that are controlled by the virtualization platform. The SLA management system interoperates with the network management tools through a custom-designed SNMP software agent that receives the SLA event notifications.

The SLA management system also interacts with the VIM through its proprietary API to associate each network SLA event to the affected virtual IT resource. The system includes a proprietary database used to store SLA events (such as virtual server and network downtimes).

The SLA management system exposes a REST API that DTGOV uses to interface with its central remote administration system. The proprietary API has a component service implementation that can be used for batch-processing with the billing management system. DTGOV utilizes this to periodically provide downtime data that translates into credit applied to cloud consumer usage fees.

9.4 Billing Management System

The *billing management system* mechanism is dedicated to the collection and processing of usage data as it pertains to cloud provider accounting and cloud consumer billing. Specifically, the billing management system relies on pay-per-use monitors to gather runtime usage data that is stored in a repository that the system components then draw from for billing, reporting, and invoicing purposes (Figures 9.9 and 9.10).

Figure 9.9

A billing management system comprised of a pricing and contract manager and a pay-per-use measurements repository.

The billing management system allows for the definition of different pricing policies, as well as custom pricing models on a per cloud consumer and/or per IT resource basis. Pricing models can vary from the traditional pay-per-use models, to flat-rate or pay-per-allocation modes, or combinations thereof.

Billing arrangements be based on pre-usage and post-usage payments. The latter type can include pre-defined limits or it can be set up (with the mutual agreement of the cloud consumer) to allow for unlimited usage (and, consequently, no limit on subsequent billing). When limits are established, they are usually in the form of usage quotas. When quotas are exceeded, the billing management system can block further usage requests by cloud consumers.

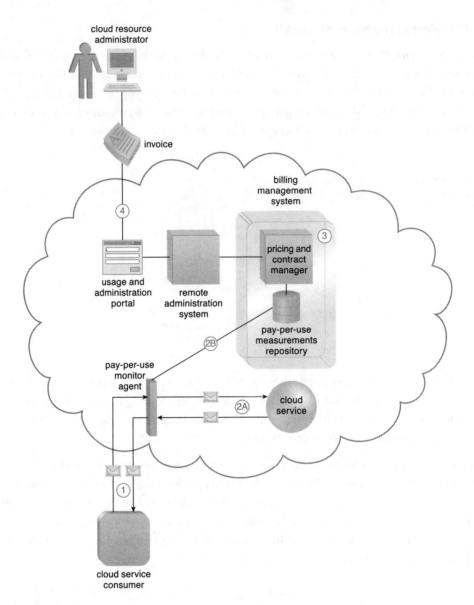

Figure 9.10

A cloud service consumer exchanges messages with a cloud service (1). A pay-per-use monitor keeps track of the usage and collects data relevant to billing (2A), which is forwarded to a repository that is part of the billing management system (2B). The system periodically calculates the consolidated cloud service usage fees and generates an invoice for the cloud consumer (3). The invoice may be provided to the cloud consumer through the usage and administration portal (4).

CASE STUDY EXAMPLE

DTGOV decides to establish a billing management system that enables them to create invoices for custom-defined billable events, such as subscriptions and IT resource volume usage. The billing management system is customized with the necessary events and pricing scheme metadata.

It includes the following two corresponding proprietary databases:

- billable event repository

- pricing scheme repository

Usage events are collected from pay-per-use monitors that are implemented as extensions to the VIM platform. Thin-granularity usage events, such as virtual server starting, stopping, up-down scaling, and decommissioning, are stored in a repository managed by the VIM platform.

The pay-per-use monitors further regularly supply the billing management system with the appropriate billable events. A standard pricing model is applied to most cloud consumer contracts, although it can be customized when special terms are negotiated.

Chapter 10

Cloud Security Mechanisms

This chapter establishes a set of fundamental cloud security mechanisms, several of which can be used to counter the security threats described in Chapter 6.

10.1 Encryption

Data, by default, is coded in a readable format known as *plaintext*. When transmitted over a network, plaintext is vulnerable to unauthorized and potentially malicious access. The *encryption* mechanism is a digital coding system dedicated to preserving the confidentiality and integrity of data. It is used for encoding plaintext data into a protected and unreadable format.

Encryption technology commonly relies on a standardized algorithm called a *cipher* to transform original plaintext data into encrypted data, referred to as *ciphertext*. Access to ciphertext does not divulge the original plaintext data, apart from some forms of metadata, such as message length and creation date. When encryption is applied to plaintext data, the data is paired with a string of characters called an *encryption key*, a secret message that is established by and shared among authorized parties. The encryption key is used to decrypt the ciphertext back into its original plaintext format.

The encryption mechanism can help counter the traffic eavesdropping, malicious intermediary, insufficient authorization, and overlapping trust boundaries security threats. For example, malicious service agents that attempt traffic eavesdropping are unable to decrypt messages in transit if they do not have the encryption key (Figure 10.1).

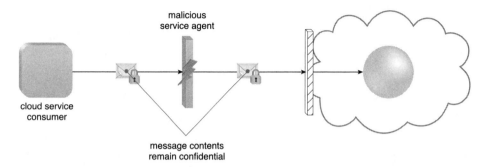

Figure 10.1

A malicious service agent is unable to retrieve data from an encrypted message. The retrieval attempt may furthermore be revealed to the cloud service consumer. (Note the use of the lock symbol to indicate that a security mechanism has been applied to the message contents.)

There are two common forms of encryption known as *symmetric encryption* and *asymmetric encryption.*

Symmetric Encryption

Symmetric encryption uses the same key for both encryption and decryption, both of which are performed by authorized parties that use the one shared key. Also known as *secret key cryptography*, messages that are encrypted with a specific key can be decrypted by only that same key. Parties that rightfully decrypt the data are provided with evidence that the original encryption was performed by parties that rightfully possess the key. A basic authentication check is always performed, because only authorized parties that own the key can create messages. This maintains and verifies data confidentiality.

Note that symmetrical encryption does not have the characteristic of non-repudiation, since determining exactly which party performed the message encryption or decryption is not possible if more than one party is in possession of the key.

Asymmetric Encryption

Asymmetric encryption relies on the use of two different keys, namely a private key and a public key. With asymmetric encryption (which is also referred to as *public key cryptography*), the private key is known only to its owner while the public key is commonly available. A document that was encrypted with a private key can only be correctly decrypted with the corresponding public key. Conversely, a document that was encrypted with a public key can be decrypted only using its private key counterpart. As a result of two different keys being used instead of just the one, asymmetric encryption is almost always computationally slower than symmetric encryption.

The level of security that is achieved is dictated by whether a private key or public key was used to encrypt the plaintext data. As every asymmetrically encrypted message has its own private-public key pair, messages that were encrypted with a private key can be correctly decrypted by any party with the corresponding public key. This method of encryption does not offer any confidentiality protection, even though successful decryption proves that the text was encrypted by the rightful private key owner. Private key encryption therefore offers integrity protection in addition to authenticity and non-repudiation. A message that was encrypted with a public key can only be decrypted by the rightful private key owner, which provides confidentiality protection. However, any party that has the public key can generate the ciphertext, meaning this method provides neither message integrity nor authenticity protection due to the communal nature of the public key.

> **NOTE**
>
> The encryption mechanism, when used to secure Web-based data transmissions, is most commonly applied via HTTPS, which refers to the use of SSL/TLS as an underlying encryption protocol for HTTP. TLS (transport layer security) is the successor to the SSL (secure sockets layer) technology. Because asymmetric encryption is usually more time-consuming than symmetric encryption, TLS uses the former only for its key exchange method. TLS systems then switch to symmetric encryption once the keys have been exchanged.
>
> Most TLS implementations primarily support RSA as the chief asymmetrical encryption cipher, while ciphers such as RC4, Triple-DES, and AES are supported for symmetrical encryption.

CASE STUDY EXAMPLE

Innovartus has recently learned that users who access their User Registration Portal via public Wi-Fi hot zones and unsecured LANs may be transmitting personal user profile details via plaintext. Innovartus immediately remedies this vulnerability by applying the encryption mechanism to its Web portal via the use of HTTPS (Figure 10.2).

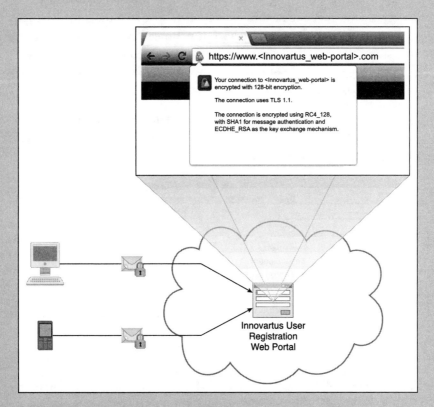

Figure 10.2

The encryption mechanism is added to the communication channel between outside users and Innovartus' User Registration Portal. This safeguards message confidentiality via the use of HTTPS.

10.2 Hashing

The *hashing* mechanism is used when a one-way, non-reversible form of data protection is required. Once hashing has been applied to a message, it is locked and no key is provided for the message to be unlocked. A common application of this mechanism is the storage of passwords.

Hashing technology can be used to derive a hashing code or *message digest* from a message, which is often of a fixed length and smaller than the original message. The message sender can then utilize the hashing mechanism to attach the message digest to the message. The recipient applies the same hash function to the message to verify that the produced message digest is identical to the one that accompanied the message. Any alteration to the original data results in an entirely different message digest and clearly indicates that tampering has occurred.

In addition to its utilization for protecting stored data, the cloud threats that can be mitigated by the hashing mechanism include malicious intermediary and insufficient authorization. An example of the former is illustrated in Figure 10.3.

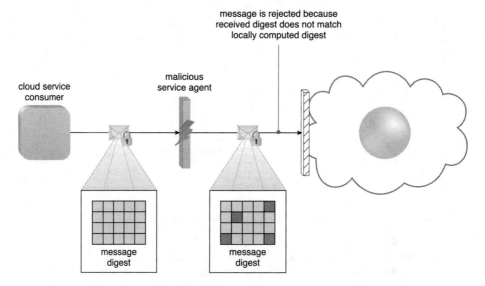

Figure 10.3

A hashing function is applied to protect the integrity of a message that is intercepted and altered by a malicious service agent, before it is forwarded. The firewall can be configured to determine that the message has been altered, thereby enabling it to reject the message before it can proceed to the cloud service.

CASE STUDY EXAMPLE

A subset of the applications that have been selected to be ported to ATN's PaaS platform allows users to access and alter highly sensitive corporate data. This information is being hosted on a cloud to enable access by trusted partners who may use it for critical calculation and assessment purposes. Concerned that the data could be tampered with, ATN decides to apply the hashing mechanism as a means of protecting and preserving the data's integrity.

ATN cloud resource administrators work with the cloud provider to incorporate a digest-generating procedure with each application version that is deployed in the cloud. Current values are logged to a secure on-premise database and the procedure is regularly repeated with the results analyzed. Figure 10.4 illustrates how ATN implements hashing to determine whether any non-authorized actions have been performed against the ported applications.

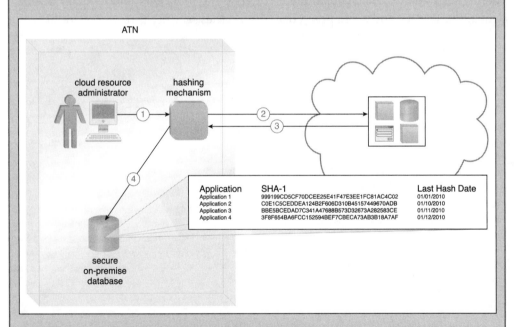

Figure 10.4

A hashing procedure is invoked when the PaaS environment is accessed (1). The applications that were ported to this environment are checked (2) and their message digests are calculated (3). The message digests are stored in a secure on-premise database (4), and a notification is issued if any of their values are not identical to the ones in storage.

10.3 Digital Signature

The *digital signature* mechanism is a means of providing data authenticity and integrity through authentication and non-repudiation. A message is assigned a digital signature prior to transmission, which is then rendered invalid if the message experiences any subsequent, unauthorized modifications. A digital signature provides evidence that the message received is the same as the one created by its rightful sender.

Both hashing and asymmetrical encryption are involved in the creation of a digital signature, which essentially exists as a message digest that was encrypted by a private key and appended to the original message. The recipient verifies the signature validity and uses the corresponding public key to decrypt the digital signature, which produces the message digest. The hashing mechanism can also be applied to the original message to produce this message digest. Identical results from the two different processes indicate that the message maintained its integrity.

The digital signature mechanism helps mitigate the malicious intermediary, insufficient authorization, and overlapping trust boundaries security threats (Figure 10.5).

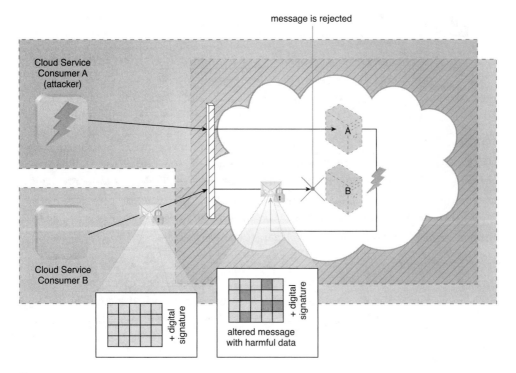

Figure 10.5

Cloud Service Consumer B sends a message that was digitally signed but was altered by trusted attacker Cloud Service Consumer A. Virtual Server B is configured to verify digital signatures before processing incoming messages even if they are within its trust boundary. The message is revealed as illegitimate due to its invalid digital signature, and is therefore rejected by Virtual Server B.

CASE STUDY EXAMPLE

With DTGOV's client portfolio expanding to include public-sector organizations, many of its cloud computing policies have become unsuitable and require modification. Considering that public-sector organizations frequently handle strategic information, security safeguards need to be established to protect data manipulation and to establish a means of auditing activities that may impact government operations.

DTGOV proceeds to implement the digital signature mechanism specifically to protect its Web-based management environment (Figure 10.6). Virtual server self-provisioning inside the IaaS environment and the tracking functionality of realtime SLA and billing are all performed via Web portals. As a result, user error or malicious actions could result in legal and financial consequences.

Digital signatures provide DTGOV with the guarantee that every action performed is linked to its legitimate originator. Unauthorized access is expected to become highly improbable, since digital signatures are only accepted if the encryption key is identical to the secret key held by the rightful owner. Users will not have grounds to deny attempts at message adulteration because the digital signatures will confirm message integrity.

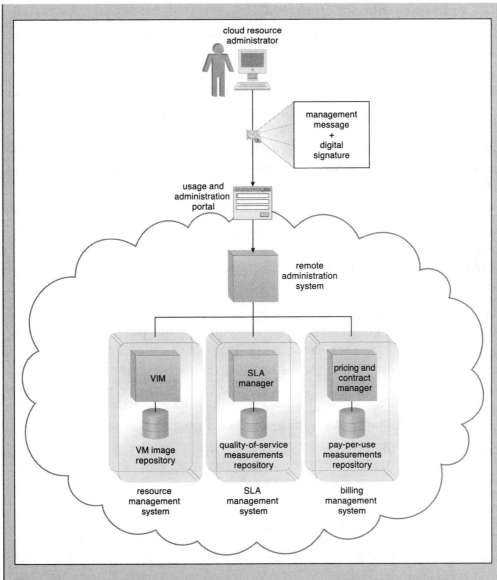

Figure 10.6

Whenever a cloud consumer performs a management action that is related to IT resources provisioned by DTGOV, the cloud service consumer program must include a digital signature in the message request to prove the legitimacy of its user.

10.4 Public Key Infrastructure (PKI)

A common approach for managing the issuance of asymmetric keys is based on the *public key infrastructure (PKI)* mechanism, which exists as a system of protocols, data formats, rules, and practices that enable large-scale systems to securely use public key cryptography. This system is used to associate public keys with their corresponding key owners (known as *public key identification*) while enabling the verification of key validity. PKIs rely on the use of digital certificates, which are digitally signed data structures that bind public keys to certificate owner identities, as well as to related information, such as validity periods. Digital certificates are usually digitally signed by a third-party certificate authority (CA), as illustrated in Figure 10.7.

Other methods of generating digital signatures can be employed, even though the majority of digital certificates are issued by only a handful of trusted CAs like VeriSign and Comodo. Larger organizations, such as Microsoft, can act as their own CA and issue certificates to their clients and the public, since even individual users can generate certificates as long as they have the appropriate software tools.

Building up an acceptable level of trust for a CA is time-intensive but necessary. Rigorous security measures, substantial infrastructure investments, and stringent operational processes all contribute to establishing the credibility of a CA. The higher its level of trust and reliability, the more esteemed and reputable its certificates. The PKI is a dependable method for implementing asymmetric encryption, managing cloud consumer and cloud provider identity information, and helping to defend against the malicious intermediary and insufficient authorization threats.

The PKI mechanism is primarily used to counter the insufficient authorization threat.

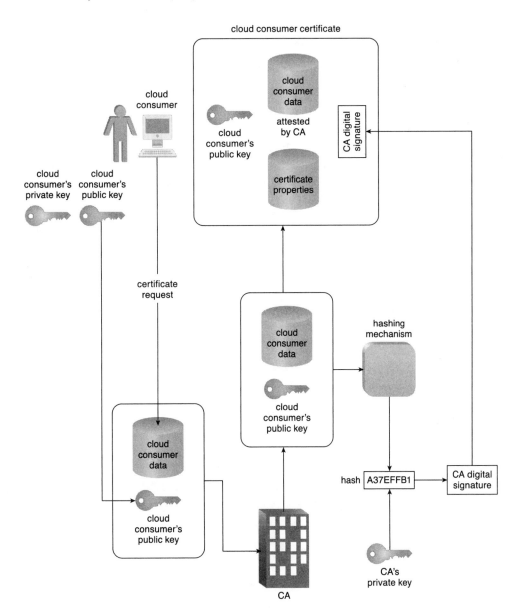

Figure 10.7

The common steps involved during the generation of certificates by a certificate authority.

CASE STUDY EXAMPLE

DTGOV requires that its clients use digital signatures to access its Web-based management environment. These are to be generated from public keys that have been certified by a recognized certificate authority (Figure 10.8).

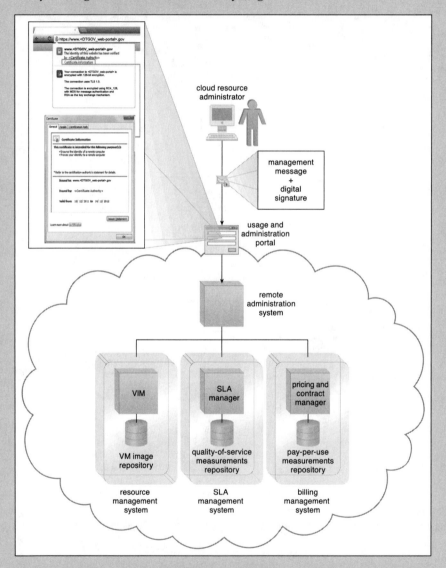

Figure 10.8

An external cloud resource administrator uses a digital certificate to access the Web-based management environment. DTGOV's digital certificate is used in the HTTPS connection and then signed by a trusted CA.

10.5 **Identity and Access Management (IAM)**

The *identity and access management (IAM)* mechanism encompasses the components and policies necessary to control and track user identities and access privileges for IT resources, environments, and systems.

Specifically, IAM mechanisms exist as systems comprised of four main components:

- *Authentication* – Username and password combinations remain the most common forms of user authentication credentials managed by the IAM system, which also can support digital signatures, digital certificates, biometric hardware (fingerprint readers), specialized software (such as voice analysis programs), and locking user accounts to registered IP or MAC addresses.

- *Authorization* – The authorization component defines the correct granularity for access controls and oversees the relationships between identities, access control rights, and IT resource availability.

- *User Management* – Related to the administrative capabilities of the system, the user management program is responsible for creating new user identities and access groups, resetting passwords, defining password policies, and managing privileges.

- *Credential Management* – The credential management system establishes identities and access control rules for defined user accounts, which mitigates the threat of insufficient authorization.

Although its objectives are similar to those of the PKI mechanism, the IAM mechanism's scope of implementation is distinct because its structure encompasses access controls and policies in addition to assigning specific levels of user privileges.

The IAM mechanism is primarily used to counter the insufficient authorization, denial of service, and overlapping trust boundaries threats.

CASE STUDY EXAMPLE

As a result of several past corporate acquisitions, ATN's legacy landscape has become complex and highly heterogeneous. Maintenance costs have increased due to redundant and similar applications and databases running concurrently. Legacy repositories of user credentials are just as assorted.

Now that ATN has ported several applications to a PaaS environment, new identities are created and configured in order to grant users access. The CloudEnhance consultants suggest that ATN capitalize on this opportunity by starting a pilot IAM system initiative, especially since a new group of cloud-based identities is needed.

ATN agrees, and a specialized IAM system is designed specifically to regulate the security boundaries within their new PaaS environment. With this system, the identities assigned to cloud-based IT resources differ from corresponding on-premise identities, which were originally defined according to ATN's internal security policies.

10.6 Single Sign-On (SSO)

Propagating the authentication and authorization information for a cloud service consumer across multiple cloud services can be a challenge, especially if numerous cloud services or cloud-based IT resources need to be invoked as part of the same overall runtime activity. The *single sign-on (SSO)* mechanism enables one cloud service consumer to be authenticated by a security broker, which establishes a security context that is persisted while the cloud service consumer accesses other cloud services or cloud-based IT resources. Otherwise, the cloud service consumer would need to re-authenticate itself with every subsequent request.

The SSO mechanism essentially enables mutually independent cloud services and IT resources to generate and circulate runtime authentication and authorization credentials. The credentials initially provided by the cloud service consumer remain valid for the duration of a session, while its security context information is shared (Figure 10.9). The SSO mechanism's security broker is especially useful when a cloud service consumer needs to access cloud services residing on different clouds (Figure 10.10).

This mechanism does not directly counter any of the cloud security threats listed in Chapter 6. It primarily enhances the usability of cloud-based environments for access and management of distributed IT resources and solutions.

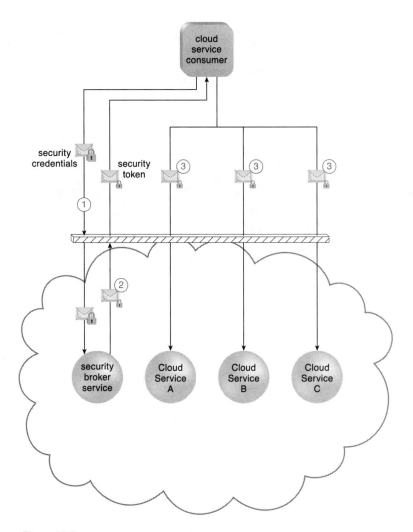

Figure 10.9

A cloud service consumer provides the security broker with login credentials (1). The security broker responds with an authentication token (message with small lock symbol) upon successful authentication, which contains cloud service consumer identity information (2) that is used to automatically authenticate the cloud service consumer acoss Cloud Services A, B, and C (3).

CASE STUDY EXAMPLE

The migration of applications to ATN's new PaaS platform was successful, but also raised a number of new concerns pertaining to the responsiveness and availability of PaaS-hosted IT resources. ATN intends to move more applications to a PaaS platform, but decides to do so by establishing a second PaaS environment with a different cloud provider. This will allow them to compare cloud providers during a three-month assessment period.

To accommodate this distributed cloud architecture, the SSO mechanism is used to establish a security broker capable of propagating login credentials across both clouds (Figure 10.10). This enables a single cloud resource administrator to access IT resources on both PaaS environments without having to log in separately to each one.

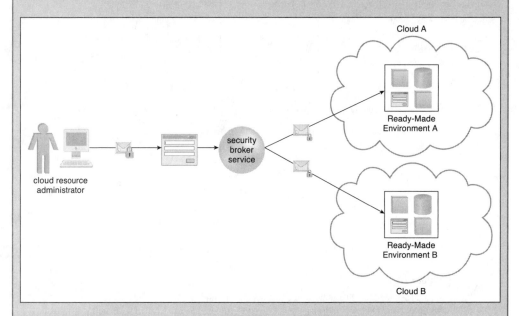

Figure 10.10

The credentials received by the security broker are propagated to ready-made environments across two different clouds. The security broker is responsible for selecting the appropriate security procedure with which to contact each cloud.

10.7 Cloud-Based Security Groups

Similar to constructing dykes and levees that separate land from water, data protection is increased by placing barriers between IT resources. Cloud resource segmentation is a process by which separate physical and virtual IT environments are created for different users and groups. For example, an organization's WAN can be partitioned according to individual network security requirements. One network can be established with a resilient firewall for external Internet access, while a second is deployed without a firewall because its users are internal and unable to access the Internet.

Resource segmentation is used to enable virtualization by allocating a variety of physical IT resources to virtual machines. It needs to be optimized for public cloud environments, since organizational trust boundaries from different cloud consumers overlap when sharing the same underlying physical IT resources.

The cloud-based resource segmentation process creates *cloud-based security group* mechanisms that are determined through security policies. Networks are segmented into logical cloud-based security groups that form logical network perimeters. Each cloud-based IT resource is assigned to at least one logical cloud-based security group. Each logical cloud-based security group is assigned specific rules that govern the communication between the security groups.

Multiple virtual servers running on the same physical server can become members of different logical cloud-based security groups (Figure 10.11). Virtual servers can further be separated into public-private groups, development-production groups, or any other designation configured by the cloud resource administrator.

Cloud-based security groups delineate areas where different security measures can be applied. Properly implemented cloud-based security groups help limit unauthorized access to IT resources in the event of a security breach. This mechanism can be used to help counter the denial of service, insufficient authorization, and overlapping trust boundaries threats, and is closely related to the logical network perimeter mechanism.

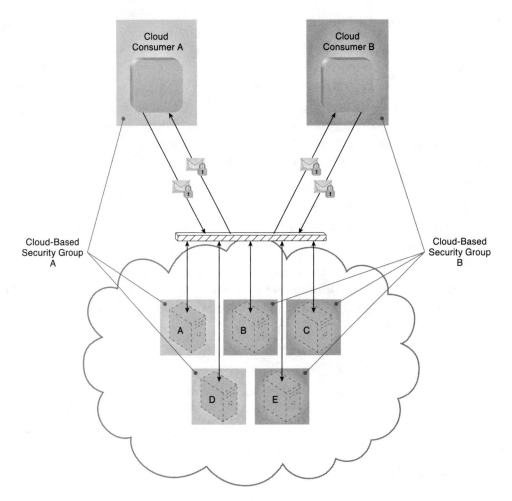

Figure 10.11

Cloud-Based Security Group A encompasses Virtual Servers A and D and is assigned to Cloud Consumer A. Cloud-Based Security Group B is comprised of Virtual Servers B, C, and E and is assigned to Cloud Consumer B. If Cloud Service Consumer A's credentials are compromised, the attacker would only be able to access and damage the virtual servers in Cloud-Based Security Group A, thereby protecting Virtual Servers B, C, and E.

CASE STUDY EXAMPLE

Now that DTGOV has itself become a cloud provider, security concerns are raised pertaining to its hosting of public-sector client data. A team of cloud security specialists is brought in to define cloud-based security groups together with the digital signature and PKI mechanisms.

Security policies are classified into levels of resource segmentation before being integrated into DTGOV's Web portal management environment. Consistent with the security requirements guaranteed by its SLAs, DTGOV maps IT resource allocation to the appropriate logical cloud-based security group (Figure 10.12), which has its own security policy that clearly stipulates its IT resource isolation and control levels.

DTGOV informs its clients about the availability of these new security policies. Cloud consumers can optionally choose to utilize them and doing so results in increased fees.

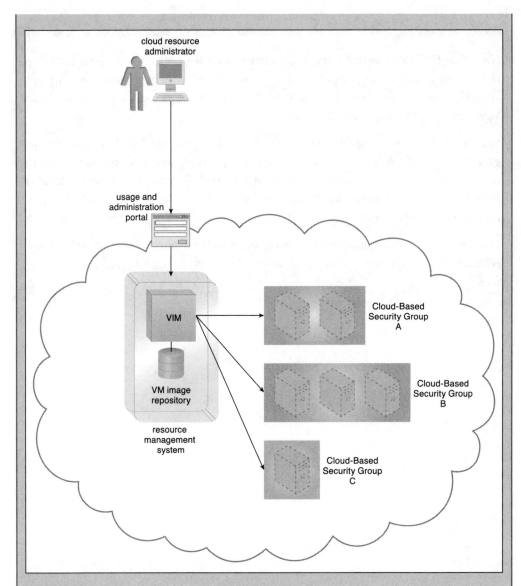

Figure 10.12

When an external cloud resource administrator accesses the Web portal to allocate a virtual server, the requested security credentials are assessed and mapped to an internal security policy that assigns a corresponding cloud-based security group to the new virtual server.

10.8 Hardened Virtual Server Images

As previously discussed, a virtual server is created from a template configuration called a virtual server image (or virtual machine image). Hardening is the process of stripping unnecessary software from a system to limit potential vulnerabilities that can be exploited by attackers. Removing redundant programs, closing unnecessary server ports, and disabling unused services, internal root accounts, and guest access are all examples of hardening.

A *hardened virtual server image* is a template for virtual service instance creation that has been subjected to a hardening process (Figure 10.13). This generally results in a virtual server template that is significantly more secure than the original standard image.

Hardened virtual server images help counter the denial of service, insufficient authorization, and overlapping trust boundaries threats.

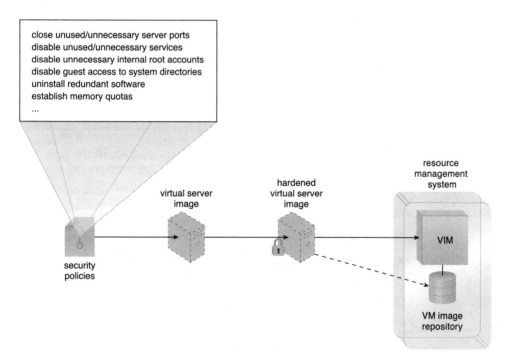

Figure 10.13

A cloud provider applies its security policies to harden its standard virtual server images. The hardened image template is saved in the VM images repository as part of a resource management system.

CASE STUDY EXAMPLE

One of the security features made available to cloud consumers as part of DTGOV adoption of cloud-based security groups is an option to have some or all virtual servers within a given group hardened (Figure 10.14). Each hardened virtual server image results in an extra fee but spares cloud consumers from having to carry out the hardening process themselves.

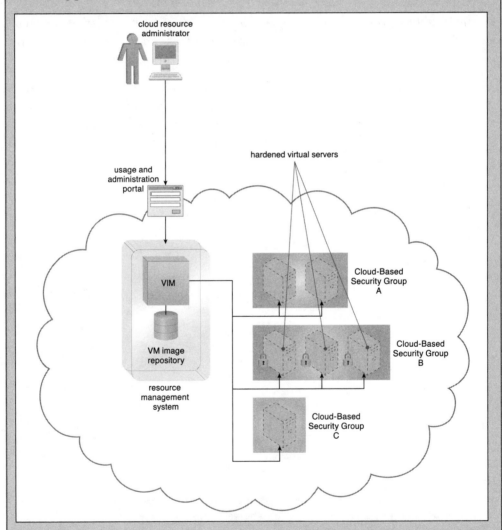

Figure 10.14

The cloud resource administrator chooses the hardened virtual server image option for the virtual servers provisioned for Cloud-Based Security Group B.

Part III

Cloud Computing Architecture

Cloud technology architectures formalize functional domains within cloud environments by establishing well-defined solutions comprised of interactions, behaviors, and distinct combinations of cloud computing mechanisms and other specialized cloud technology components.

The fundamental cloud architectural models covered in Chapter 11 establish foundational layers of technology architecture common to most clouds. Many of the advanced and specialized models described in Chapters 12 and 13 build upon these foundations to add complex and narrower-focused solution architectures.

Notably absent from the upcoming chapters are security architectures or architectural models that involve the cloud security mechanisms from Chapter 10. These are covered separately in a series title dedicated to cloud security.

> **NOTE**
>
> The 29 cloud architectures described over the next three chapters are further explored in a formal cloud computing design patterns catalog authored by Thomas Erl and Amin Naserpour. Visit www.cloudpatterns.org to read the official pattern profile for each cloud architecture. The cloud computing design patterns catalog organizes these and several other design patterns into compound patterns that correspond to cloud delivery models, cloud deployment models, and feature-sets that represent elastic, resilient, and multitenant environments.

Chapter 11

Fundamental Cloud Architectures

This chapter introduces and describes several of the more common foundational cloud architectural models, each exemplifying a common usage and characteristic of contemporary cloud-based environments. The involvement and importance of different combinations of cloud computing mechanisms in relation to these architectures are explored.

11.1 Workload Distribution Architecture

IT resources can be horizontally scaled via the addition of one or more identical IT resources, and a load balancer that provides runtime logic capable of evenly distributing the workload among the available IT resources (Figure 11.1). The resulting *workload distribution architecture* reduces both IT resource over-utilization and under-utilization to an extent dependent upon the sophistication of the load balancing algorithms and runtime logic.

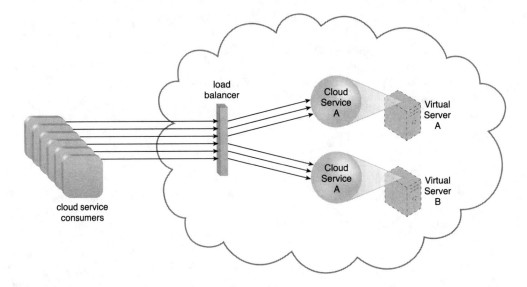

Figure 11.1

A redundant copy of Cloud Service A is implemented on Virtual Server B. The load balancer intercepts cloud service consumer requests and directs them to both Virtual Servers A and B to ensure even workload distribution.

This fundamental architectural model can be applied to any IT resource, with workload distribution commonly carried out in support of distributed virtual servers, cloud storage devices, and cloud services. Load balancing systems applied to specific IT resources usually produce specialized variations of this architecture that incorporate aspects of load balancing, such as:

- the service load balancing architecture explained later in this chapter

- the load balanced virtual server architecture covered in Chapter 12

- the load balanced virtual switches architecture described in Chapter 13

In addition to the base load balancer mechanism, and the virtual server and cloud storage device mechanisms to which load balancing can be applied, the following mechanisms can also be part of this cloud architecture:

- *Audit Monitor* – When distributing runtime workloads, the type and geographical location of the IT resources that process the data can determine whether monitoring is necessary to fulfill legal and regulatory requirements.

- *Cloud Usage Monitor* – Various monitors can be involved to carry out runtime workload tracking and data processing.

- *Hypervisor* – Workloads between hypervisors and the virtual servers that they host may require distribution.

- *Logical Network Perimeter* – The logical network perimeter isolates cloud consumer network boundaries in relation to how and where workloads are distributed.

- *Resource Cluster* – Clustered IT resources in active/active mode are commonly used to support workload balancing between different cluster nodes.

- *Resource Replication* – This mechanism can generate new instances of virtualized IT resources in response to runtime workload distribution demands.

11.2 Resource Pooling Architecture

A *resource pooling architecture* is based on the use of one or more resource pools, in which identical IT resources are grouped and maintained by a system that automatically ensures that they remain synchronized.

Provided here are common examples of resource pools:

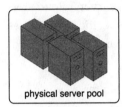

physical server pool

Physical server pools are composed of networked servers that have been installed with operating systems and other necessary programs and/or applications and are ready for immediate use.

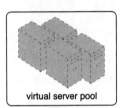

virtual server pool

Virtual server pools are usually configured using one of several available templates chosen by the cloud consumer during provisioning. For example, a cloud consumer can set up a pool of mid-tier Windows servers with 4 GB of RAM or a pool of low-tier Ubuntu servers with 2 GB of RAM.

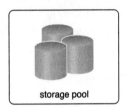

storage pool

Storage pools, or cloud storage device pools, consist of file-based or block-based storage structures that contain empty and/or filled cloud storage devices.

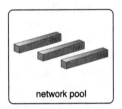

network pool

Network pools (or interconnect pools) are composed of different preconfigured network connectivity devices. For example, a pool of virtual firewall devices or physical network switches can be created for redundant connectivity, load balancing, or link aggregation.

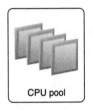

CPU pool

CPU pools are ready to be allocated to virtual servers, and are typically broken down into individual processing cores.

memory pool

Pools of physical RAM can be used in newly provisioned physical servers or to vertically scale physical servers.

Dedicated pools can be created for each type of IT resource and individual pools can be grouped into a larger pool, in which case each individual pool becomes a sub-pool (Figure 11.2).

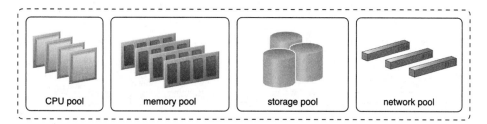

CPU pool   memory pool   storage pool   network pool

Figure 11.2

A sample resource pool that is comprised of four sub-pools of CPUs, memory, cloud storage devices, and virtual network devices.

Resource pools can become highly complex, with multiple pools created for specific cloud consumers or applications. A hierarchical structure can be established to form parent, sibling, and nested pools in order to facilitate the organization of diverse resource pooling requirements (Figure 11.3).

Sibling resource pools are usually drawn from physically grouped IT resources, as opposed to IT resources that are spread out over different data centers. Sibling pools are isolated from one another so that each cloud consumer is only provided access to its respective pool.

In the nested pool model, larger pools are divided into smaller pools that individually group the same type of IT resources together (Figure 11.4). Nested pools can be used to assign resource pools to different departments or groups in the same cloud consumer organization.

After resources pools have been defined, multiple instances of IT resources from each pool can be created to provide an in-memory pool of "live" IT resources.

In addition to cloud storage devices and virtual servers, which are commonly pooled mechanisms, the following mechanisms can also be part of this cloud architecture:

- *Audit Monitor* – This mechanism monitors resource pool usage to ensure compliance with privacy and regulation requirements, especially when pools contain cloud storage devices or data loaded into memory.

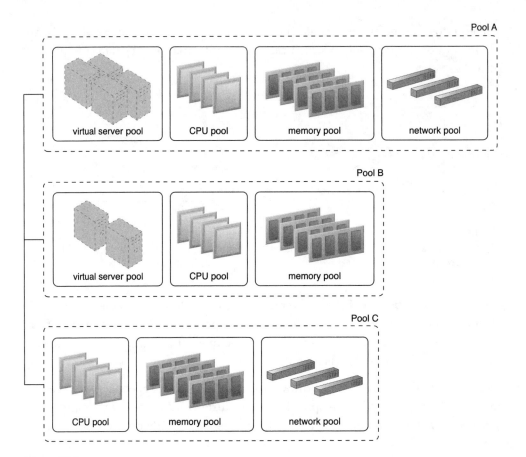

Figure 11.3

Pools B and C are sibling pools that are taken from the larger Pool A, which has been allocated to a cloud consumer. This is an alternative to taking the IT resources for Pool B and Pool C from a general reserve of IT resources that is shared throughout the cloud.

- *Cloud Usage Monitor* – Various cloud usage monitors are involved in the runtime tracking and synchronization that are required by the pooled IT resources and any underlying management systems.

- *Hypervisor* – The hypervisor mechanism is responsible for providing virtual servers with access to resource pools, in addition to hosting the virtual servers and sometimes the resource pools themselves.

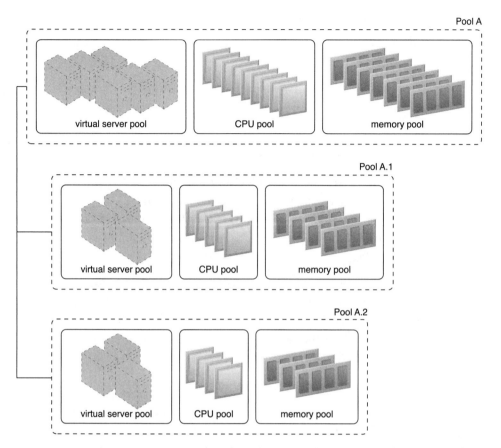

Figure 11.4

Nested Pools A.1 and Pool A.2 are comprised of the same IT resources as Pool A, but in different quantities. Nested pools are typically used to provision cloud services that need to be rapidly instantiated using the same type of IT resources with the same configuration settings.

- *Logical Network Perimeter* – The logical network perimeter is used to logically organize and isolate resource pools.

- *Pay-Per-Use Monitor* – The pay-per-use monitor collects usage and billing information on how individual cloud consumers are allocated and use IT resources from various pools.

- *Remote Administration System* – This mechanism is commonly used to interface with backend systems and programs in order to provide resource pool administration features via a front-end portal.

- *Resource Management System* – The resource management system mechanism supplies cloud consumers with the tools and permission management options for administering resource pools.

- *Resource Replication* – This mechanism is used to generate new instances of IT resources for resource pools.

11.3 Dynamic Scalability Architecture

The *dynamic scalability architecture* is an architectural model based on a system of predefined scaling conditions that trigger the dynamic allocation of IT resources from resource pools. Dynamic allocation enables variable utilization as dictated by usage demand fluctuations, since unnecessary IT resources are efficiently reclaimed without requiring manual interaction.

The automated scaling listener is configured with workload thresholds that dictate when new IT resources need to be added to the workload processing. This mechanism can be provided with logic that determines how many additional IT resources can be dynamically provided, based on the terms of a given cloud consumer's provisioning contract.

The following types of dynamic scaling are commonly used:

- *Dynamic Horizontal Scaling* – IT resource instances are scaled out and in to handle fluctuating workloads. The automatic scaling listener monitors requests and signals resource replication to initiate IT resource duplication, as per requirements and permissions.

- *Dynamic Vertical Scaling* – IT resource instances are scaled up and down when there is a need to adjust the processing capacity of a single IT resource. For example, a virtual server that is being overloaded can have its memory dynamically increased or it may have a processing core added.

- *Dynamic Relocation* – The IT resource is relocated to a host with more capacity. For example, a database may need to be moved from a tape-based SAN storage device with 4 GB per second I/O capacity to another disk-based SAN storage device with 8 GB per second I/O capacity.

Figures 11.5 to 11.7 illustrate the process of dynamic horizontal scaling.

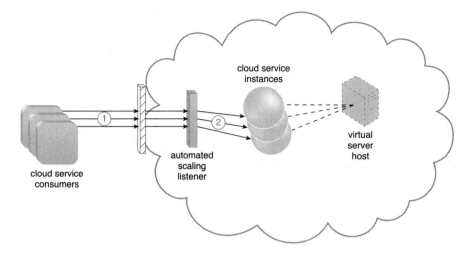

Figure 11.5

Cloud service consumers are sending requests to a cloud service (1). The automated scaling listener monitors the cloud service to determine if predefined capacity thresholds are being exceeded (2).

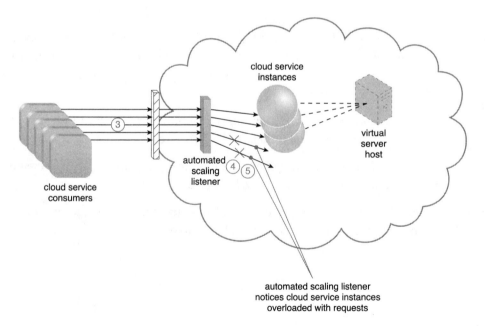

automated scaling listener
notices cloud service instances
overloaded with requests

Figure 11.6

The number of requests coming from cloud service consumers increases (3). The workload exceeds the performance thresholds. The automated scaling listener determines the next course of action based on a predefined scaling policy (4). If the cloud service implementation is deemed eligible for additional scaling, the automated scaling listener initiates the scaling process (5).

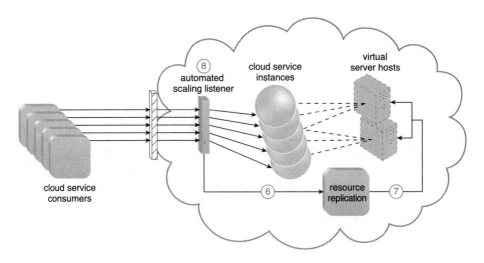

Figure 11.7

The automated scaling listener sends a signal to the resource replication mechanism (6), which creates more instances of the cloud service (7). Now that the increased workload has been accommodated, the automated scaling listener resumes monitoring and detracting and adding IT resources, as required (8).

The dynamic scalability architecture can be applied to a range of IT resources, including virtual servers and cloud storage devices. Besides the core automated scaling listener and resource replication mechanisms, the following mechanisms can also be used in this form of cloud architecture:

- *Cloud Usage Monitor* – Specialized cloud usage monitors can track runtime usage in response to dynamic fluctuations caused by this architecture.

- *Hypervisor* – The hypervisor is invoked by a dynamic scalability system to create or remove virtual server instances, or to be scaled itself.

- *Pay-Per-Use Monitor* – The pay-per-use monitor is engaged to collect usage cost information in response to the scaling of IT resources.

11.4 Elastic Resource Capacity Architecture

The *elastic resource capacity architecture* is primarily related to the dynamic provisioning of virtual servers, using a system that allocates and reclaims CPUs and RAM in immediate response to the fluctuating processing requirements of hosted IT resources (Figures 11.8 and 11.9).

Resource pools are used by scaling technology that interacts with the hypervisor and/or VIM to retrieve and return CPU and RAM resources at runtime. The runtime processing of the virtual server is monitored so that additional processing power can be leveraged from the resource pool via dynamic allocation, before capacity thresholds are met. The virtual server and its hosted applications and IT resources are vertically scaled in response.

This type of cloud architecture can be designed so that the intelligent automation engine script sends its scaling request via the VIM instead of to the hypervisor directly. Virtual servers that participate in elastic resource allocation systems may require rebooting in order for the dynamic resource allocation to take effect.

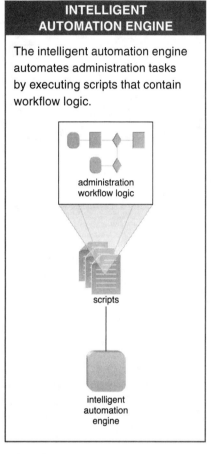

INTELLIGENT AUTOMATION ENGINE

The intelligent automation engine automates administration tasks by executing scripts that contain workflow logic.

administration workflow logic

scripts

intelligent automation engine

Some additional mechanisms that can be included in this cloud architecture are the following:

- *Cloud Usage Monitor* – Specialized cloud usage monitors collect resource usage information on IT resources before, during, and after scaling, to help define the future processing capacity thresholds of the virtual servers.

- *Pay-Per-Use Monitor* – The pay-per-use monitor is responsible for collecting resource usage cost information as it fluctuates with the elastic provisioning.

- *Resource Replication* – Resource replication is used by this architectural model to generate new instances of the scaled IT resources.

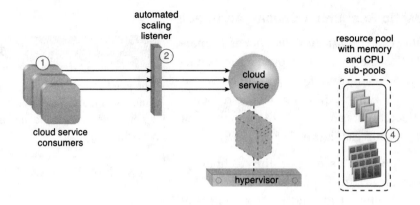

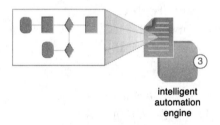

Figure 11.8

Cloud service consumers are actively sending requests to a cloud service (1), which are
monitored by an automated scaling listener (2). An intelligent automation engine script is
deployed with workflow logic (3) that is capable of notifying the resource pool using allocation
requests (4).

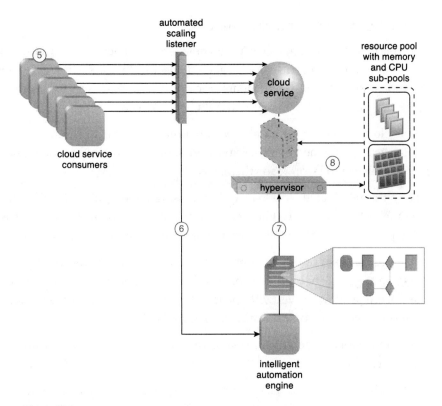

Figure 11.9

Cloud service consumer requests increase (5), causing the automated scaling listener to signal the intelligent automation engine to execute the script (6). The script runs the workflow logic that signals the hypervisor to allocate more IT resources from the resource pools (7). The hypervisor allocates additional CPU and RAM to the virtual server, enabling the increased workload to be handled (8).

11.5 Service Load Balancing Architecture

The *service load balancing architecture* can be considered a specialized variation of the workload distribution architecture that is geared specifically for scaling cloud service implementations. Redundant deployments of cloud services are created, with a load balancing system added to dynamically distribute workloads.

The duplicate cloud service implementations are organized into a resource pool, while the load balancer is positioned as either an external or built-in component to allow the host servers to balance the workloads themselves.

Depending on the anticipated workload and processing capacity of host server environments, multiple instances of each cloud service implementation can be generated as part of a resource pool that responds to fluctuating request volumes more efficiently.

The load balancer can be positioned either independent of the cloud services and their host servers (Figure 11.10), or built-in as part of the application or server's environment. In the latter case, a primary server with the load balancing logic can communicate with neighboring servers to balance the workload (Figure 11.11).

The service load balancing architecture can involve the following mechanisms in addition to the load balancer:

- *Cloud Usage Monitor* – Cloud usage monitors may be involved with monitoring cloud service instances and their respective IT resource consumption levels, as well as various runtime monitoring and usage data collection tasks.

- *Resource Cluster* – Active-active cluster groups are incorporated in this architecture to help balance workloads across different members of the cluster.

- *Resource Replication* – The resource replication mechanism is utilized to generate cloud service implementations in support of load balancing requirements.

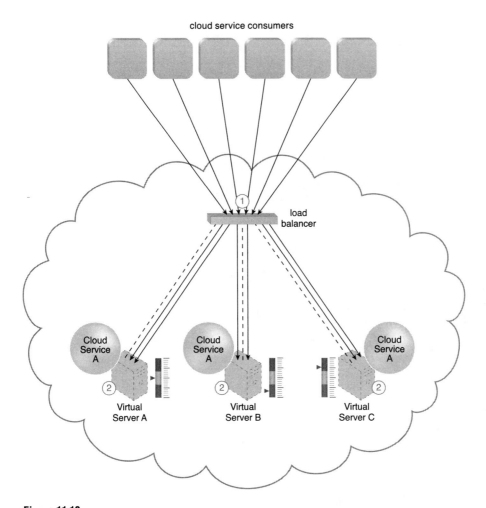

Figure 11.10

The load balancer intercepts messages sent by cloud service consumers (1) and forwards them to the virtual servers so that the workload processing is horizontally scaled (2).

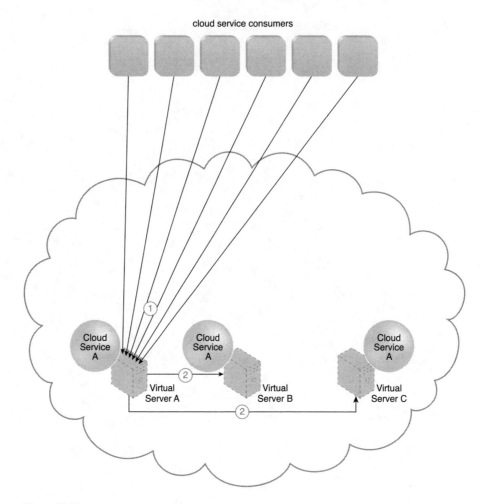

Figure 11.11

Cloud service consumer requests are sent to Cloud Service A on Virtual Server A (1). The cloud service implementation includes built-in load balancing logic that is capable of distributing requests to the neighboring Cloud Service A implementations on Virtual Servers B and C (2).

11.6 Cloud Bursting Architecture

The *cloud bursting architecture* establishes a form of dynamic scaling that scales or "bursts out" on-premise IT resources into a cloud whenever predefined capacity thresholds have been reached. The corresponding cloud-based IT resources are redundantly pre-deployed but remain inactive until cloud bursting occurs. After they are no longer required, the cloud-based IT resources are released and the architecture "bursts in" back to the on-premise environment.

Cloud bursting is a flexible scaling architecture that provides cloud consumers with the option of using cloud-based IT resources only to meet higher usage demands. The foundation of this architectural model is based on the automated scaling listener and resource replication mechanisms.

The automated scaling listener determines when to redirect requests to cloud-based IT resources, and resource replication is used to maintain synchronicity between on-premise and cloud-based IT resources in relation to state information (Figure 11.12).

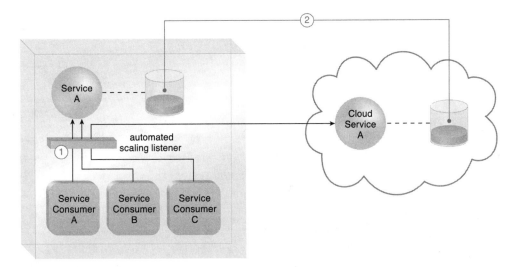

Figure 11.12

An automated scaling listener monitors the usage of on-premise Service A, and redirects Service Consumer C's request to Service A's redundant implementation in the cloud (Cloud Service A) once Service A's usage threshold has been exceeded (1). A resource replication system is used to keep state management databases synchronized (2).

In addition to the automated scaling listener and resource replication, numerous other mechanisms can be used to automate the burst in and out dynamics for this architecture, depending primarily on the type of IT resource being scaled.

11.7 Elastic Disk Provisioning Architecture

Cloud consumers are commonly charged for cloud-based storage space based on fixed-disk storage allocation, meaning the charges are predetermined by disk capacity and not aligned with actual data storage consumption. Figure 11.13 demonstrates this by illustrating a scenario in which a cloud consumer provisions a virtual server with the Windows Server operating system and three 150 GB hard drives. The cloud consumer is billed for using 450 GB of storage space after installing the operating system, even though it has not yet installed any software.

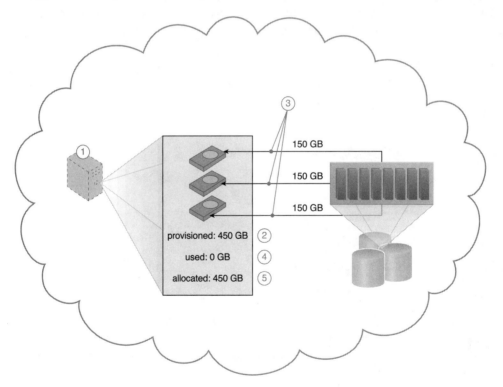

Figure 11.13

The cloud consumer requests a virtual server with three hard disks, each with a capacity of 150 GB (1). The virtual server is provisioned according to the elastic disk provisioning architecture, with a total of 450 GB of disk space (2). The 450 GB is allocated to the virtual server by the cloud provider (3). The cloud consumer has not installed any software yet, meaning the actual used space is currently 0 GB (4). Because the 450 GB are already allocated and reserved for the cloud consumer, it will be charged for 450 GB of disk usage as of the point of allocation (5).

The *elastic disk provisioning architecture* establishes a dynamic storage provisioning system that ensures that the cloud consumer is granularly billed for the exact amount of storage that it actually uses. This system uses thin-provisioning technology for the dynamic allocation of storage space, and is further supported by runtime usage monitoring to collect accurate usage data for billing purposes (Figure 11.14).

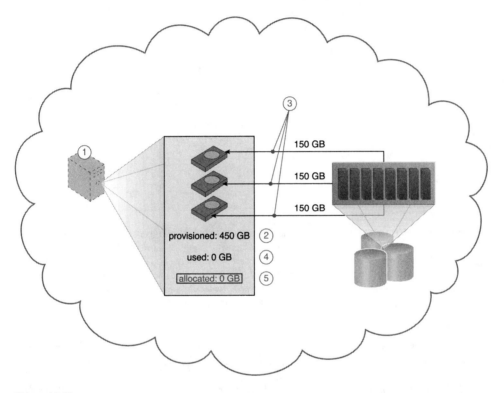

Figure 11.14

The cloud consumer requests a virtual server with three hard disks, each with a capacity of 150 GB (1). The virtual server is provisioned by this architecture with a total of 450 GB of disk space (2). The 450 GB are set as the maximum disk usage that is allowed for this virtual server, although no physical disk space has been reserved or allocated yet (3). The cloud consumer has not installed any software, meaning the actual used space is currently at 0 GB (4). Because the allocated disk space is equal to the actual used space (which is currently at zero), the cloud consumer is not charged for any disk space usage (5).

Thin-provisioning software is installed on virtual servers that process dynamic storage allocation via the hypervisor, while the pay-per-use monitor tracks and reports granular billing-related disk usage data (Figure 11.15).

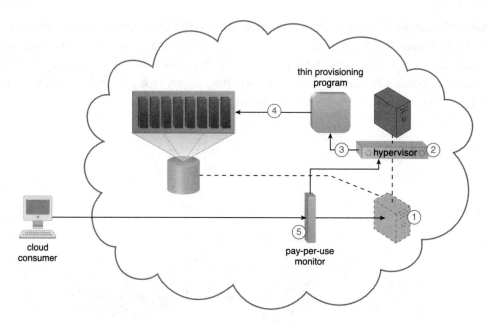

Figure 11.15

A request is received from a cloud consumer, and the provisioning of a new virtual server instance begins (1). As part of the provisioning process, the hard disks are chosen as dynamic or thin-provisioned disks (2). The hypervisor calls a dynamic disk allocation component to create thin disks for the virtual server (3). Virtual server disks are created via the thin-provisioning program and saved in a folder of near-zero size. The size of this folder and its files grow as operating applications are installed and additional files are copied onto the virtual server (4). The pay-per-use monitor tracks the actual dynamically allocated storage for billing purposes (5).

The following mechanisms can be included in this architecture in addition to the cloud storage device, virtual server, hypervisor, and pay-per-use monitor:

- *Cloud Usage Monitor* – Specialized cloud usage monitors can be used to track and log storage usage fluctuations.

- *Resource Replication* – Resource replication is part of an elastic disk provisioning system when conversion of dynamic thin-disk storage into static thick-disk storage is required.

11.8 Redundant Storage Architecture

Cloud storage devices are occasionally subject to failure and disruptions that are caused by network connectivity issues, controller or general hardware failure, or security breaches. A compromised cloud storage device's reliability can have a ripple effect and cause impact failure across all of the services, applications, and infrastructure components in the cloud that are reliant on its availability.

The *redundant storage architecture* introduces a secondary duplicate cloud storage device as part of a failover system that synchronizes its data with the data in the primary cloud storage device. A storage service gateway diverts cloud consumer requests to the secondary device whenever the primary device fails (Figures 11.16 and 11.17).

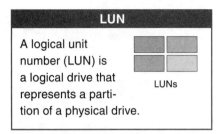

LUN

A logical unit number (LUN) is a logical drive that represents a partition of a physical drive.

LUNs

STORAGE SERVICE GATEWAY

The storage service gateway is a component that acts as the external interface to cloud storage services, and is capable of automatically redirecting cloud consumer requests whenever the location of the requested data has changed.

storage service gateway

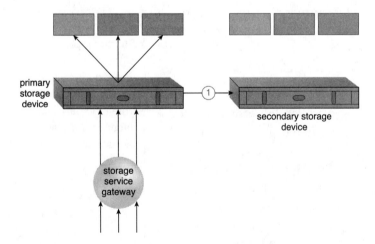

Figure 11.16

The primary cloud storage device is routinely replicated to the secondary cloud storage device (1).

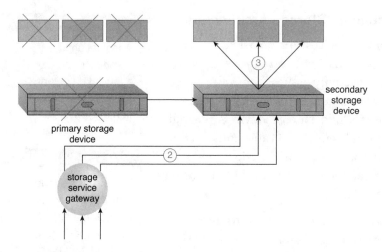

Figure 11.17

The primary storage becomes unavailable and the storage service gateway forwards
the cloud consumer requests to the secondary storage device (2). The secondary
storage device forwards the requests to the LUNs, allowing cloud consumers to
continue to access their data (3).

This cloud architecture primarily relies on a storage replication system that keeps the primary cloud storage device synchronized with its duplicate secondary cloud storage devices (Figure 11.18).

Cloud providers may locate secondary cloud storage devices in a different geographical region than the primary cloud storage device, usually for economic reasons. However, this can introduce legal concerns for some types of data. The location of the secondary cloud storage devices can dictate the protocol and method used for synchronization, as some replication transport protocols have distance restrictions.

STORAGE REPLICATION

Storage replication is a variation of the resource replication mechanisms used to synchronously or asynchronously replicate data from a primary storage device to a secondary storage device. It can be used to replicate partial and entire LUNs.

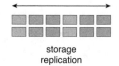

storage
replication

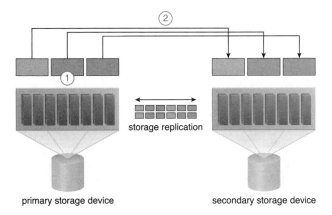

Figure 11.18

Storage replication is used to keep the redundant storage device synchronized with the primary storage device.

Some cloud providers use storage devices with dual array and storage controllers to improve device redundancy, and place secondary storage devices in a different physical location for cloud balancing and disaster recovery purposes. In this case, cloud providers may need to lease a network connection via a third-party cloud provider in order to establish the replication between the two devices.

11.9 CASE STUDY EXAMPLE

An in-house solution that ATN did not migrate to the cloud is the Remote Upload Module, a program that is used by their clients to upload accounting and legal documents to a central archive on a daily basis. Usage peaks occur without warning, since the quantity of documents received on a day-by-day basis is unpredictable.

The Remote Upload Module currently rejects upload attempts when it is operating at capacity, which is problematic for users that need to archive certain documents before the end of a business day or prior to a deadline.

ATN decides to take advantage of its cloud-based environment by creating a cloud-bursting architecture around the on-premise Remote Upload Module service implementation. This enables it to burst out into the cloud whenever on-premise processing thresholds are exceeded (Figures 11.19 and 11.20).

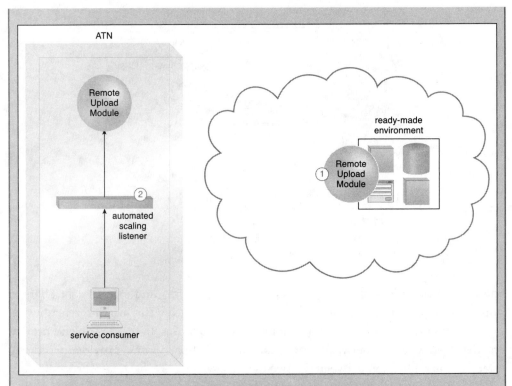

Figure 11.19
A cloud-based version of the on-premise Remote Upload Module service is deployed on ATN's leased ready-made environment (1). The automated scaling listener monitors service consumer requests (2).

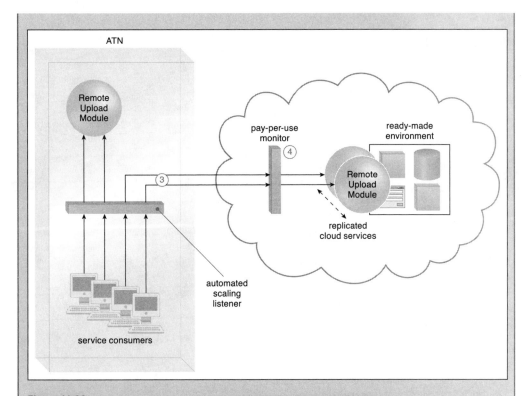

Figure 11.20

The automated scaling listener detects that service consumer usage has exceeded the local Remote Upload Module service's usage threshold, and begins diverting excess requests to the cloud-based Remote Upload Module implementation (3). The cloud provider's pay-per-use monitor tracks the requests received from the on-premise automated scaling listener to collect billing data, and Remote Upload Module cloud service instances are created on-demand via resource replication (4).

A "burst in" system is invoked after the service usage has decreased enough so that service consumer requests can be processed by the on-premise Remote Upload Module implementation again. Instances of the cloud services are released, and no additional cloud-related usage fees are incurred.

Chapter 12

Advanced Cloud Architectures

The cloud technology architectures explored in this chapter represent distinct and sophisticated architectural layers, several of which can be built upon the more foundational environments established by the architectural models covered in Chapter 11.

12.1 Hypervisor Clustering Architecture

Hypervisors can be responsible for creating and hosting multiple virtual servers. Because of this dependency, any failure conditions that affect a hypervisor can cascade to its virtual servers (Figure 12.1).

HEARTBEATS

Heartbeats are system-level messages exchanged between hypervisors, hypervisors and virtual servers, and hypervisors and VIMs.

heartbeat

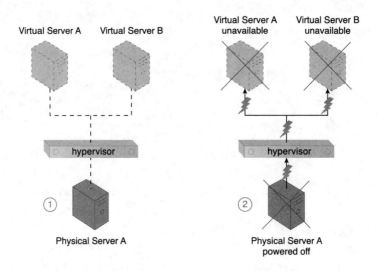

Figure 12.1

Physical Server A is hosting a hypervisor that hosts Virtual Servers A and B (1). When Physical Server A fails, the hypervisor and two virtual servers consequently fail as well (2).

The *hypervisor clustering architecture* establishes a high-availability cluster of hypervisors across multiple physical servers. If a given hypervisor or its underlying physical server becomes unavailable, the hosted virtual servers can be moved to another physical server or hypervisor to maintain runtime operations (Figure 12.2).

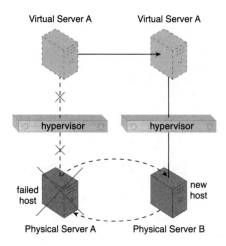

Figure 12.2

Physical Server A becomes unavailable and causes its hypervisor to fail. Virtual Server A is migrated to Physical Server B, which has another hypervisor that is part of the cluster to which Physical Server A belongs.

The hypervisor cluster is controlled via a central VIM, which sends regular heartbeat messages to the hypervisors to confirm that they are up and running. Unacknowledged heartbeat messages cause the VIM to initiate the live VM migration program, in order to dynamically move the affected virtual servers to a new host.

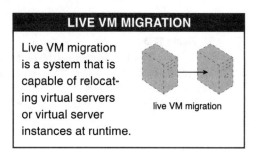

LIVE VM MIGRATION

Live VM migration is a system that is capable of relocating virtual servers or virtual server instances at runtime.

live VM migration

The hypervisor cluster uses a shared cloud storage device to live-migrate virtual servers, as illustrated in Figures 12.3 to 12.6.

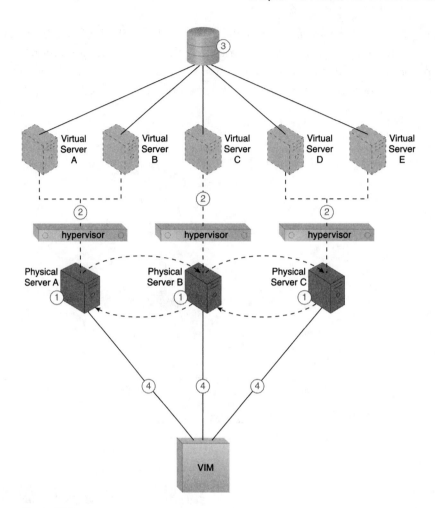

Figure 12.3

Hypervisors are installed on Physical Servers A, B, and C (1). Virtual servers are created by the hypervisors (2). A shared cloud storage device containing virtual server configuration files is positioned in a shared cloud storage device for access by all hypervisors (3). The hypervisor cluster is enabled on the three physical server hosts via a central VIM (4).

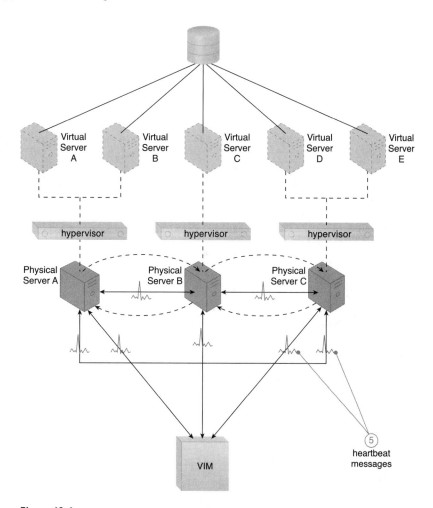

Figure 12.4

The physical servers exchange heartbeat messages with one another and the VIM according to a pre-defined schedule (5).

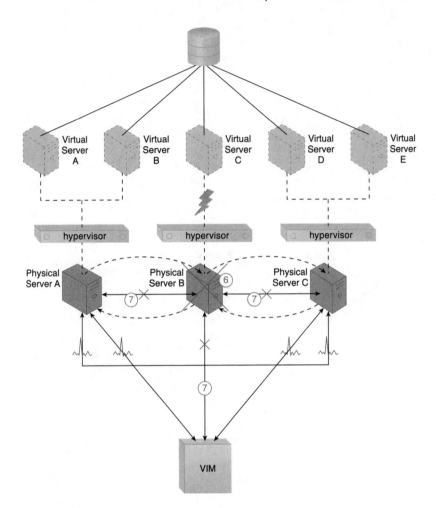

Figure 12.5

Physical Server B fails and becomes unavailable, jeopardizing Virtual Server C (6). The other physical servers and the VIM stop receiving heartbeat messages from Physical Server B (7).

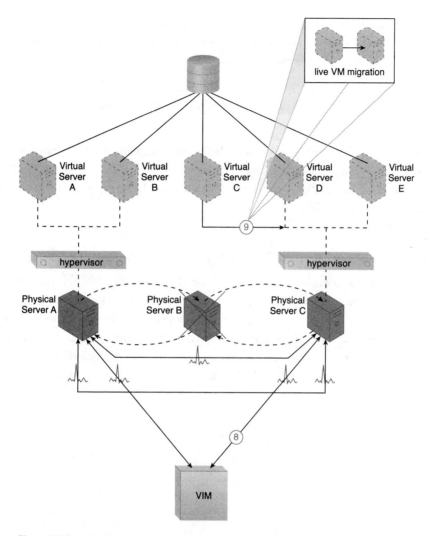

Figure 12.6

The VIM chooses Physical Server C as the new host to take ownership of Virtual Server C after assessing the available capacity of other hypervisors in the cluster (8). Virtual Server C is live-migrated to the hypervisor running on Physical Server C, where restarting may be necessary before normal operations can be resumed (9).

In addition to the hypervisor and resource cluster mechanisms that form the core of this architectural model and the virtual servers that are protected by the clustered environment, the following mechanisms can be incorporated:

- *Logical Network Perimeter* – The logical boundaries created by this mechanism ensure that none of the hypervisors of other cloud consumers are accidentally included in a given cluster.

- *Resource Replication* – Hypervisors in the same cluster inform one another about their status and availability. Updates on any changes that occur in the cluster, such as the creation or deletion of a virtual switch, need to be replicated to all of the hypervisors via the VIM.

12.2 Load Balanced Virtual Server Instances Architecture

Keeping cross-server workloads evenly balanced between physical servers whose operation and management are isolated can be challenging. A physical server can easily end up hosting more virtual servers or receive larger workloads than its neighboring physical servers (Figure 12.7). Both physical server over and under-utilization can increase dramatically over time, leading to on-going performance challenges (for over-utilized servers) and constant waste (for the lost processing potential of under-utilized servers).

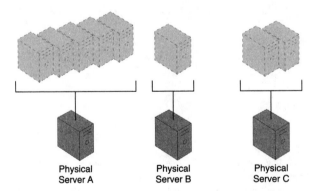

Physical   Physical   Physical
Server A   Server B   Server C

Figure 12.7

Three physical servers have to host different quantities of virtual server instances, leading to both over-utilized and under-utilized servers.

The *load balanced virtual server instances architecture* establishes a capacity watchdog system that dynamically calculates virtual server instances and associated workloads, before distributing the processing across available physical server hosts (Figure 12.8).

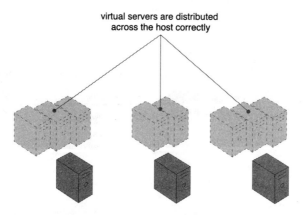

virtual servers are distributed
across the host correctly

Figure 12.8

The virtual server instances are more evenly distributed across the physical server hosts.

The capacity watchdog system is comprised of a capacity watchdog cloud usage monitor, the live VM migration program, and a capacity planner. The capacity watchdog monitor tracks physical and virtual server usage and reports any significant fluctuations to the capacity planner, which is responsible for dynamically calculating physical server computing capacities against virtual server capacity requirements. If the capacity planner decides to move a virtual server to another host to distribute the workload, the live VM migration program is signaled to move the virtual server (Figures 12.9 to 12.11).

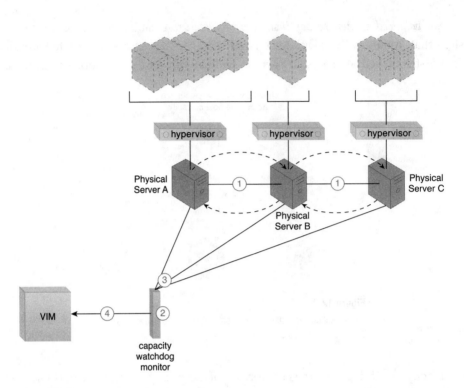

Figure 12.9

The hypervisor cluster architecture provides the foundation upon which the load-balanced virtual server architecture is built (1). Policies and thresholds are defined for the capacity watchdog monitor (2), which compares physical server capacities with virtual server processing (3). The capacity watchdog monitor reports an over-utilization to the VIM (4).

The following mechanisms can be included in this architecture, in addition to the hypervisor, resource clustering, virtual server, and (capacity watchdog) cloud usage monitor:

- *Automated Scaling Listener* – The automated scaling listener may be used to initiate the process of load balancing and to dynamically monitor workload coming to the virtual servers via the hypervisors.

- *Load Balancer* – The load balancer mechanism is responsible for distributing the workload of the virtual servers between the hypervisors.

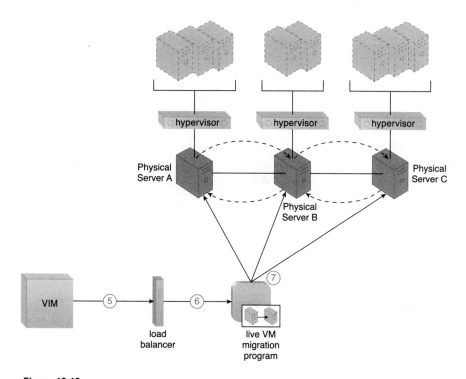

Figure 12.10

The VIM signals the load balancer to redistribute the workload based on pre-defined thresholds (5). The load balancer initiates the live VM migration program to move the virtual servers (6). Live VM migration moves the selected virtual servers from one physical host to another (7).

- *Logical Network Perimeter* – A logical network perimeter ensures that the destination of a given relocated virtual server is in compliance with SLA and privacy regulations.

- *Resource Replication* – The replication of virtual server instances may be required as part of the load balancing functionality.

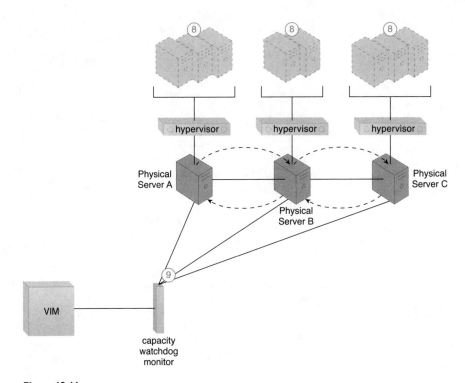

Figure 12.11

The workload is balanced across the physical servers in the cluster (8). The capacity watchdog continues to monitor the workload and resource consumption (9).

12.3 Non-Disruptive Service Relocation Architecture

A cloud service can become unavailable for a number of reasons, such as:

- runtime usage demands that exceed its processing capacity

- a maintenance update that mandates a temporary outage

- permanent migration to a new physical server host

Cloud service consumer requests are usually rejected if a cloud service becomes unavailable, which can potentially result in exception conditions. Rendering the cloud service temporarily unavailable to cloud consumers is not preferred even if the outage is planned.

The *non-disruptive service relocation architecture* establishes a system by which a predefined event triggers the duplication or migration of a cloud service implementation at runtime, thereby avoiding any disruption. Instead of scaling cloud services in or out with redundant implementations, cloud service activity can be temporarily diverted to another hosting environment at runtime by adding a duplicate implementation onto a new host. Similarly, cloud service consumer requests can be temporarily redirected to a duplicate implementation when the original implementation needs to undergo a maintenance outage. The relocation of the cloud service implementation and any cloud service activity can also be permanent to accommodate cloud service migrations to new physical server hosts.

A key aspect of the underlying architecture is that the new cloud service implementation is guaranteed to be successfully receiving and responding to cloud service consumer requests *before* the original cloud service implementation is deactivated or removed. A common approach is for live VM migration to move the entire virtual server instance that is hosting the cloud service. The automated scaling listener and/or load balancer mechanisms can be used to trigger a temporary redirection of cloud service consumer requests, in response to scaling and workload distribution requirements. Either mechanism can contact the VIM to initiate the live VM migration process, as shown in Figures 12.12 to 12.14.

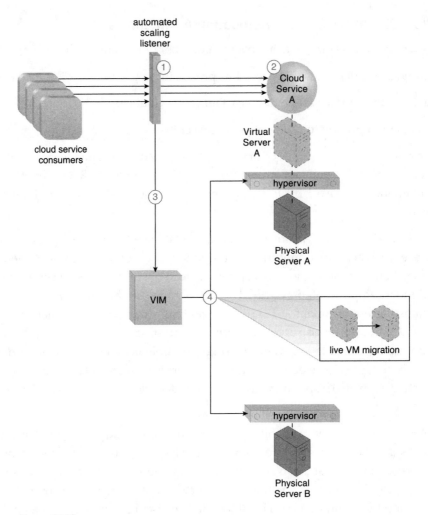

Figure 12.12

The automated scaling listener monitors the workload for a cloud service (1). The cloud service's pre-defined threshold is reached as the workload increases (2), causing the automated scaling listener to signal the VIM to initiate relocation (3). The VIM uses the live VM migration program to instruct both the origin and destination hypervisors to carry out runtime relocation (4).

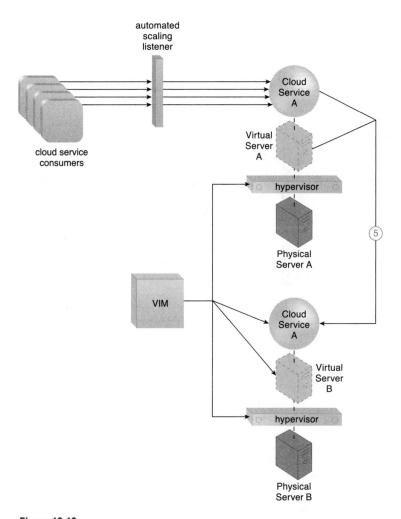

Figure 12.13

A second copy of the virtual server and its hosted cloud service are created via the destination hypervisor on Physical Server B (5).

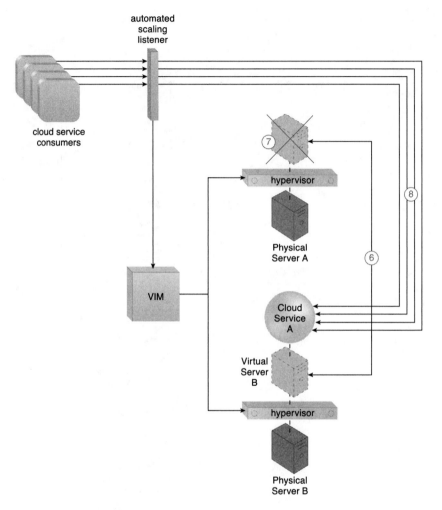

Figure 12.14

The state of both virtual server instances is synchronized (6). The first virtual server instance is removed from Physical Server A after cloud service consumer requests are confirmed to be successfully exchanged with the cloud service on Physical Server B (7). Cloud service consumer requests are now only sent to the cloud service on Physical Server B (8).

Virtual server migration can occur in one of the following two ways, depending on the location of the virtual server's disks and configuration:

- A copy of the virtual server disks is created on the destination host, if the virtual server disks are stored on a local storage device or non-shared remote storage devices attached to the source host. After the copy has been created, both virtual server instances are synchronized and virtual server files are removed from the origin host.

- Copying the virtual server disks is unnecessary if the virtual server's files are stored on a remote storage device that is shared between origin and destination hosts. Ownership of the virtual server is simply transferred from the origin to the destination physical server host, and the virtual server's state is automatically synchronized.

This architecture can be supported by the persistent virtual network configurations architecture, so that the defined network configurations of migrated virtual servers are preserved to retain connection with the cloud service consumers.

Besides the automated scaling listener, load balancer, cloud storage device, hypervisor, and virtual server, other mechanisms that can be part of this architecture include the following:

- *Cloud Usage Monitor* – Different types of cloud usage monitors can be used to continuously track IT resource usage and system activity.

- *Pay-Per-Use Monitor* – The pay-per-use monitor is used to collect data for service usage cost calculations for IT resources at both source and destination locations.

- *Resource Replication* – The resource replication mechanism is used to instantiate the shadow copy of the cloud service at its destination.

- *SLA Management System* – This management system is responsible for processing SLA data provided by the SLA monitor to obtain cloud service availability assurances, both during and after cloud service duplication or relocation.

- *SLA Monitor* – This monitoring mechanism collects the SLA information required by the SLA management system, which may be relevant if availability guarantees rely on this architecture.

NOTE

The non-disruptive service relocation technology architecture conflicts and cannot be applied together with the direct I/O access architecture covered in Chapter 13. A virtual server with direct I/O access is locked into its physical server host and cannot be moved to other hosts in this fashion.

12.4 Zero Downtime Architecture

A physical server naturally acts as a single point of failure for the virtual servers it hosts. As a result, when the physical server fails or is compromised, the availability of any (or all) hosted virtual servers can be affected. This makes the issuance of zero downtime guarantees by a cloud provider to cloud consumers challenging.

The *zero downtime architecture* establishes a sophisticated failover system that allows virtual servers to be dynamically moved to different physical server hosts, in the event that their original physical server host fails (Figure 12.15).

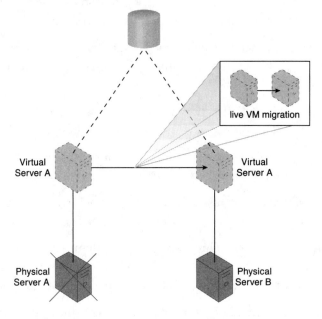

Figure 12.15

Physical Server A fails triggering the live VM migration program to dynamically move Virtual Server A to Physical Server B.

Multiple physical servers are assembled into a group that is controlled by a fault tolerance system capable of switching activity from one physical server to another, without interruption. The live VM migration component is typically a core part of this form of high availability cloud architecture.

The resulting fault tolerance assures that, in case of physical server failure, hosted virtual servers will be migrated to a secondary physical server. All virtual servers are stored on a shared volume (as per the persistent virtual network configuration architecture) so that other physical server hosts in the same group can access their files.

Besides the failover system, cloud storage device, and virtual server mechanisms, the following mechanisms can be part of this architecture:

- *Audit Monitor* – This mechanism may be required to check whether the relocation of virtual servers also relocates hosted data to prohibited locations.

- *Cloud Usage Monitor* – Incarnations of this mechanism are used to monitor the actual IT resource usage of cloud consumers to help ensure that virtual server capacities are not exceeded.

- *Hypervisor* – The hypervisor of each affected physical server hosts the affected virtual servers.

- *Logical Network Perimeter* – Logical network perimeters provide and maintain the isolation that is required to ensure that each cloud consumer remains within its own logical boundary subsequent to virtual server relocation.

- *Resource Cluster* – The resource cluster mechanism is applied to create different types of active-active cluster groups that collaboratively improve the availability of virtual server-hosted IT resources.

- *Resource Replication* – This mechanism can create the new virtual server and cloud service instances upon primary virtual server failure.

12.5 Cloud Balancing Architecture

The *cloud balancing architecture* establishes a specialized architectural model in which IT resources can be load-balanced across multiple clouds.

The cross-cloud balancing of cloud service consumer requests can help:

- improve the performance and scalability of IT resources

- increase the availability and reliability of IT resources

- improve load-balancing and IT resource optimization

Cloud balancing functionality is primarily based on the combination of the automated scaling listener and failover system mechanisms (Figure 12.16). Many more components (and possibly other mechanisms) can be part of a complete cloud balancing architecture.

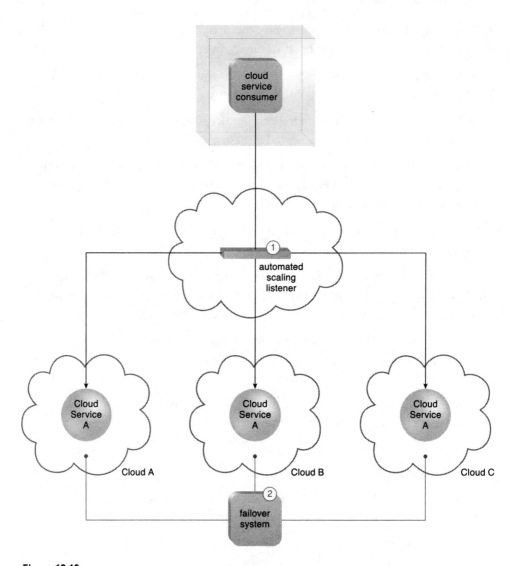

Figure 12.16

An automated scaling listener controls the cloud balancing process by routing cloud service consumer requests to redundant implementations of Cloud Service A distributed across multiple clouds (1). The failover system instills resiliency within this architecture by providing cross-cloud failover (2).

As a starting point, the two mechanisms are utilized as follows:

- The automated scaling listener redirects cloud service consumer requests to one of several redundant IT resource implementations, based on current scaling and performance requirements.

- The failover system ensures that redundant IT resources are capable of cross-cloud failover in the event of a failure within an IT resource or its underlying hosting environment. IT resource failures are announced so that the automated scaling listener can avoid inadvertently routing cloud service consumer requests to unavailable or unstable IT resources.

For a cloud balancing architecture to function effectively, the automated scaling listener needs to be aware of all redundant IT resource implementations within the scope of the cloud balanced architecture.

Note that if the manual synchronization of cross-cloud IT resource implementations is not possible, the resource replication mechanism may need to be incorporated to automate the synchronization.

12.6 Resource Reservation Architecture

Depending on how IT resources are designed for shared usage and depending on their available levels of capacity, concurrent access can lead to a runtime exception condition called *resource constraint*. A resource constraint is a condition that occurs when two or more cloud consumers have been allocated to share an IT resource that does not have the capacity to accommodate the total processing requirements of the cloud consumers. As a result, one or more of the cloud consumers encounter degraded performance or may be rejected altogether. The cloud service itself may go down, resulting in all cloud consumers being rejected.

Other types of runtime conflicts can occur when an IT resource (especially one not specifically designed to accommodate sharing) is concurrently accessed by different cloud service consumers. For example, nested and sibling resource pools introduce the notion of *resource borrowing*, whereby one pool can temporarily borrow IT resources from other pools. A runtime conflict can be triggered when the borrowed IT resource is not returned due to prolonged usage by the cloud service consumer that is borrowing it. This can inevitably lead back to the occurrence of resource constraints.

The *resource reservation architecture* establishes a system whereby one of the following is set aside exclusively for a given cloud consumer (Figures 12.17 to 12.19):

- single IT resource
- portion of an IT resource
- multiple IT resources

This protects cloud consumers from each other by avoiding the aforementioned resource constraint and resource borrowing conditions.

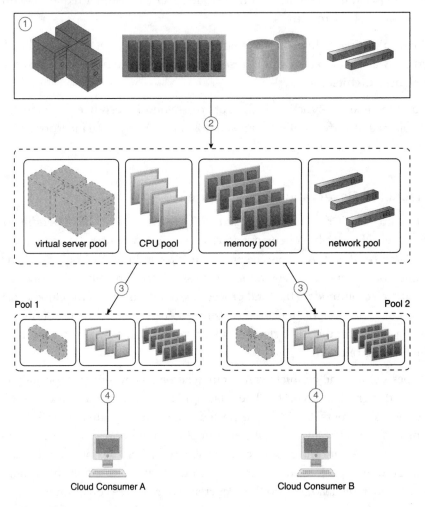

Figure 12.17

A physical resource group is created (1), from which a parent resource pool is created as per the resource pooling architecture (2). Two smaller child pools are created from the parent resource pool, and resource limits are defined using the resource management system (3). Cloud consumers are provided with access to their own exclusive resource pools (4).

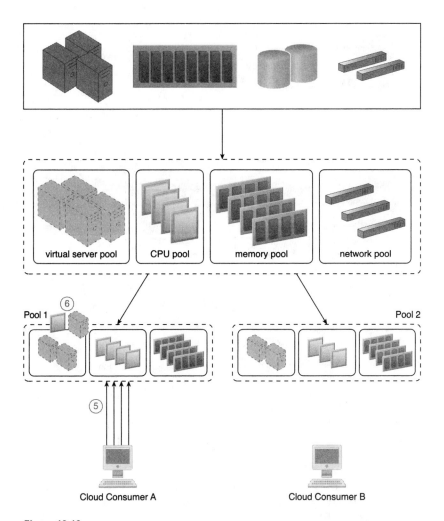

Figure 12.18

An increase in requests from Cloud Consumer A results in more IT resources being allocated to that cloud consumer (5), meaning some IT resources need to be borrowed from Pool 2. The amount of borrowed IT resources is confined by the resource limit that was defined in Step 3, to ensure that Cloud Consumer B will not face any resource constraints (6).

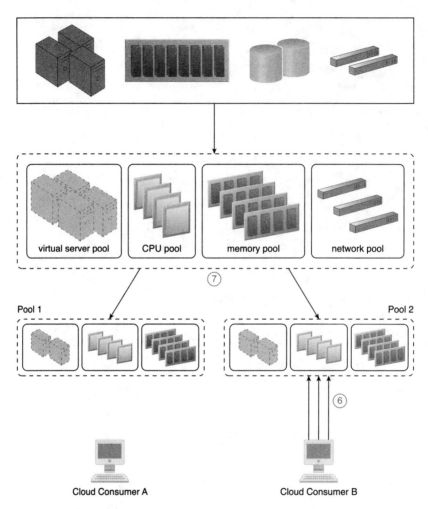

Figure 12.19

Cloud Consumer B now imposes more requests and usage demands and may soon need to utilize all available IT resources in the pool (6). The resource management system forces Pool 1 to release the IT resources and move them back to Pool 2 to become available for Cloud Consumer B (7).

The creation of an IT resource reservation system can require involving the resource management system mechanism, which is used to define the usage thresholds for individual IT resources and resource pools. Reservations lock the amount of IT resources that each pool needs to keep, with the balance of the pool's IT resources still available for sharing and borrowing. The remote administration system mechanism is also used to enable front-end customization, so that cloud consumers have administration controls for the management of their reserved IT resource allocations.

The types of mechanisms that are commonly reserved within this architecture are cloud storage devices and virtual servers. Other mechanisms that may be part of the architecture can include:

- *Audit Monitor* – The audit monitor is used to check whether the resource reservation system is complying with cloud consumer auditing, privacy, and other regulatory requirements. For example, it may track the geographical location of reserved IT resources.

- *Cloud Usage Monitor* – A cloud usage monitor may oversee the thresholds that trigger the allocation of reserved IT resources.

- *Hypervisor* – The hypervisor mechanism may apply reservations for different cloud consumers to ensure that they are correctly allocated to their guaranteed IT resources.

- *Logical Network Perimeter* – This mechanism establishes the boundaries necessary to ensure that reserved IT resources are made exclusively available to cloud consumers.

- *Resource Replication* – This component needs to stay informed about each cloud consumer's limits for IT resource consumption, in order to replicate and provision new IT resource instances expediently.

12.7 Dynamic Failure Detection and Recovery Architecture

Cloud-based environments can be comprised of vast quantities of IT resources that are simultaneously accessed by numerous cloud consumers. Any of those IT resources can experience failure conditions that require more than manual intervention to resolve. Manually administering and solving IT resource failures is generally inefficient and impractical.

The *dynamic failure detection and recovery architecture* establishes a resilient watchdog system to monitor and respond to a wide range of pre-defined failure scenarios (Figures 12.20 and 12.21). This system notifies and escalates the failure conditions that it cannot automatically resolve itself. It relies on a specialized cloud usage monitor called the intelligent watchdog monitor to actively track IT resources and take pre-defined actions in response to pre-defined events.

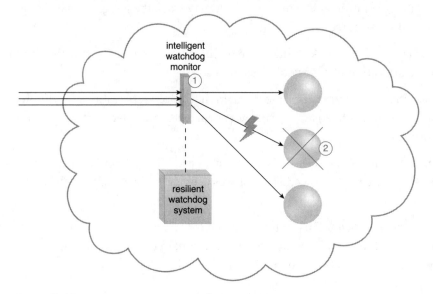

Figure 12.20

The intelligent watchdog monitor keeps track of cloud consumer requests (1) and detects that a cloud service has failed (2).

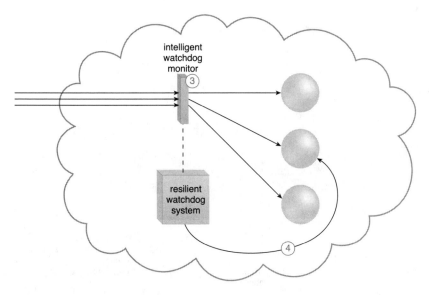

Figure 12.21

The intelligent watchdog monitor notifies the watchdog system (3), which restores the cloud service based on pre-defined policies. The cloud service resumes its runtime operation (4).

The resilient watchdog system performs the following five core functions:

- watching
- deciding upon an event
- acting upon an event
- reporting
- escalating

Sequential recovery policies can be defined for each IT resource to determine the steps that the intelligent watchdog monitor needs to take when a failure condition occurs. For example, a recovery policy can state that one recovery attempt needs to be automatically carried out before issuing a notification (Figure 12.22).

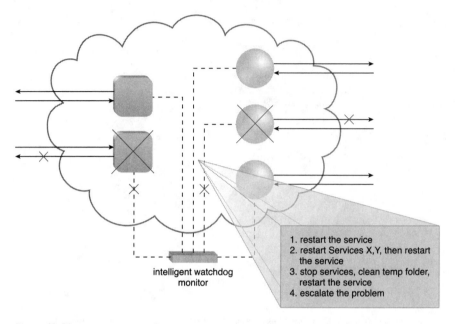

Figure 12.22

In the event of a failure, the intelligent watchdog monitor refers to its pre-defined policies to recover the cloud service step-by-step, escalating the process when a problem proves to be deeper than expected.

Some of the actions the intelligent watchdog monitor commonly takes to escalate an issue include:

- running a batch file
- sending a console message
- sending a text message
- sending an email message
- sending an SNMP trap
- logging a ticket

There are varieties of programs and products that can act as intelligent watchdog monitors. Most can be integrated with standard ticketing and event management systems.

This architectural model can further incorporate the following mechanisms:

- *Audit Monitor* – This mechanism is used to track whether data recovery is carried out in compliance with legal or policy requirements.

- *Failover System* – The failover system mechanism is usually used during the initial attempts to recover failed IT resources.

- *SLA Management System* and *SLA Monitor* – Since the functionality achieved by applying this architecture is closely associated with SLA guarantees, the system commonly relies on the information that is managed and processed by these mechanisms.

12.8 Bare-Metal Provisioning Architecture

Remotely provisioning servers is common because remote management software is usually native to the operating system of most physical servers. However, access to conventional remote management programs is unavailable for *bare-metal servers*—physical servers that do not have pre-installed operating systems or any other software.

Most contemporary physical servers provide the option of installing remote management support in the server's ROM. This is offered by some vendors through an expansion card while others have the components already integrated into the chipset. The *bare-metal provisioning architecture* establishes a system that utilizes this feature with specialized service agents, which are used to discover and effectively provision entire operating systems remotely.

The remote management software that is integrated with the server's ROM becomes available upon server start-up. A Web-based or proprietary user-interface, like the portal provided by the remote administration system, is usually used to connect to the physical server's native remote management interface. The IP address of the remote management interface can be configured manually, through the default IP, or alternatively set through the configuration of a DHCP service. IP addresses in IaaS platforms can be forwarded directly to cloud consumers so that they can perform bare-metal operating system installations independently.

Although remote management software is used to enable connections to physical server consoles and deploy operating systems, there are two common concerns about its usage:

- Manual deployment on multiple servers can be vulnerable to inadvertent human and configuration errors.

- Remote management software can be time-intensive and require significant runtime IT resource processing.

The bare-metal provisioning system addresses these issues by using the following components:

- *Discovery Agent* – A type of monitoring agent that searches and finds available physical servers to be assigned to cloud consumers.

- *Deployment Agent* – A management agent that is installed into a physical server's memory, to be positioned as a client for the bare-metal provisioning deployment system.

- *Discovery Section* – A software component that scans the network and locates available physical servers with which to connect.

- *Management Loader* – The component that connects to the physical server and loads the management options for the cloud consumer.

- *Deployment Component* – The component responsible for installing the operating system on the selected physical servers.

The bare-metal provisioning system provides an auto-deployment feature that allows cloud consumers to connect to the deployment software and provision more than one server or operating system at the same time. The central deployment system connects to the servers via their management interfaces, and uses the same protocol to upload and operate as an agent in the physical server's RAM. The bare-metal server then becomes a raw client with a management agent installed, and the deployment software uploads the required setup files to deploy the operating system (Figures 12.23 and 12.24).

Deployment images, operating system deployment automation, or unattended deployment and post installation configuration scripts can be used via the intelligent automation engine and self-service portal to extend this functionality.

The following additional mechanisms can be part of this architecture:

- *Cloud Storage Device* – This mechanism stores operating system templates and installation files, as well as deployment agents and deployment packages for the provisioning system.

- *Hypervisor* – The deployment of hypervisors on physical servers as part of the operating system provisioning can be required.

- *Logical Network Perimeter* – Logical network perimeter boundaries help ensure that raw physical servers can only be accessed by authorized cloud consumers.

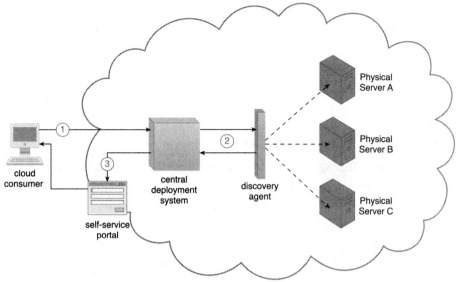

Figure 12.23

The cloud consumer connects to the deployment solution (1) to perform a search using the discovery agent (2). The available physical servers are shown to the cloud consumer (3).

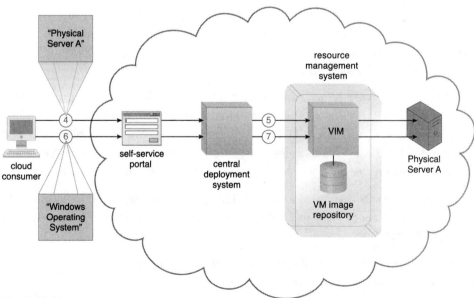

Figure 12.24

The cloud consumer selects a physical server to provision (4). The deployment agent is loaded to the physical server's RAM via the remote management system (5). The cloud consumer selects an operating system and method of configuration via the deployment solution (6). The operating system is installed and the server becomes operational (7).

- *Resource Replication* – This mechanism is implemented for the replication of IT resources by deploying a new hypervisor on a physical server to balance the hypervisor workload during or after provisioning.

- *SLA Management System* – This management system ensures that the availability of physical bare-metal servers is in accordance with pre-defined SLA stipulations.

12.9 Rapid Provisioning Architecture

A conventional provisioning process can involve a number of tasks that are traditionally completed manually by administrators and technology experts that prepare the requested IT resources as per pre-packaged specifications or custom client requests. In cloud environments, where higher volumes of customers are serviced and where the average customer requests higher volumes of IT resources, manual provisioning processes are inadequate and can even lead to unreasonable risk due to human error and inefficient response times.

For example, a cloud consumer that requests the installation, configuration, and updating of twenty-five Windows servers with several applications requires that half of the applications be identical installations, while the other half be customized. Each operating system deployment can take up to 30 minutes, followed by additional time for security patches and operating system updates that require server rebooting. The applications finally need to be deployed and configured. Using a manual or semi-automated approach requires excessive amounts of time, and introduces a probability of human error that increases with each installation.

The *rapid provisioning architecture* establishes a system that automates the provisioning of a wide range of IT resources, either individually or as a collective. The underlying technology architecture for rapid IT resource provisioning can be sophisticated and complex, and relies on a system comprised of an automated provisioning program, rapid provisioning engine, and scripts and templates for on-demand provisioning.

Beyond the components displayed in Figure 12.25, many additional architectural artifacts are available to coordinate and automate the different aspects of IT resource provisioning, such as:

- *Server Templates* – Templates of virtual image files that are used to automate the instantiation of new virtual servers.

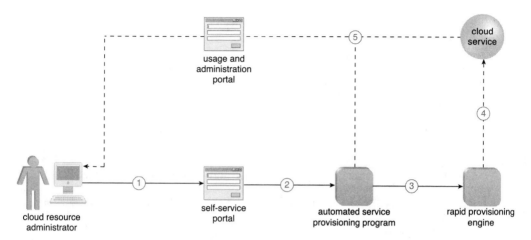

Figure 12.25

A cloud resource administrator requests a new cloud service through the self-service portal (1). The self-service portal passes the request to the automated service provisioning program installed on the virtual server (2), which passes the necessary tasks to be performed to the rapid provisioning engine (3). The rapid provisioning engine announces when the new cloud service is ready (4). The automated service provisioning program finalizes and publishes the cloud service on the usage and administration portal for cloud consumer access (5).

- *Server Images* – These images are similar to virtual server templates, but are used to provision physical servers.

- *Application Packages* – Collections of applications and other software that are packaged for automated deployment.

- *Application Packager* – The software used to create application packages.

- *Custom Scripts* – Scripts that automate administrative tasks, as part of an intelligent automation engine.

- *Sequence Manager* – A program that organizes sequences of automated provisioning tasks.

- *Sequence Logger* – A component that logs the execution of automated provisioning task sequences.

- *Operating System Baseline* – A configuration template that is applied after the operating system is installed, to quickly prepare it for usage.

- *Application Configuration Baseline* – A configuration template with the settings and environmental parameters that are needed to prepare new applications for use.

- *Deployment Data Store* – The repository that stores virtual images, templates, scripts, baseline configurations, and other related data.

The following step-by-step description helps provide some insight into the inner workings of a rapid provisioning engine, involving a number of the previously listed system components:

1. A cloud consumer requests a new server through the self-service portal.

2. The sequence manager forwards the request to the deployment engine for the preparation of an operating system.

3. The deployment engine uses the virtual server templates for provisioning if the request is for a virtual server. Otherwise, the deployment engine sends the request to provision a physical server.

4. The pre-defined image for the requested type of operating system is used for the provisioning of the operating system, if available. Otherwise, the regular deployment process is executed to install the operating system.

5. The deployment engine informs the sequence manager when the operating system is ready.

6. The sequence manager updates and sends the logs to the sequence logger for storage.

7. The sequence manager requests that the deployment engine apply the operating system baseline to the provisioned operating system.

8. The deployment engine applies the requested operating system baseline.

9. The deployment engine informs the sequence manager that the operating system baseline has been applied.

10. The sequence manager updates and sends the logs of completed steps to the sequence logger for storage.

11. The sequence manager requests that the deployment engine install the applications.

12. The deployment engine deploys the applications on the provisioned server.

13. The deployment engine informs the sequence manager that the applications have been installed.

14. The sequence manager updates and sends the logs of completed steps to the sequence logger for storage.

15. The sequence manager requests that the deployment engine apply the application's configuration baseline.

16. The deployment engine applies the configuration baseline.

17. The deployment engine informs the sequence manager that the configuration baseline has been applied.

18. The sequence manager updates and sends the logs of completed steps to the sequence logger for storage.

The cloud storage device mechanism is used to provide storage for application baseline information, templates, and scripts, while the hypervisor rapidly creates, deploys, and hosts the virtual servers that are either provisioned themselves, or host other provisioned IT resources. The resource replication mechanism is usually used to generate replicated instances of IT resources in response to rapid provisioning requirements.

12.10 Storage Workload Management Architecture

Over-utilized cloud storage devices increase the workload on the storage controller and can cause a range of performance challenges. Conversely, cloud storage devices that are under-utilized are wasteful due to lost processing and storage capacity potential (Figure 12.26).

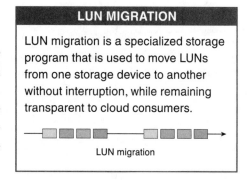

LUN MIGRATION

LUN migration is a specialized storage program that is used to move LUNs from one storage device to another without interruption, while remaining transparent to cloud consumers.

LUN migration

The *storage workload management architecture* enables LUNs to be evenly distributed across available cloud storage devices, while a storage capacity system is established to ensure that runtime workloads are evenly distributed across the LUNs (Figure 12.27).

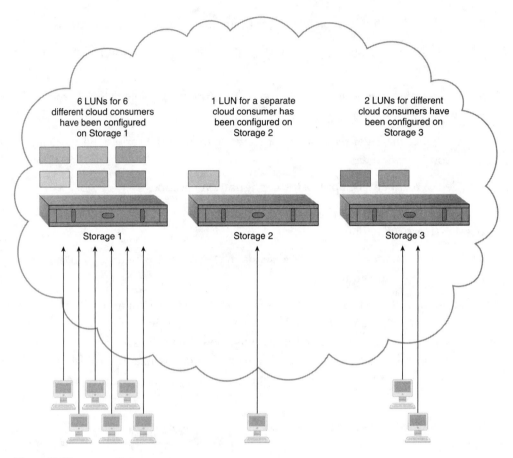

Figure 12.26

An unbalanced cloud storage architecture has six storage LUNs in Storage 1 for cloud consumers to use, while Storage 2 is hosting one LUN and Storage 3 is hosting two. The majority of the workload ends up with Storage 1, since it is hosting the most LUNs.

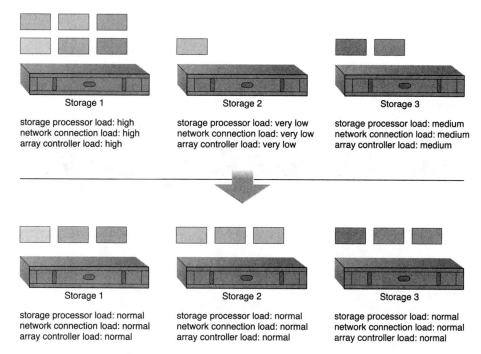

Figure 12.27

LUNs are dynamically distributed across cloud storage devices, resulting in more even distribution of associated types of workloads.

Combining cloud storage devices into a group allows LUN data to be distributed between available storage hosts equally. A storage management system is configured and an automated scaling listener is positioned to monitor and equalize runtime workloads among the grouped cloud storage devices, as illustrated in Figures 12.28 to 12.30.

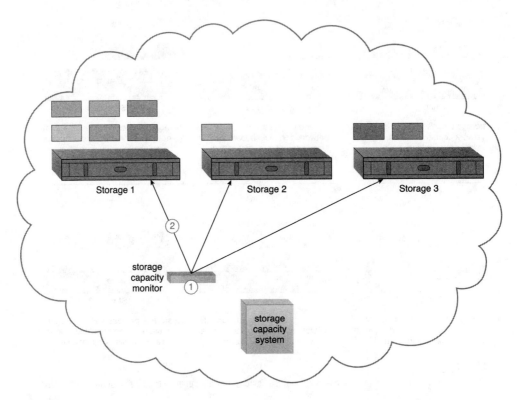

Figure 12.28

The storage capacity system and storage capacity monitor are configured to survey three storage devices in realtime, whose workload and capacity thresholds are pre-defined (1). The storage capacity monitor determines that the workload on Storage 1 is reaching its threshold (2).

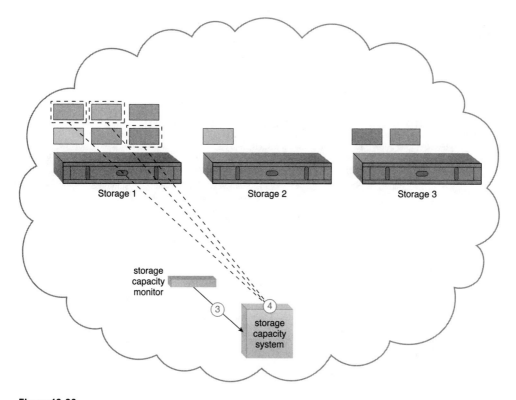

Figure 12.29

The storage capacity monitor informs the storage capacity system that Storage 1 is over-utilized (3). The storage capacity system identifies the LUNs to be moved from Storage 1 (4).

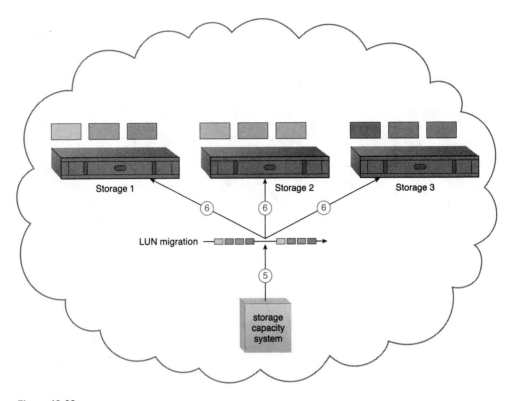

Figure 12.30
The storage capacity system calls for LUN migration to move some of the LUNs from Storage 1 to the other two storage devices (5). LUN migration transitions LUNs to Storage 2 and 3 to balance the workload (6).

The storage capacity system can keep the hosting storage device in power-saving mode for the periods when the LUNs are being accessed less frequently or only at specific times.

Some other mechanisms that can be included in the storage workload management architecture to accompany the cloud storage device are as follows:

- *Audit Monitor* – This monitoring mechanism is used to check for compliance with regulatory, privacy, and security requirements, since the system established by this architecture can physically relocate data.

- *Automated Scaling Listener* – The automated scaling listener is used to watch and respond to workload fluctuations.

- *Cloud Usage Monitor* – In addition to the capacity workload monitor, specialized cloud usage monitors are used to track LUN movements and collect workload distribution statistics.

- *Load Balancer* – This mechanism can be added to horizontally balance workloads across available cloud storage devices.

- *Logical Network Perimeter* – Logical network perimeters provide levels of isolation so that cloud consumer data that undergoes relocation remains inaccessible to unauthorized parties.

12.11 CASE STUDY EXAMPLE

Innovartus is leasing two cloud-based environments from two different cloud providers, and intends to take advantage of this opportunity to establish a pilot cloud-balancing architecture for its Role Player cloud service.

After assessing its requirements against the respective clouds, Innovartus' cloud architects produce a design specification that is based on each cloud having multiple implementations of the cloud service. This architecture incorporates separate automated scaling listener and failover system implementations, together with a central load balancer mechanism (Figure 12.31).

The load balancer distributes cloud service consumer requests across clouds using a workload distribution algorithm, while each cloud's automated scaling listener routes requests to local cloud service implementations. The failover systems can failover to the redundant cloud service implementations that are both within and across clouds. Inter-cloud failover is carried out primarily when local cloud service implementations are nearing their processing thresholds, or if a cloud is encountering a severe platform failure.

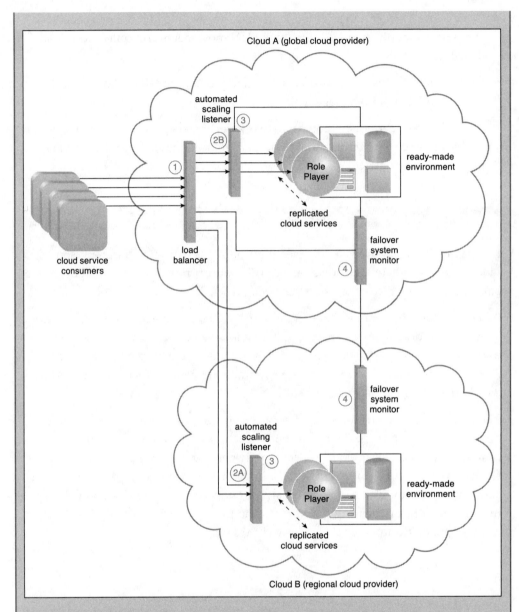

Figure 12.31

A load-balancing service agent routes cloud service consumer requests according to a pre-defined algorithm (1). Requests are received by the local or external automated scaling listener (2A, 2B), which forward each request to a cloud service implementation (3). Failover system monitors are used to detect and respond to cloud service failure (4).

Chapter 13

Specialized Cloud Architectures

The architectural models that are covered in this chapter span a broad range of functional areas and topics to offer creative combinations of mechanisms and specialized components.

13.1 Direct I/O Access Architecture

Access to the physical I/O cards that are installed on a physical server is usually provided to hosted virtual servers via a hypervisor-based layer of processing called I/O virtualization. However, virtual servers sometimes need to connect to and use I/O cards without any hypervisor interaction or emulation.

With the *direct I/O access architecture*, virtual servers are allowed to circumvent the hypervisor and directly access the physical server's I/O card as an alternative to emulating a connection via the hypervisor (Figures 13.1 to 13.3).

To achieve this solution and access the physical I/O card without hypervisor interaction, the host CPU needs to support this type of access with the appropriate drivers installed on the virtual server. The virtual server can then recognize the I/O card as a hardware device after the drivers are installed.

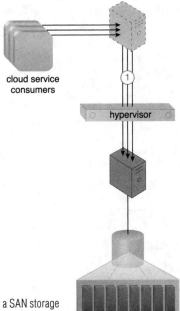

Figure 13.1
Cloud service consumers access a virtual server, which accesses a database on a SAN storage LUN (1). Connectivity from the virtual server to the database occurs via a virtual switch.

Figure 13.2

There is an increase in the amount of cloud service consumer requests (2), causing the bandwidth and performance of the virtual switch to become inadequate (3).

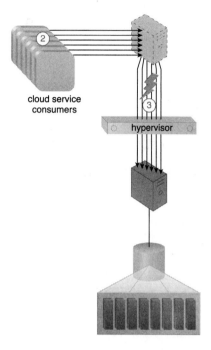

Figure 13.3

The virtual server bypasses the hypervisor to connect to the database server via a direct physical link to the physical server (4). The increased workload can now be properly handled.

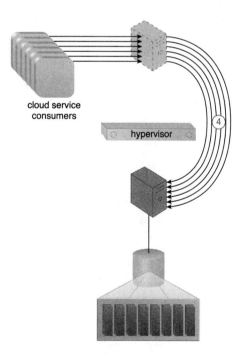

Other mechanisms that can be involved in this architecture in addition to the virtual server and hypervisor include:

- *Cloud Usage Monitor* – The cloud service usage data that is collected by runtime monitors can include and separately classify direct I/O access.

- *Logical Network Perimeter* – The logical network perimeter ensures that the allocated physical I/O card does not allow cloud consumers to access other cloud consumers' IT resources.

- *Pay-Per-Use Monitor* – This monitor collects usage cost information for the allocated physical I/O card.

- *Resource Replication* – Replication technology is used to replace virtual I/O cards with physical I/O cards.

13.2 Direct LUN Access Architecture

Storage LUNs are typically mapped via a host bus adapter (HBA) on the hypervisor, with the storage space emulated as file-based storage to virtual servers (Figure 13.4). However, virtual servers sometimes need direct access to RAW block-based storage. For example, access via an emulated adapter is insufficient when a cluster is implemented and a LUN is used as the shared cluster storage device between two virtual servers.

The *direct LUN access architecture* provides virtual servers with LUN access via a physical HBA card, which is effective because virtual servers in the same cluster can use the LUN as a shared volume for clustered databases. After implementing this solution, the virtual servers' physical connectivity to the LUN and cloud storage device is enabled by the physical hosts.

The LUNs are created and configured on the cloud storage device for LUN presentation to the hypervisors. The cloud storage device needs to be configured using raw device mapping to make the LUNs visible to the virtual servers as a block-based RAW SAN LUN, which is unformatted, un-partitioned storage. The LUN needs to be represented with a unique LUN ID to be used by all of the virtual servers as shared storage. Figures 13.5 and 13.6 illustrate how virtual servers are given direct access to block-based storage LUNs.

Figure 13.4

The cloud storage device is installed and configured (1). The LUN mapping is defined so that each hypervisor has access to its own LUN and can also see all of the mapped LUNs (2). The hypervisor shows the mapped LUNs to the virtual servers as normal file-based storage to be used as such (3).

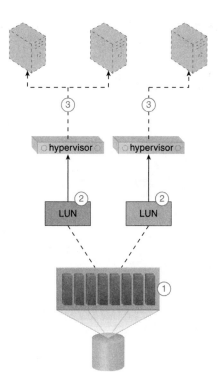

Besides the virtual server, hypervisor, and cloud storage device, the following mechanisms can be incorporated into this architecture:

- *Cloud Usage Monitor* – This monitor tracks and collects storage usage information that pertains to the direct usage of LUNs.

- *Pay-Per-Use Monitor* – The pay-per-use monitor collects and separately classifies usage cost information for direct LUN access.

- *Resource Replication* – This mechanism relates to how virtual servers directly access block-based storage in replacement of file-based storage.

Figure 13.5

The cloud storage device is installed and configured (1). The required LUNs are created and presented to the hypervisors (2), which map the presented LUNs directly to the virtual servers (3). The virtual servers can see the LUNs as RAW block-based storage and can access them directly (4).

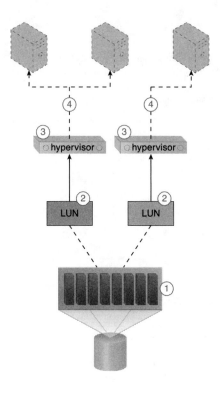

Figure 13.6

The virtual servers' storage commands are received by the hypervisors (5), which process and forward the requests to the storage processor (6).

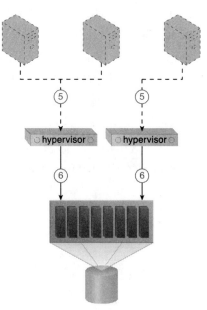

13.3 Dynamic Data Normalization Architecture

Redundant data can cause a range of issues in cloud-based environments, such as:

- increased time required to store and catalog files

- increased required storage and backup space

- increased costs due to increased data volume

- increased time required for replication to secondary storage

- increased time required to backup data

For example, if a cloud consumer copies 100 MB of files onto a cloud storage device and the data is redundantly copied ten times, the consequences can be considerable:

- The cloud consumer will be charged for using 10 x 100 MB of storage space, even though only 100 MB of unique data was actually stored.

- The cloud provider needs to provide an unnecessary 900 MB of space in the online cloud storage device and any backup storage systems.

- Significantly more time is required to store and catalog data.

- Data replication duration and performance are unnecessarily taxed whenever the cloud provider performs a site recovery, since 1,000 MB need to be replicated instead of 100 MB.

These impacts can be significantly amplified in multitenant public clouds.

The *dynamic data normalization architecture* establishes a de-duplication system, which prevents cloud consumers from inadvertently saving redundant copies of data by detecting and eliminating redundant data on cloud storage devices. This system can be applied to both block and file-based storage devices, although it is most effective on the former. This de-duplication system checks each received block to determine whether it is redundant with a block that has already been received. Redundant blocks are replaced with pointers to the equivalent blocks that are already in storage (Figure 13.7).

The de-duplication system examines received data prior to passing it to storage controllers. As part of the examination process, a hash code is assigned to every piece of data that has been processed and stored. An index of hashes and pieces is also maintained. As a result, the generated hash of a newly received block of data is compared with the hashes in storage to determine whether it is a new or duplicate data block. New blocks

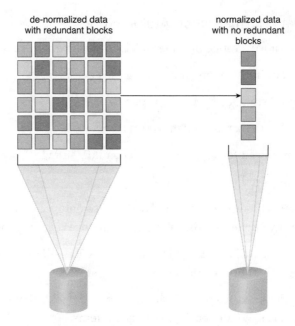

Figure 13.7

Data sets containing redundant data are unnecessarily bloating
storage (left). The data de-duplication system normalizes the
data, so that only unique data is stored (right).

are saved, while duplicate data is eliminated and a pointer to the original data block is
created and saved instead.

This architectural model can be used for both disk storage and backup tape drives.
One cloud provider can decide to prevent redundant data only on backup cloud storage
devices, while another can more aggressively implement the data de-duplication system
on all of its cloud storage devices. There are different methods and algorithms for comparing blocks of data to confirm their duplicity with other blocks.

13.4 Elastic Network Capacity Architecture

Even if IT resources are scaled on-demand by a cloud platform, performance and scalability can still be inhibited when remote access to the IT resources is impacted by
network bandwidth limitations (Figure 13.8).

The *elastic network capacity architecture* establishes a system in which additional bandwidth is allocated dynamically to the network to avoid runtime bottlenecks. This

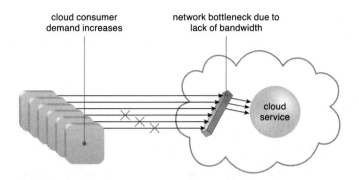

Figure 13.8
A lack of available bandwidth causes performance issues for cloud consumer requests.

system ensures that each cloud consumer is using a different set of network ports to isolate individual cloud consumer traffic flows.

The automated scaling listener and intelligent automation engine scripts are used to detect when traffic reaches the bandwidth threshold, and to dynamically allocate additional bandwidth and/or network ports when required.

The cloud architecture can be equipped with a network resource pool containing network ports that are made available for shared usage. The automated scaling listener monitors workload and network traffic, and signals the intelligent automation engine to modify the number of allocated network ports and/or bandwidth in response to usage fluctuations.

Note that when this architectural model is implemented at the virtual switch level, the intelligent automation engine may need to run a separate script that adds physical uplinks to the virtual switch specifically. Alternatively, the direct I/O access architecture can also be incorporated to increase network bandwidth that is allocated to the virtual server.

In addition to the automated scaling listener, the following mechanisms can be part of this architecture:

- *Cloud Usage Monitor* – These monitors are responsible for tracking elastic network capacity before, during, and after scaling.

- *Hypervisor* – The hypervisor provides virtual servers with access to the physical network, via virtual switches and physical uplinks.

- *Logical Network Perimeter* – This mechanism establishes the boundaries that are needed to provide individual cloud consumers with their allocated network capacity.

- *Pay-Per-Use Monitor* – This monitor keeps track of any billing-related data that pertains to dynamic network bandwidth consumption.

- *Resource Replication* – Resource replication is used to add network ports to physical and virtual servers, in response to workload demands.

- *Virtual Server* – Virtual servers host the IT resources and cloud services to which network resources are allocated and are themselves affected by the scaling of network capacity.

13.5 Cross-Storage Device Vertical Tiering Architecture

Cloud storage devices are sometimes unable to accommodate the performance requirements of cloud consumers, and have more data processing power or bandwidth added to increase IOPS. These conventional methods of vertical scaling are usually inefficient and time-consuming to implement, and can become wasteful when the increased capacity is no longer required.

The scenario in Figures 13.9 and 13.10 depicts an approach in which a number of requests for access to a LUN has increased, requiring its manual transfer to a high-performance cloud storage device.

The *cross-storage device vertical tiering architecture* establishes a system that survives bandwidth and data processing power constraints by vertically scaling between storage devices that have different capacities. LUNs can automatically scale up and down across multiple devices in this system so that requests can use the appropriate storage device level to perform cloud consumer tasks.

New cloud storage devices with increased capacity can also be made available, even if the automated tiering technology can move data to cloud storage devices with the same storage processing capacity. For example, solid-state drives (SSDs) can be suitable devices for data processing power upgrades.

Figure 13.9

A cloud provider installs and configures a cloud storage device (1) and creates LUNs that are made available to the cloud service consumers for usage (2). The cloud service consumers initiate data access requests to the cloud storage device (3), which forwards the requests to one of the LUNs (4).

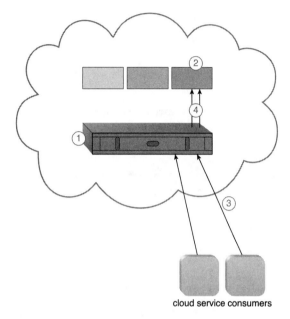

cloud service consumers

Figure 13.10

The number of requests increases, resulting in high storage bandwidth and performance demands (5). Some of the requests are rejected, or time out due to performance capacity limitations within the cloud storage device (6).

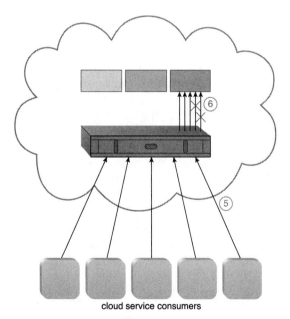

cloud service consumers

The automated scaling listener monitors the requests that are sent to specific LUNs, and signals the storage management program to move the LUN to a higher capacity device once it identifies a predefined threshold has been reached. Service interruption is prevented because there is never a disconnection during the transfer. The original device remains up and running, while the LUN data scales up to another device. Cloud consumer requests are automatically redirected to the new cloud storage device as soon as the scaling is completed (Figures 13.11 to 13.13).

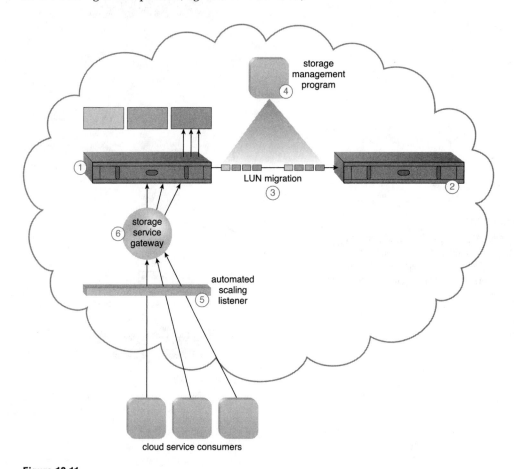

Figure 13.11

The lower capacity primary cloud storage device is responding to cloud service consumer storage requests (1). A secondary cloud storage device with higher capacity and performance is installed (2). The LUN migration (3) is configured via the storage management program that is configured to categorize the storage based on device performance (4). Thresholds are defined in the automated scaling listener that is monitoring the requests (5). Cloud service consumer requests are received by the storage service gateway and sent to the primary cloud storage device (6).

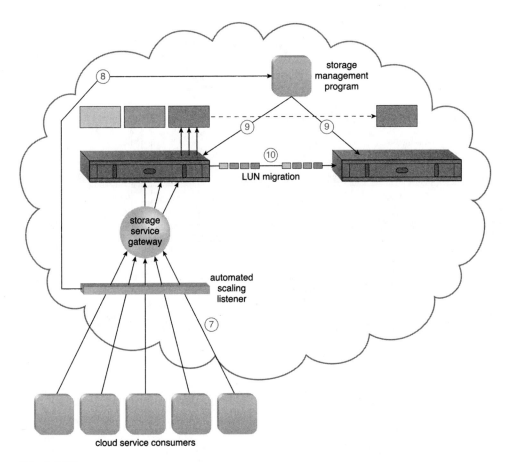

Figure 13.12

The number of cloud service consumer requests reaches the predefined threshold (7), and the automated scaling listener notifies the storage management program that scaling is required (8). The storage management program calls LUN migration to move the cloud consumer's LUN to the secondary, higher capacity storage device (9) and the LUN migration performs this move (10).

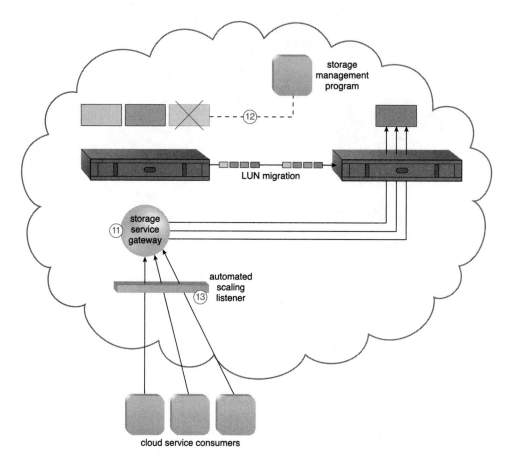

Figure 13.13

The storage service gateway forwards the cloud service consumer requests from the LUN to the new cloud storage device (11). The original LUN is deleted from the lower capacity device via the storage management program and LUN migration (12). The automated scaling listener monitors cloud service consumer requests to ensure that the request volume continues to require access to the higher capacity secondary storage for the migrated LUN (13).

In addition to the automated scaling listener and cloud storage device, the mechanisms that can be incorporated in this technology architecture include:

- *Audit Monitor* – The auditing performed by this monitor checks whether the relocation of cloud consumer data does not conflict with any legal or data privacy regulations or policies.

- *Cloud Usage Monitor* – This infrastructure mechanism represents various runtime monitoring requirements for tracking and recording data transfer and usage, at both source and destination storage locations.

- *Pay-Per-Use Monitor* – Within the context of this architecture, the pay-per-use monitor collects storage usage information on both source and destination locations, as well as IT resource usage information for carrying out cross-storage tiering functionality.

13.6 Intra-Storage Device Vertical Data Tiering Architecture

Some cloud consumers may have distinct data storage requirements that restrict the data's physical location to a single cloud storage device. Distribution across other cloud storage devices may be disallowed due to security, privacy, or various legal reasons. This type of limitation can impose severe scalability limitations upon the device's storage and performance capacity. These limitations can further cascade to any cloud services or applications that are dependent upon the use of the cloud storage device.

The *intra-storage device vertical data tiering architecture* establishes a system to support vertical scaling within a single cloud storage device. This intra-device scaling system optimizes the availability of different disk types with different capacities (Figure 13.14).

Figure 13.14

The cloud intra-storage device system vertically scales through disk types graded into different tiers (1). Each LUN is moved to a tier that corresponds to its processing and storage requirements (2).

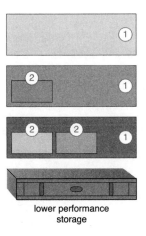

lower performance
storage

This cloud storage architecture requires the use of a complex storage device that supports different types of hard disks, especially high-performance disks like SATAs, SASs, and SSDs. The disk types are organized into graded tiers so that LUN migration can vertically scale the device based on the allocation of disk types, which align with the processing and capacity requirements.

Data load conditions and definitions are set after disk categorization so that the LUNs can move to either a higher or lower grade, depending on which predefined conditions are met. These thresholds and conditions are used by the automated scaling listener when monitoring runtime data processing traffic (Figures 13.15 to 13.17).

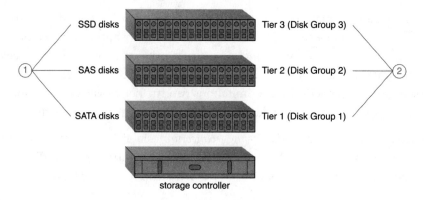

Figure 13.15

Different types of hard disks are installed in the enclosures of a cloud storage device (1). Similar disk types are grouped into tiers to create different grades of disk groups based on I/O performance (2).

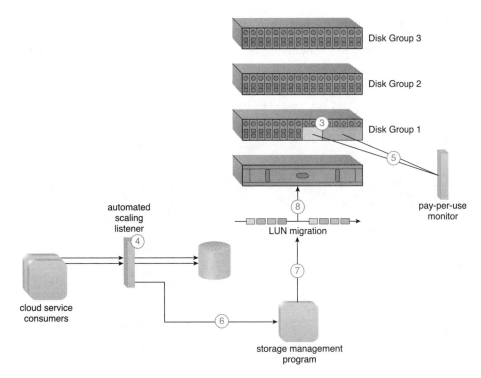

Figure 13.16

Two LUNs have been created on Disk Group 1 (3). The automated scaling listener monitors the requests in relation to pre-defined thresholds (4). The pay-per-use monitor tracks the actual amount of disk usage, based on free space and disk group performance (5). The automated scaling listener determines that the number of requests is reaching a threshold, and informs the storage management program that the LUN needs to be moved to a higher performance disk group (6). The storage management program signals the LUN migration program to perform the required move (7). The LUN migration program works with the storage controller to move the LUN to the higher capacity Disk Group 2 (8).

Figure 13.17

The usage price of the migrated LUN in Disk Group 2 is now higher than before, because a higher performance disk group is being used (9).

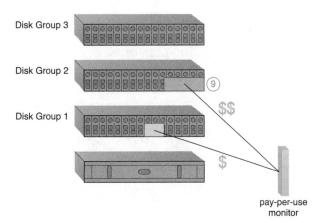

13.7 Load Balanced Virtual Switches Architecture

Virtual servers are connected to the outside world via virtual switches, which send and receive traffic with the same uplink. Bandwidth bottlenecks form when the network traffic on the uplink's port increases to a point that it causes transmission delays, performance issues, packet loss, and lag time (Figures 13.18 and 13.19).

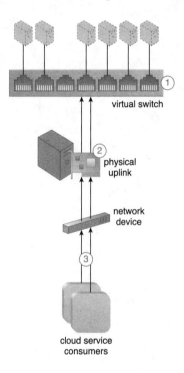

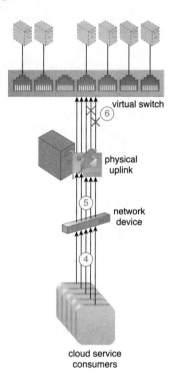

Figure 13.18

A virtual switch is interconnecting virtual servers (1). A physical network adapter has been attached to the virtual switch to be used as an uplink to the physical (external) network, connecting the virtual servers to cloud consumers (2). Cloud service consumers send requests via the physical uplink (3).

Figure 13.19

The amount of traffic passing through the physical uplink grows in parallel with the increasing number of requests. The number of packets that need to be processed and forwarded by the physical network adapter also increases (4). The physical adapter cannot handle the workload, now that the network traffic has exceeded its capacity (5). The network forms a bottleneck that results in performance degradation and the loss of delay-sensitive data packets (6).

The *load balanced virtual switches architecture* establishes a load balancing system where multiple uplinks are provided to balance network traffic workloads across multiple uplinks or redundant paths, which can help avoid slow transfers and data loss (Figure 13.20). Link aggregation can be executed to balance the traffic, which allows the workload to be distributed across multiple uplinks at the same time so that none of the network cards are overloaded.

The virtual switch needs to be configured to support multiple physical uplinks, which are usually configured as an NIC team that has defined traffic-shaping policies.

The following mechanisms can be incorporated into this architecture:

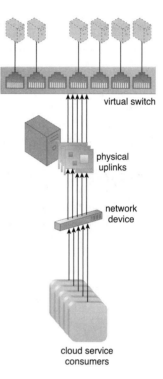

Figure 13.20
Additional physical uplinks are added to distribute and balance network traffic.

- *Cloud Usage Monitor* – Cloud usage monitors are used to monitor network traffic and bandwidth usage.

- *Hypervisor* – This mechanism hosts and provides the virtual servers with access to both the virtual switches and external network.

- *Load Balancer* – The load balancer distributes the network workload across the different uplinks.

- *Logical Network Perimeter* – The logical network perimeter creates boundaries that protect and limit the bandwidth usage for each cloud consumer.

- *Resource Replication* – This mechanism is used to generate additional uplinks to the virtual switch.

- *Virtual Server* – Virtual servers host the IT resources that benefit from the additional uplinks and bandwidth via virtual switches.

13.8 Multipath Resource Access Architecture

Certain IT resources can only be accessed using an assigned path (or hyperlink) that leads to their exact location. This path can be lost or incorrectly defined by the cloud consumer or changed by the cloud provider. An IT resource whose hyperlink is no longer in the possession of the cloud consumer becomes inaccessible and unavailable (Figure 13.21). Exception conditions that result from IT resource unavailability can compromise the stability of larger cloud solutions that depend on the IT resource.

Figure 13.21

Physical Server A is connected to LUN A via a single fiber channel, and uses the LUN to store different types of data. The fiber channel connection becomes unavailable due to a HBA card failure and invalidates the path used by Physical Server A, which has now lost access to LUN A and all of its stored data.

The *multipath resource access architecture* establishes a multipathing system with alternative paths to IT resources, so that cloud consumers have the means to programmatically or manually overcome path failures (Figure 13.22).

This technology architecture requires the use of a multipathing system and the creation of alternative physical or virtual hyperlinks that are assigned to specific IT resources. The multipathing system resides on the server or hypervisor, and ensures that each IT resource can be seen via each alternative path identically (Figure 13.23).

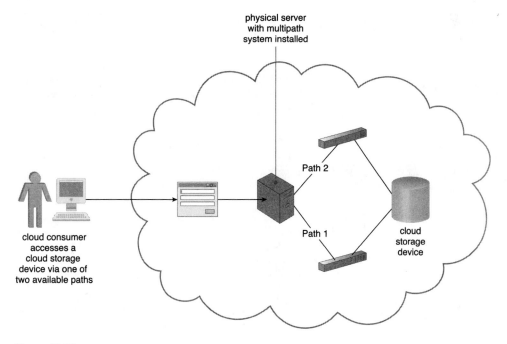

Figure 13.22
A multipathing system is providing alternative paths to a cloud storage device.

This architecture can involve the following mechanisms:

- *Cloud Storage Device* – The cloud storage device is a common IT resource that requires the creation of alternative paths in order to remain accessible to solutions that rely on data access.

- *Hypervisor* – Alternative paths to a hypervisor are required in order to have redundant links to the hosted virtual servers.

- *Logical Network Perimeter* – This mechanism guarantees the maintenance of cloud consumer privacy, even when multiple paths to the same IT resource are created.

- *Resource Replication* – The resource replication mechanism is required when a new instance of an IT resource needs to be created to generate the alternative path.

- *Virtual Server* – These servers host the IT resources that have multipath access via different links or virtual switches. Hypervisors can provide multipath access to the virtual servers.

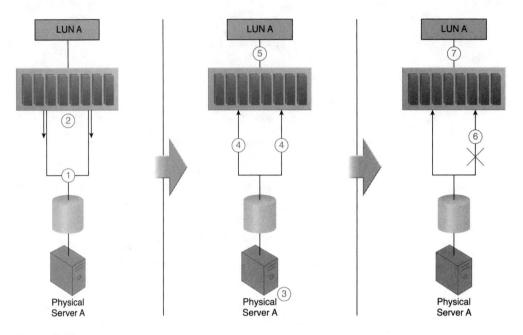

Figure 13.23

Physical Server A is connected to the LUN A cloud storage device via two different paths (1). LUN A is seen as different LUNs from each of the two paths (2). The multipathing system is configured (3). LUN A is seen as one identical LUN from both paths (4), and Physical Server A has access to LUN A from two different paths (5). A link failure occurs and one of the paths becomes unavailable (6). Physical Server A can still use LUN A because the other link remains active (7).

13.9 Persistent Virtual Network Configuration Architecture

Network configurations and port assignments for virtual servers are generated during the creation of the virtual switch on the host physical server and the hypervisor hosting the virtual server. These configurations and assignments reside in the virtual server's immediate hosting environment, meaning a virtual server that is moved or migrated to another host will lose network connectivity because destination hosting environments do not have the required port assignments and network configuration information (Figure 13.24).

In the *persistent virtual network configuration architecture*, network configuration information is stored in a centralized location and replicated to physical server hosts. This allows the destination host to access the configuration information when a virtual server is moved from one host to another.

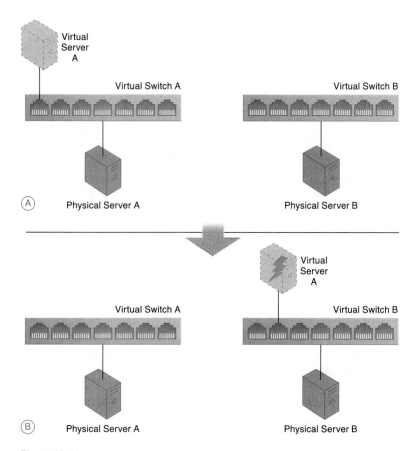

Figure 13.24

Part A shows Virtual Server A connected to the network through Virtual Switch A, which was
created on Physical Server A. In Part B, Virtual Server A is connected to Virtual Switch B after
being moved to Physical Server B. The virtual server cannot connect to the network because its
configuration settings are missing.

The system established with this architecture includes a centralized virtual switch,
VIM, and configuration replication technology. The centralized virtual switch is shared
by physical servers and configured via the VIM, which initiates replication of the configuration settings to the physical servers (Figure 13.25).

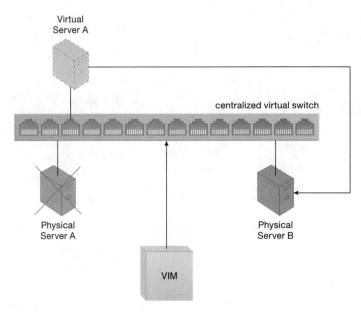

Figure 13.25

A virtual switch's configuration settings are maintained by the VIM, which ensures that these settings are replicated to other physical servers. The centralized virtual switch is published, and each host physical server is assigned some of its ports. Virtual Server A is moved to Physical Server B when Physical Server A fails. The virtual server's network settings are retrievable, since they are stored on a centralized virtual switch that is shared by both physical servers. Virtual Server A maintains network connectivity on its new host, Physical Server B.

In addition to the virtual server mechanism for which this architecture provides a migration system, the following mechanisms can be included:

- *Hypervisor* – The hypervisor hosts the virtual servers that require the configuration settings to be replicated across the physical hosts.

- *Logical Network Perimeter* – The logical network perimeter helps ensure that access to the virtual server and its IT resources is isolated to the rightful cloud consumer, before and after a virtual server is migrated.

- *Resource Replication* – The resource replication mechanism is used to replicate the virtual switch configurations and network capacity allocations across the hypervisors, via the centralized virtual switch.

13.10 Redundant Physical Connection for Virtual Servers Architecture

A virtual server is connected to an external network via a virtual switch uplink port, meaning the virtual server will become isolated and disconnected from the external network if the uplink fails (Figure 13.26).

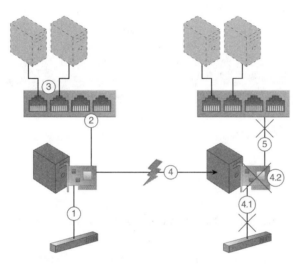

Figure 13.26

A physical network adapter installed on the host physical server is connected to the physical switch on the network (1). A virtual switch is created for use by two virtual servers. The physical network adapter is attached to the virtual switch to act as an uplink, since it requires access to the physical (external) network (2). The virtual servers communicate with the external network via the attached physical uplink network card (3). A connection failure occurs, either because of a physical link connectivity issue between the physical adapter and the physical switch (4.1), or because of a physical network card failure (4.2). The virtual servers lose access to the physical external network and are no longer accessible to their cloud consumers (5).

The *redundant physical connection for virtual servers architecture* establishes one or more redundant uplink connections and positions them in standby mode. This architecture ensures that a redundant uplink connection is available to connect the active uplink, whenever the primary uplink connection becomes unavailable (Figure 13.27).

Figure 13.27

Redundant uplinks are installed on a physical server that is hosting several virtual servers. When an uplink fails, another uplink takes over to maintain the virtual servers' active network connections.

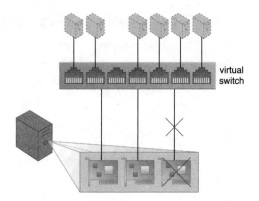

In a process that is transparent to both virtual servers and their users, a standby uplink automatically becomes the active uplink as soon as the main uplink fails, and the virtual servers use the newly active uplink to sends packets externally.

The second NIC does not forward any traffic while the primary uplink is alive, even though it receives the virtual server's packets. However, the secondary uplink will start forwarding packets immediately if the primary uplink were to fail (Figures 13.28 to 13.30). The failed uplink becomes the primary uplink again after it returns to operation, while the second NIC returns to standby mode.

Figure 13.28

A new network adapter is added to support a redundant uplink (1). Both network cards are connected to the physical external switch (2), and both physical network adapters are configured to be used as uplink adapters for the virtual switch (3).

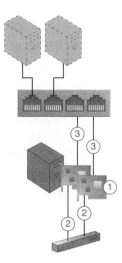

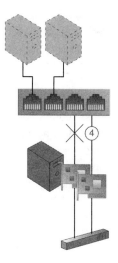

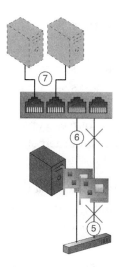

Figure 13.29

One physical network adapter is designated as the primary adapter (4), while the other is designated as the secondary adapter providing the standby uplink. The secondary adapter does not forward any packets.

Figure 13.30

The primary uplink becomes unavailable (5). The secondary standby uplink automatically takes over and uses the virtual switch to forward the virtual servers' packets to the external network (6). The virtual servers do not experience interruptions and remain connected to the external network (7).

The following mechanisms are commonly part of this architecture, in addition to the virtual server:

- *Failover System* – The failover system performs the transition of unavailable uplinks to standby uplinks.

- *Hypervisor* – This mechanism hosts virtual servers and some virtual switches, and provides virtual networks and virtual switches with access to the virtual servers.

- *Logical Network Perimeter* – Logical network perimeters ensure that the virtual switches that are allocated or defined for each cloud consumer remain isolated.

- *Resource Replication* – Resource replication is used to replicate the current status of active uplinks to standby uplinks so as to maintain the network connection.

13.11 Storage Maintenance Window Architecture

Cloud storage devices that are subject to maintenance and administrative tasks sometimes need to be temporarily shut down, meaning cloud service consumers and IT resources consequently lose access to these devices and their stored data (Figure 13.31).

The data of a cloud storage device that is about to undergo a maintenance outage can be temporarily moved to a secondary duplicate cloud storage

LIVE STORAGE MIGRATION

The live storage migration program is a sophisticated system that utilizes the LUN migration component to reliably move LUNs by enabling the original copy to remain active until after the destination copy has been verified as being fully functional.

live storage migration

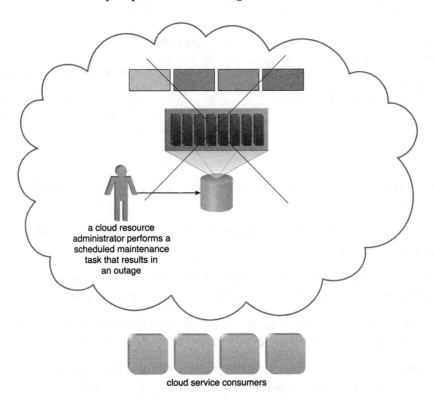

a cloud resource administrator performs a scheduled maintenance task that results in an outage

cloud service consumers

Figure 13.31

A pre-scheduled maintenance task carried out by a cloud resource administrator causes an outage for the cloud storage device, which becomes unavailable to cloud service consumers. Because cloud consumers were previously notified of the outage, cloud consumers do not attempt any data access.

device. The *storage maintenance window architecture* enables cloud service consumers to be automatically and transparently redirected to the secondary cloud storage device, without becoming aware that their primary storage device has been taken offline.

This architecture uses a live storage migration program, as demonstrated in Figures 13.32 to 13.37.

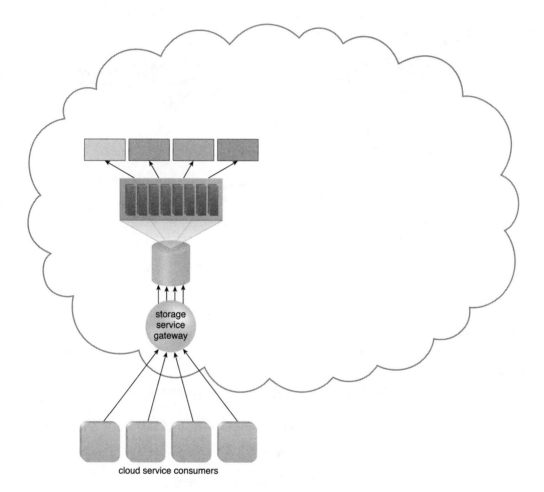

Figure 13.32

The cloud storage device is scheduled to undergo a maintenance outage, but unlike the scenario depicted in Figure 13.31, the cloud service consumers were not notified of the outage and continue to access the cloud storage device.

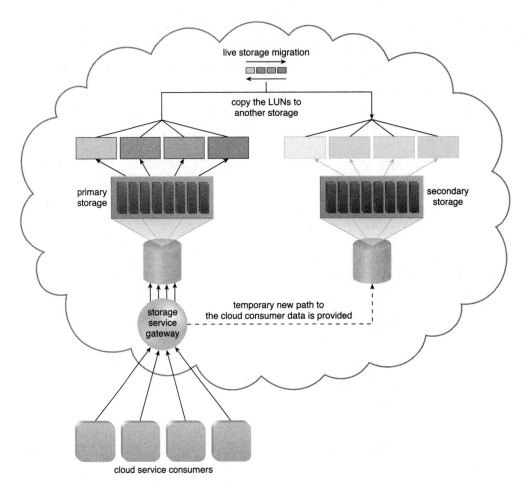

Figure 13.33

Live storage migration moves the LUNs from the primary storage device to a secondary storage device.

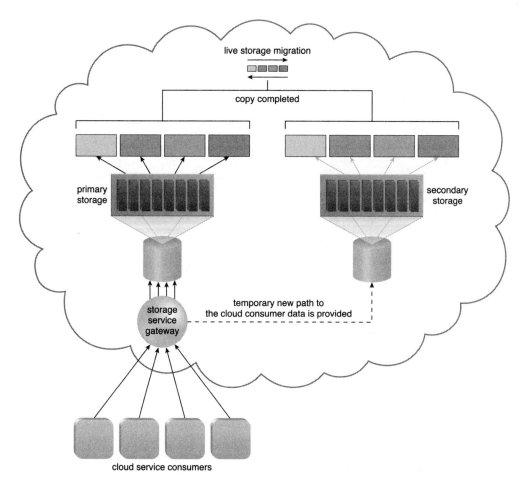

Figure 13.34

Requests for the data are forwarded to the duplicate LUNs on the secondary storage device, once the LUN's data has been migrated.

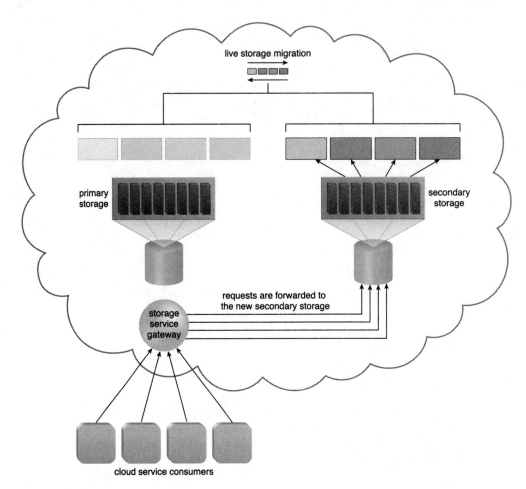

Figure 13.35

The primary storage is powered off for maintenance.

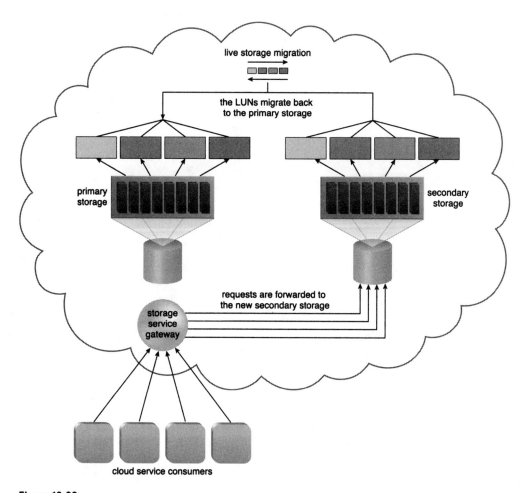

Figure 13.36

The primary storage is brought back online, after the maintenance task is finished. Live storage migration restores the LUN data from the secondary storage device to the primary storage device.

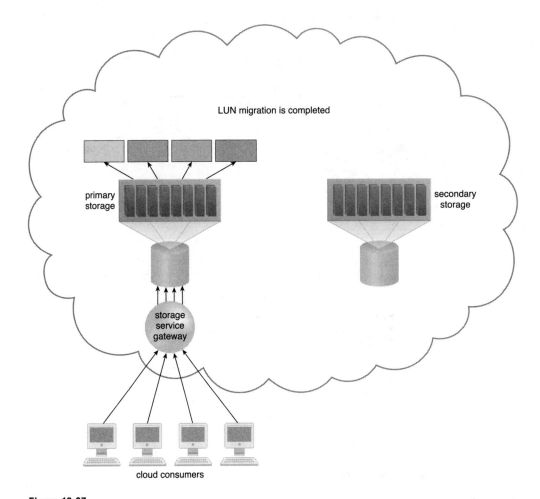

Figure 13.37
The live storage migration process is completed and all of the data access requests are forwarded back to the primary cloud storage device.

In addition to the cloud storage device mechanism that is principal to this architecture, the resource replication mechanism is used to keep the primary and secondary storage devices synchronized. Both manually and automatically initiated failover can also be incorporated into this cloud architecture via the failover system mechanism, even though the migration is often pre-scheduled.

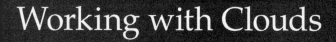

Working with Clouds

Each of the chapters in this part of the book addresses a different topic area that pertains to planning or using cloud environments and cloud-based technologies. The numerous considerations, strategies, and metrics provided in these chapters help associate topics covered in preceding chapters with real-world requirements and constraints.

Chapter 14

Cloud Delivery Model Considerations

M̲ost of the preceding chapters have been focused on technologies and models used to define and implement infrastructure and architecture layers within cloud environments. This chapter revisits the cloud delivery models that were introduced in Chapter 4 in order to address a number of real world considerations within the context of IaaS, PaaS, and SaaS-based environments.

The chapter is organized into two primary sections that explore cloud delivery model issues pertaining to cloud providers and cloud consumers respectively.

14.1 Cloud Delivery Models: The Cloud Provider Perspective

This section explores the architecture and administration of IaaS, PaaS, and SaaS cloud delivery models from the point of view of the cloud provider. The integration and management of these cloud-based environments as part of greater environments and how they can relate to different technologies and cloud mechanism combinations are examined.

Building IaaS Environments

The virtual server and cloud storage device mechanisms represent the two most fundamental IT resources that are delivered as part of a standard rapid provisioning architecture within IaaS environments. They are offered in various standardized configurations that are defined by the following properties:

- operating system
- primary memory capacity
- processing capacity
- virtualized storage capacity

Memory and virtualized storage capacity is usually allocated with increments of 1 GB to simplify the provisioning of underlying physical IT resources. When limiting cloud consumer access to virtualized environments, IaaS offerings are preemptively assembled by cloud providers via virtual server images that capture the pre-defined configurations. Some cloud providers may offer cloud consumers direct administrative access to physical IT resources, in which case the bare-metal provisioning architecture may come into play.

Snapshots can be taken of a virtual server to record its current state, memory, and configuration of a virtualized IaaS environment for backup and replication purposes, in support of horizontal and vertical scaling requirements. For example, a virtual server can use its snapshot to become reinitialized in another hosting environment after its capacity has been increased to allow for vertical scaling. The snapshot can alternatively be used to duplicate a virtual server. The management of custom virtual server images is a vital feature that is provided via the remote administration system mechanism. Most cloud providers also support importing and exporting options for custom-built virtual server images in both proprietary and standard formats.

Data Centers

Cloud providers can offer IaaS-based IT resources from multiple geographically diverse data centers, which provides the following primary benefits:

- Multiple data centers can be linked together for increased resiliency. Each data center is placed in a different location to lower the chances of a single failure forcing all of the data centers to go offline simultaneously.

- Connected through high-speed communications networks with low latency, data centers can perform load balancing, IT resource backup and replication, and increase storage capacity, while improving availability and reliability. Having multiple data centers spread over a greater area further reduces network latency.

- Data centers that are deployed in different countries make access to IT resources more convenient for cloud consumers that are constricted by legal and regulatory requirements.

Figure 14.1 provides an example of a cloud provider that is managing four data centers that are split between two different geographic regions.

When an IaaS environment is used to provide cloud consumers with virtualized network environments, each cloud consumer is segregated into a tenant environment that isolates IT resources from the rest of the cloud through the Internet. VLANs and network access control software collaboratively realize the corresponding logical network perimeters.

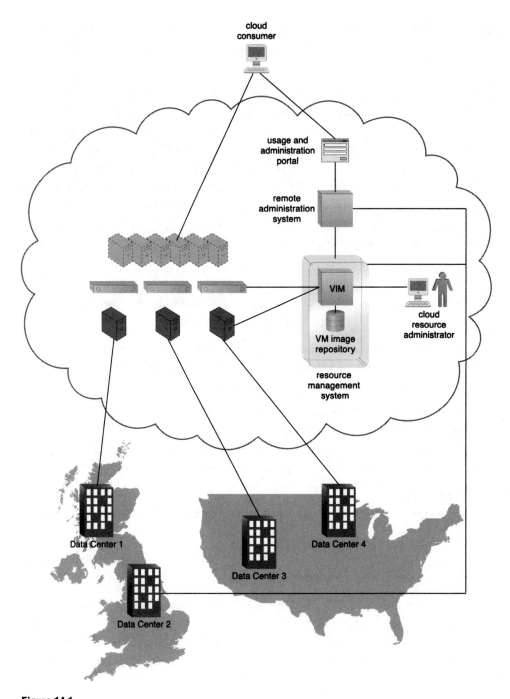

Figure 14.1

A cloud provider is provisioning and managing an IaaS environment with IT resources from different data centers in the United States and the United Kingdom.

Scalability and Reliability

Within IaaS environments, cloud providers can automatically provision virtual servers via the dynamic vertical scaling type of the dynamic scalability architecture. This can be performed through the VIM, as long as the host physical servers have sufficient capacity. The VIM can scale virtual servers out using resource replication as part of a resource pool architecture, if a given physical server has insufficient capacity to support vertical scaling. The load balancer mechanism, as part of a workload distribution architecture, can be used to distribute the workload among IT resources in a pool to complete the horizontal scaling process.

Manual scalability requires the cloud consumer to interact with a usage and administration program to explicitly request IT resource scaling. In contrast, automatic scalability requires the automated scaling listener to monitor the workload and reactively scale the resource capacity. This mechanism typically acts as a monitoring agent that tracks IT resource usage in order to notify the resource management system when capacity has been exceeded.

Replicated IT resources can be arranged in high-availability configuration that forms a failover system for implementation via standard VIM features. Alternatively, a high-availability/high-performance resource cluster can be created at the physical or virtual server level, or both simultaneously. The multipath resource access architecture is commonly employed to enhance reliability via the use of redundant access paths, and some cloud providers further offer the provisioning of dedicated IT resources via the resource reservation architecture.

Monitoring

Cloud usage monitors in an IaaS environment can be implemented using the VIM or specialized monitoring tools that directly comprise and/or interface with the virtualization platform. Several common capabilities of the IaaS platform involve monitoring:

- *Virtual Server Lifecycles* – Recording and tracking uptime periods and the allocation of IT resources, for pay-per-use monitors and time-based billing purposes.

- *Data Storage* – Tracking and assigning the allocation of storage capacity to cloud storage devices on virtual servers, for pay-per-use monitors that record storage usage for billing purposes.

- *Network Traffic* – For pay-per-use monitors that measure inbound and outbound network usage and SLA monitors that track QoS metrics, such as response times and network losses.

- *Failure Conditions* – For SLA monitors that track IT resource and QoS metrics to provide warning in times of failure.

- *Event Triggers* – For audit monitors that appraise and evaluate the regulatory compliance of select IT resources.

Monitoring architectures within IaaS environments typically involve service agents that communicate directly with backend management systems.

Security

Cloud security mechanisms that are relevant for securing IaaS environments include:

- encryption, hashing, digital signature, and PKI mechanisms for overall protection of data transmission

- IAM and SSO mechanisms for accessing services and interfaces in security systems that rely on user identification, authentication, and authorization capabilities

- cloud-based security groups for isolating virtual environments through hypervisors and network segments via network management software

- hardened virtual server images for internal and externally available virtual server environments

- various cloud usage monitors to track provisioned virtual IT resources to detect abnormal usage patterns

---

NOTE

The public cloud vendor IaaS offerings table maintained on
www.servicetechbooks.com/cloud summarizes the configuration
information of several commercial public cloud providers that offer IaaS
products, and further lists the physical locations of their data centers.

Equipping PaaS Environments

PaaS environments typically need to be outfitted with a selection of application development and deployment platforms in order to accommodate different programming models, languages, and frameworks. A separate ready-made environment is usually created for each programming stack that contains the necessary software to run applications specifically developed for the platform.

Each platform is accompanied by a matching SDK and IDE, which can be custom-built or enabled by IDE plugins supplied by the cloud provider. IDE toolkits can simulate the cloud runtime locally within the PaaS environment and usually include executable application servers. The security restrictions that are inherent to the runtime are also simulated in the development environment, including checks for unauthorized attempts to access system IT resources.

Cloud providers often offer a resource management system mechanism that is customized for the PaaS platform so that cloud consumers can create and control customized virtual server images with ready-made environments. This mechanism also provides features specific to the PaaS platform, such as managing deployed applications and configuring multitenancy. Cloud providers further rely on a variation of the rapid provisioning architecture known as platform provisioning, which is designed specifically to provision ready-made environments.

Scalability and Reliability

The scalability requirements of cloud services and applications that are deployed within PaaS environments are generally addressed via dynamic scalability and workload distribution architectures that rely on the use of native automated scaling listeners and load balancers. The resource pooling architecture is further utilized to provision IT resources from resource pools made available to multiple cloud consumers.

Cloud providers can evaluate network traffic and server-side connection usage against the instance's workload, when determining how to scale an overloaded application as per parameters and cost limitations provided by the cloud consumer. Alternatively, cloud consumers can configure the application designs to customize the incorporation of available mechanisms themselves.

The reliability of ready-made environments and hosted cloud services and applications can be supported with standard failover system mechanisms (Figure 14.2), as well as the non-disruptive service relocation architecture, so as to shield cloud consumers from failover conditions. The resource reservation architecture may also be in place to offer exclusive access to PaaS-based IT resources. As with other IT resources, ready-made environments can also span multiple data centers and geographical regions to further increase availability and resiliency.

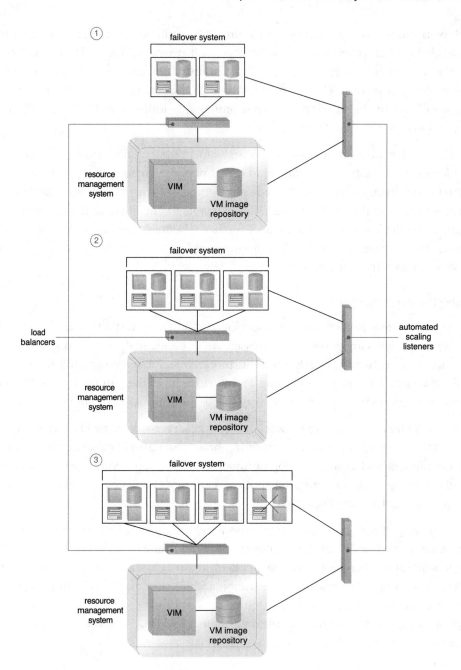

Figure 14.2

Load balancers are used to distribute ready-made environment instances that are part of a failover
system, while automated scaling listeners are used to monitor the network and instance workloads (1).
The ready-made environments are scaled out in response to an increase in workload (2), and the failover
system detects a failure condition and stops replicating a failed ready-made environment (3).

Monitoring

Specialized cloud usage monitors in PaaS environments are used to monitor the following:

- *Ready-Made Environment Instances* – The applications of these instances are recorded by pay-per-use monitors for the calculation of time-based usage fees.

- *Data Persistence* – This statistic is provided by pay-per-use monitors that record the number of objects, individual occupied storage sizes, and database transactions per billing period.

- *Network Usage* – Inbound and outbound network usage is tracked for pay-per-use monitors and SLA monitors that track network-related QoS metrics.

- *Failure Conditions* – SLA monitors that track the QoS metrics of IT resources need to capture failure statistics.

- *Event Triggers* – This metric is primarily used by audit monitors that need to respond to certain types of events.

Security

The PaaS environment, by default, does not usually introduce the need for new cloud security mechanisms beyond those that are already provisioned for IaaS environments.

Optimizing SaaS Environments

In SaaS implementations, cloud service architectures are generally based on multitenant environments that enable and regulate concurrent cloud consumer access (Figure 14.3). SaaS IT resource segregation does not typically occur at the infrastructure level in SaaS environments, as it does in IaaS and PaaS environments.

SaaS implementations rely heavily on the features provided by the native dynamic scalability and workload distribution architectures, as well as non-disruptive service relocation to ensure that failover conditions do not impact the availability of SaaS-based cloud services.

However, it is vital to acknowledge that, unlike the relatively vanilla designs of IaaS and PaaS products, each SaaS deployment will bring with it unique architectural, functional, and runtime requirements. These requirements are specific to the nature of the business logic the SaaS-based cloud service is programmed with, as well as the distinct usage patterns it is subjected to by its cloud service consumers.

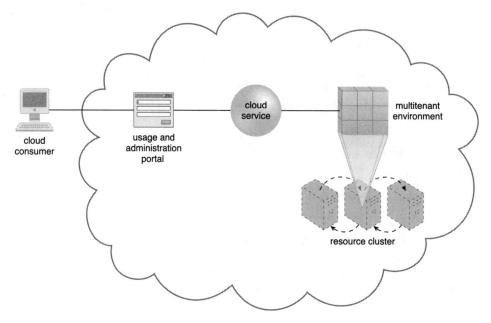

Figure 14.3

The SaaS-based cloud service is hosted by a multitenant environment deployed in a high-performance virtual server cluster. A usage and administration portal is used by the cloud consumer to access and configure the cloud service.

For example, consider the diversity in functionality and usage of the following recognized online SaaS offerings:

- collaborative authoring and information-sharing (Wikipedia, Blogger)

- collaborative management (Zimbra, Google Apps)

- conferencing services for instant messaging, audio/video communications (Skype, Google Talk)

- enterprise management systems (ERP, CRM, CM)

- file-sharing and content distribution (YouTube, Dropbox)

- industry-specific software (engineering, bioinformatics)

- messaging systems (e-mail, voicemail)

- mobile application marketplaces (Android Play Store, Apple App Store)

- office productivity software suites (Microsoft Office, Adobe Creative Cloud)

- search engines (Google, Yahoo)
- social networking media (Twitter, LinkedIn)

Now consider that many of the previously listed cloud services are offered in one or more of the following implementation mediums:

- mobile application
- REST service
- Web service

Each of these SaaS implementation mediums provide Web-based APIs for interfacing by cloud consumers. Examples of online SaaS-based cloud services with Web-based APIs include:

- electronic payment services (PayPal)
- mapping and routing services (Google Maps)
- publishing tools (WordPress)

Mobile-enabled SaaS implementations are commonly supported by the multi-device broker mechanism, unless the cloud service is intended exclusively for access by specific mobile devices.

The potentially diverse nature of SaaS functionality, the variation in implementation technology, and the tendency to offer a SaaS-based cloud service redundantly with multiple different implementation mediums makes the design of SaaS environments highly specialized. Though not essential to a SaaS implementation, specialized processing requirements can prompt the need to incorporate architectural models, such as:

- *Service Load Balancing* – for workload distribution across redundant SaaS-based cloud service implementations
- *Dynamic Failure Detection and Recovery* – to establish a system that can automatically resolve some failure conditions without disruption in service to the SaaS implementation
- *Storage Maintenance Window* – to allow for planned maintenance outages that do not impact SaaS implementation availability
- *Elastic Resource Capacity/Elastic Network Capacity* – to establish inherent elasticity within the SaaS-based cloud service architecture that enables it to automatically accommodate a range of runtime scalability requirements

- *Cloud Balancing* – to instill broad resiliency within the SaaS implementation, which can be especially important for cloud services subjected to extreme concurrent usage volumes

Specialized cloud usage monitors can be used in SaaS environments to track the following types of metrics:

- *Tenant Subscription Period* – This metric is used by pay-per-use monitors to record and track application usage for time-based billing. This type of monitoring usually incorporates application licensing and regular assessments of leasing periods that extend beyond the hourly periods of IaaS and PaaS environments.

- *Application Usage* – This metric, based on user or security groups, is used with pay-per-use monitors to record and track application usage for billing purposes.

- *Tenant Application Functional Module* – This metric is used by pay-per-use monitors for function-based billing. Cloud services can have different functionality tiers according to whether the cloud consumer is free-tier or a paid subscriber.

Similar to the cloud usage monitoring that is performed in IaaS and PaaS implementations, SaaS environments are also commonly monitored for data storage, network traffic, failure conditions, and event triggers.

Security

SaaS implementations generally rely on a foundation of security controls inherent to their deployment environment. Distinct business processing logic will then add layers of additional cloud security mechanisms or specialized security technologies.

14.2 Cloud Delivery Models: The Cloud Consumer Perspective

This section raises various considerations concerning the different ways in which cloud delivery models are administered and utilized by cloud consumers.

Working with IaaS Environments

Virtual servers are accessed at the operating system level through the use of remote terminal applications. Accordingly, the type of client software used directly depends on the type of operating system that is running at the virtual server, of which two common options are:

- *Remote Desktop (or Remote Desktop Connection) Client* – for Windows-based environments and presents a Windows GUI desktop

- *SSH Client* – for Mac and other Linux-based environments to allow for secure channel connections to text-based shell accounts running on the server OS

Figure 14.4 illustrates a typical usage scenario for virtual servers that are being offered as IaaS services after having been created with management interfaces.

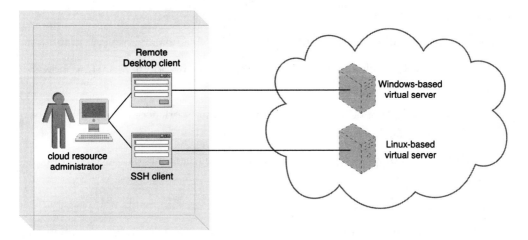

Figure 14.4

A cloud resource administrator uses the Windows-based Remote Desktop client to administer a Windows-based virtual server and the SSH client for the Linux-based virtual server.

A cloud storage device can be attached directly to the virtual servers and accessed through the virtual servers' functional interface for management by the operating system. Alternatively, a cloud storage device can be attached to an IT resource that is being hosted outside of the cloud, such as an on-premise device over a WAN or VPN. In these cases, the following formats for the manipulation and transmission of cloud storage data are commonly used:

- *Networked File System* – System-based storage access, whose rendering of files is similar to how folders are organized in operating systems (NFS, CIFS)

- *Storage Area Network Devices* – Block-based storage access collates and formats geographically diverse data into cohesive files for optimal network transmission (iSCSI, Fibre Channel)

- *Web-Based Resources* – Object-based storage access by which an interface that is not integrated into the operating system logically represents files, which can be accessed through a Web-based interface (Amazon S3)

IT Resource Provisioning Considerations

Cloud consumers have a high degree of control over how and to what extent IT resources are provisioned as part of their IaaS environments.

For example:

- controlling scalability features (automated scaling, load balancing)
- controlling the lifecycle of virtual IT resources (shutting down, restarting, powering up of virtual devices)
- controlling the virtual network environment and network access rules (firewalls, logical network perimeters)
- establishing and displaying service provisioning agreements (account conditions, usage terms)
- managing the attachment of cloud storage devices
- managing the pre-allocation of cloud-based IT resources (resource reservation)
- managing credentials and passwords for cloud resource administrators
- managing credentials for cloud-based security groups that access virtualized IT resources through an IAM
- managing security-related configurations
- managing customized virtual server image storage (importing, exporting, backup)
- selecting high-availability options (failover, IT resource clustering)
- selecting and monitoring SLA metrics
- selecting basic software configurations (operating system, pre-installed software for new virtual servers)
- selecting IaaS resource instances from a number of available hardware-related configurations and options (processing capabilities, RAM, storage)

- selecting the geographical regions in which cloud-based IT resources should be hosted

- tracking and managing costs

The management interface for these types of provisioning tasks is usually a usage and administration portal, but may also be offered via the use of command line interface (CLI) tools that can simplify the execution of many scripted administrative actions.

Even though standardizing the presentation of administrative features and controls is typically preferred, using different tools and user-interfaces can sometimes be justified. For example, a script can be made to turn virtual servers on and off nightly through a CLI, while adding or removing storage capacity can be more easily carried out using a portal.

Working with PaaS Environments

A typical PaaS IDE can offer a wide range of tools and programming resources, such as software libraries, class libraries, frameworks, APIs, and various runtime capabilities that emulate the intended cloud-based deployment environment. These features allow developers to create, test, and run application code within the cloud or locally (on-premise) while using the IDE to emulate the cloud deployment environment. Compiled or completed applications are then bundled and uploaded to the cloud, and deployed via the ready-made environments. This deployment process can also be controlled through the IDE.

PaaS also allows for applications to use cloud storage devices as independent data storing systems for holding development-specific data (for example in a repository that is available outside of the cloud environment). Both SQL and NoSQL database structures are generally supported.

IT Resource Provisioning Considerations

PaaS environments provide less administrative control than IaaS environments, but still offer a significant range of management features.

For example:

- establishing and displaying service provisioning agreements, such as account conditions and usage terms

- selecting software platform and development frameworks for ready-made environments

- selecting instance types, which are most commonly frontend or backend instances

- selecting cloud storage devices for use in ready-made environments

- controlling the lifecycle of PaaS-developed applications (deployment, starting, shutdown, restarting, and release)

- controlling the versioning of deployed applications and modules

- configuring availability and reliability-related mechanisms

- managing credentials for developers and cloud resource administrators using IAM

- managing general security settings, such as accessible network ports

- selecting and monitoring PaaS-related SLA metrics

- managing and monitoring usage and IT resource costs

- controlling scalability features such as usage quotas, active instance thresholds, and the configuration and deployment of the automated scaling listener and load balancer mechanisms

The usage and administration portal that is used to access PaaS management features can provide the feature of pre-emptively selecting the times at which an IT resource is started and stopped. For example, a cloud resource administrator can set a cloud storage device to turn itself on at 9:00AM then turn off twelve hours later. Building on this system can enable the option of having the ready-made environment self-activate upon receiving data requests for a particular application and turn off after an extended period of inactivity.

Working with SaaS Services

Because SaaS-based cloud services are almost always accompanied by refined and generic APIs, they are usually designed to be incorporated as part of larger distributed solutions. A common example of this is Google Maps, which offers a comprehensive API that enables mapping information and images to be incorporated into Web sites and Web-based applications.

Many SaaS offerings are provided free of charge, although these cloud services often come with data collecting sub-programs that harvest usage data for the benefit of the cloud provider. When using any SaaS product that is sponsored by third parties, there is a reasonable chance that it is performing a form of background information gathering. Reading the cloud provider's agreement will usually help shed light on any secondary activity that the cloud service is designed to perform.

Cloud consumers using SaaS products supplied by cloud providers are relieved of the responsibilities of implementing and administering their underlying hosting environments. Customization options are usually available to cloud consumers; however, these options are generally limited to the runtime usage control of the cloud service instances that are generated specifically by and for the cloud consumer.

For example:

- managing security-related configurations

- managing select availability and reliability options

- managing usage costs

- managing user accounts, profiles, and access authorization

- selecting and monitoring SLAs

- setting manual and automated scalability options and limitations

---

14.3 CASE STUDY EXAMPLE

DTGOV discovers that a number of additional mechanisms and technologies need to be assembled in order to complete its IaaS management architecture (Figure 14.5):

- Network virtualization is incorporated into logical network topologies, and logical network perimeters are established using different firewalls and virtual networks.

- The VIM is positioned as the central tool for controlling the IaaS platform and equipping it with self-provisioning capabilities.

- Additional virtual server and cloud storage device mechanisms are implemented through the virtualization platform, while several virtual server images that provide base template configurations for virtual servers are created.

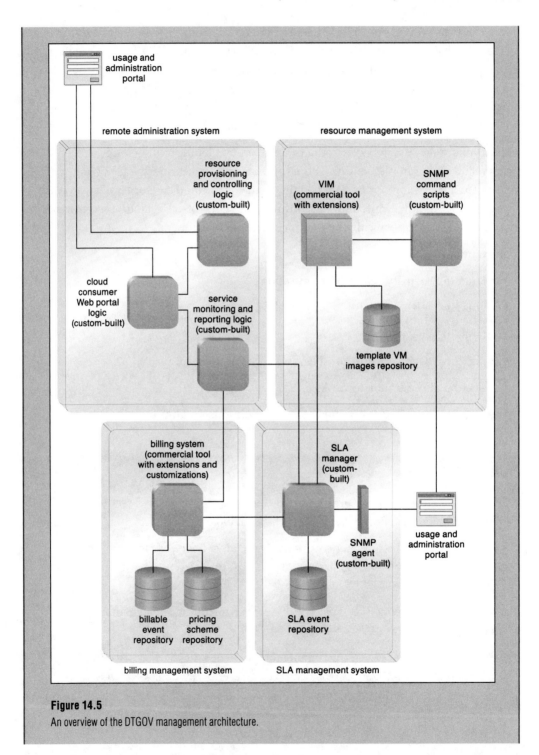

Figure 14.5

An overview of the DTGOV management architecture.

- Dynamic scaling is added using the VIM's API through the use of automated scaling listeners.

- High-availability virtual server clusters are created using the resource replication, load balancer, failover system, and resource cluster mechanisms.

- A customized application that directly uses the SSO and IAM system mechanisms is built to enable interoperability between the remote administration system, network management tools, and VIM.

DTGOV uses a powerful commercial network management tool that is customized to store event information gathered by the VIM and SLA monitoring agents in an SLA measurements database. The management tool and database are used as part of a greater SLA management system. In order to enable billing processing, DTGOV expands a proprietary software tool that is based on a set of usage measurements from a database populated by pay-per-use monitors. The billing software is used as the base implementation for the billing management system mechanism.

Chapter 15

Cost Metrics and Pricing Models

Reducing operating costs and optimizing IT environments are pivotal to understanding and being able to compare the cost models behind provisioning on-premise and cloud-based environments. The pricing structures used by public clouds are typically based on utility-centric pay-per-usage models, enabling organizations to avoid up-front infrastructure investments. These models need to be assessed against the financial implications of on-premise infrastructure investments and associated total cost-of-ownership commitments.

The following chapter provides metrics, formulas, and practices to assist cloud consumers in performing accurate financial analysis of cloud adoption plans.

15.1 Business Cost Metrics

This section begins by describing the common types of metrics used to evaluate the estimated costs and business value of leasing cloud-based IT resources when compared to the purchase of on-premise IT resources.

Up-Front and On-Going Costs

Up-front costs are associated with the initial investments that organizations need to make in order to fund the IT resources they intend to use. This includes both the costs associated with obtaining the IT resources, as well as expenses required to deploy and administer them.

- Up-front costs for the purchase and deployment of on-premise IT resources tend to be high. Examples of up-front costs for on-premise environments can include hardware, software, and the labor required for deployment.

- Up-front costs for the leasing of cloud-based IT resources tend to be low. Examples of up-front costs for cloud-based environments can include the labor costs required to assess and set up a cloud environment.

On-going costs represent the expenses required by an organization to run and maintain IT resources it uses.

- On-going costs for the operation of on-premise IT resources can vary. Examples include licensing fees, electricity, insurance, and labor.

- On-going costs for the operation of cloud-based IT resources can also vary, but often exceed the on-going costs of on-premise IT resources (especially over a longer period of time). Examples include virtual hardware leasing fees, bandwidth usage fees, licensing fees, and labor.

Additional Costs

To supplement and extend a financial analysis beyond the calculation and comparison of standard up-front and on-going business cost metrics, several other more specialized business cost metrics can be taken into account.

For example:

- *Cost of Capital* – The *cost of capital* is a value that represents the cost incurred by raising required funds. For example, it will generally be more expensive to raise an initial investment of $150,000 than it will be to raise this amount over a period of three years. The relevancy of this cost depends on how the organization goes about gathering the funds it requires. If the cost of capital for an initial investment is high, then it further helps justify the leasing of cloud-based IT resources.

- *Sunk Costs* – An organization will often have existing IT resources that are already paid for and operational. The prior investment that has been made in these on-premise IT resources is referred to as *sunk costs*. When comparing up-front costs together with significant sunk costs, it can be more difficult to justify the leasing of cloud-based IT resources as an alternative.

- *Integration Costs* – Integration testing is a form of testing required to measure the effort required to make IT resources compatible and interoperable within a foreign environment, such as a new cloud platform. Depending on the cloud deployment model and cloud delivery model being considered by an organization, there may be the need to further allocate funds to carry out integration testing and additional labor related to enable interoperability between cloud service consumers and cloud services. These expenses are referred to as *integration costs*. High integration costs can make the option of leasing cloud-based IT resources less appealing.

- *Locked-in Costs* – As explained in the *Risks and Challenges* section in Chapter 3, cloud environments can impose portability limitations. When performing a metrics analysis over a longer period of time, it may be necessary to take into consideration the possibility of having to move from one cloud provider to another. Due to the fact that cloud service consumers can become dependent on proprietary characteristics of a cloud environment, there are *locked-in costs* associated with this type of move. Locked-in costs can further decrease the long-term business value of leasing cloud-based IT resources.

CASE STUDY EXAMPLE

ATN performs a total cost-of-ownership (TCO) analysis on migrating two of its legacy applications to a PaaS environment. The report produced by the analysis examines comparative evaluations of on-premise and cloud-based implementations based on a three-year time frame.

The following sections provide a summary from the report for each of the two applications.

Product Catalog Browser

The Product Catalog Browser is a globally used Web application that interoperates with the ATN Web portal and several other systems. This application was deployed in a virtual server cluster that is comprised of 4 virtual servers running on 2 dedicated physical servers. The application has its own 300 GB database that resides in a separate HA cluster. Its code was recently generated from a refactoring project. Only minor portability issues needed to be addressed before it was ready to proceed with a cloud migration.

The TCO analysis reveals the following:

On-Premise Up-Front Costs

- Licensing: The purchase price for each physical server hosting the application is $7,500, while the software required to run all 4 servers totals $30,500

- Labor: Labor costs are estimated as $5,500, including setup and application deployment.

The total up-front costs are: ($7,500 x 2) + $30,500 + $5,500 = $51,000

The configuration of the servers is derived from a capacity plan that accounts for peak workloads. Storage was not assessed as part of this plan, since the application database is assumed to be only negligibly affected by the application's deployment.

On-Premise On-Going Costs

The following are monthly on-going costs:

- Environmental Fees: $750

- Licensing Fees: $520

- Hardware Maintenance: $100

- Labor: $2,600

The total on-premise on-going costs are: $750 + $520 + $100 + $2,600 = $3,970

Cloud-Based Up-Front Costs

If the servers are leased from a cloud provider, there is no up-front cost for hardware or software. Labor costs are estimated at $5,000, which includes expenses for solving interoperability issues and application setup.

Cloud-Based On-Going Costs

The following are monthly on-going costs:

- Server Instance: Usage fee is calculated per virtual server at a rate of $1.25/hour per virtual server. For 4 virtual servers, this results in: 4 x ($1.25 x 720) = $3,600. However, the application consumption is equivalent to 2.3 servers when server instance scaling is factored in, meaning the actual on-going server usage cost is: $2,070.

- Database Server and Storage: Usage fees are calculated per database size, at a rate of $1.09/GB per month = $327.

- Network: Usage fees are calculated per outbound WAN traffic at the rate of $0.10/GB and a monthly volume of 420 GB = $42.

- Labor: Estimated at $800 per month, including expenses for cloud resource administration tasks.

The total on-going costs are: $2,070 + $327 + $42 + $800 = $3,139

The TCO breakdown for the Product Catalog Browser application is provided in Table 15.1.

Up-Front Costs	Cloud Environment	On-Premise Environment
Hardware	$0	$15,000
Licensing	$0	$30,500
Labor	$5,000	$5,500
Total Up-Front Costs	**$5,000**	**$51,000**

Monthly On-Going Costs	Cloud Environment	On-Premise Environment
Application Servers	$2,070	$0
Database Servers	$327	$0
WAN Network	$42	$0
Environment	$0	$750
Software Licensing	$0	$520
Hardware Maintenance	$0	$100
Administration	$800	$2,600
Total On-Going Costs	**$3,139**	**$3,970**

Table 15.1

The TCO analysis for the Product Catalog Browser application.

A comparison of the respective TCOs over a three-year period for both approaches reveals the following:

- On-Premise TCO: $51,000 up-front + ($3,970 x 36) on-going = $193,920

- Cloud-Based TCO: $5,000 up-front + ($3,139 x 36) on-going = $118,004

Based on the results of the TCO analysis, ATN decides to migrate the application to the cloud.

Client Database

The Client Database application is deployed in a virtual server cluster comprised of 8 virtual servers running on 2 dedicated physical servers, with a 1.5 TB database on a HA cluster that is coupled with another system database. The application code is old, requiring considerable effort to port to the PaaS environment.

The TCO analysis reveals the following:

On-Premise Up-Front Costs

- Licensing: Each physical server that is used to host the application costs $7,500, while the software that is required to run all 8 virtual servers costs $15,200.

- Labor: Estimated at $5,500, the labor cost includes expenses for setting up the new environment and deploying the application on the new servers.

The total up-front costs are: ($7,500 x 2) + $15,200 + $5,500 = $35,700

On-Premise On-Going Costs

The following are monthly on-going costs:

- Environmental Fees: $1,050

- Licensing Fees: $300

- Hardware Maintenance: $100

- Administration: $4,500

The total on-going costs are: $1,050 + $300 + $100 + $4,500 = $5,950

Cloud-Based Up-Front Costs

There are no up-front hardware or software costs if the servers are leased from a cloud provider. The labor is estimated at $45,000, most of which is for integration testing and application porting tasks.

Cloud-Based On-Going Costs

The following are monthly on-going costs:

- Server Instance: Usage fees are calculated at a rate of $1.25/hour per virtual server. The estimated scaling of the virtual server means that actual service usage is equivalent to 3.8 servers, which results in a total of $3,420.

- Database Server and Storage: Usage fees are calculated per database size at a rate of $1.09/GB per month = $1,635.

- Network: Outbound WAN traffic usage is calculated at a rate of $0.10/GB, at an estimated volume of 800 GB per month = $80.

- Labor: Estimated at $1,200 when cloud resource administration tasks are included.

The total on-going costs are: $3,420 + $1,635 + $80 + $1,200 = $6,335

The TCO breakdown for the Client Database application is shown in Table 15.2.

Up-Front Costs	Cloud Environment	On-Premise Environment
Hardware	$0	$15,000
Licensing	$0	$15,200
Labor	$45,000	$5,500
Total Up-Front Costs	**$45,000**	**$35,700**

Monthly On-Going Costs	Cloud Environment	On-Premise Environment
Application Servers	$3,420	$0
Database Servers	$1,635	$0
WAN Network	$80	$0
Environment	$0	$1,050
Software Licensing	$0	$300
Hardware Maintenance	$0	$100
Administration	$1,200	$4,500
Total On-Going Costs	**$6,335**	**$5,950**

Table 15.2
The TCO analysis for the Client Database application.

A comparison of the respective TCOs over a three-year period reveals the following:

- On-Premise TCO: $35,700 up-front + ($5,950 x 36) on-going = $251,700

- Cloud-Based TCO: $45,000 up-front + ($6,335 x 36) on-going = $273,060

The decision to migrate the application to the cloud is not supported by the TCO analysis.

15.2 Cloud Usage Cost Metrics

The following sections describe a set of usage cost metrics for calculating costs associated with cloud-based IT resource usage measurements:

- *Network Usage* – inbound and outbound network traffic, as well as intra-cloud network traffic

- *Server Usage* – virtual server allocation (and resource reservation)

- *Cloud Storage Device* – storage capacity allocation

- *Cloud Service* – subscription duration, number of nominated users, number of transactions (of cloud services and cloud-based applications)

For each usage cost metric a description, measurement unit, and measurement frequency is provided, along with the cloud delivery model most applicable to the metric. Each metric is further supplemented with a brief example.

Network Usage

Defined as the amount of data that is transferred over a network connection, network usage is typically calculated using separately measured *inbound network usage traffic* and *outbound network usage traffic* metrics in relation to cloud services or other IT resources.

Inbound Network Usage Metric

- *Description* – inbound network traffic

- *Measurement* – Σ, inbound network traffic in bytes

- *Frequency* – continuous and cumulative over a predefined period

- *Cloud Delivery Model* – IaaS, PaaS, SaaS

- *Example* – up to 1 GB free, $0.001/GB up to 10 TB a month

Outbound Network Usage Metric

- *Description* – outbound network traffic

- *Measurement* – Σ, outbound network traffic in bytes

- *Frequency* – continuous and cumulative over a predefined period

- *Cloud Delivery Model* – IaaS, PaaS, SaaS

- *Example* – up to 1 GB free a month, $0.01/GB between 1 GB to 10 TB per month

Network usage metrics can be applied to WAN traffic between IT resources of one cloud that are located in different geographical regions in order to calculate costs for synchronization, data replication, and related forms of processing. Conversely, LAN usage and other network traffic among IT resources that reside at the same data center are typically not tracked.

Intra-Cloud WAN Usage Metric

- *Description* – network traffic between geographically diverse IT resources of the same cloud

- *Measurement* – Σ, intra-cloud WAN traffic in bytes

- *Frequency* – continuous and cumulative over a predefined period

- *Cloud Delivery Model* – IaaS, PaaS, SaaS

- *Example* – up to 500 MB free daily and $0.01/GB thereafter, $0.005/GB after 1 TB per month

Many cloud providers do not charge for inbound traffic in order to encourage cloud consumers to migrate data to the cloud. Some also do not charge for WAN traffic within the same cloud.

Network-related cost metrics are determined by the following properties:

- *Static IP Address Usage* – IP address allocation time (if a static IP is required)

- *Network Load-Balancing* – the amount of load-balanced network traffic (in bytes)

- *Virtual Firewall* – the amount of firewall-processed network traffic (as per allocation time)

Server Usage

The allocation of virtual servers is measured using common pay-per-use metrics in IaaS and PaaS environments that are quantified by the number of virtual servers and ready-made environments. This form of server usage measurement is divided into *on-demand virtual machine instance allocation* and *reserved virtual machine instance allocation* metrics.

The former metric measures pay-per-usage fees on a short-term basis, while the latter metric calculates up-front reservation fees for using virtual servers over extended periods. The up-front reservation fee is usually used in conjunction with the discounted pay-per-usage fees.

On-Demand Virtual Machine Instance Allocation Metric

- *Description* – uptime of a virtual server instance
- *Measurement* – Σ, virtual server start date to stop date
- *Frequency* – continuous and cumulative over a predefined period
- *Cloud Delivery Model* – IaaS, PaaS
- *Example* – \$0.10/hour small instance, \$0.20/hour medium instance, \$0.90/hour large instance

Reserved Virtual Machine Instance Allocation Metric

- *Description* – up-front cost for reserving a virtual server instance
- *Measurement* – Σ, virtual server reservation start date to expiry date
- *Frequency* – daily, monthly, yearly
- *Cloud Delivery Model* – IaaS, PaaS
- *Example* – \$55.10/small instance, \$99.90/medium instance, \$249.90/large instance

Another common cost metric for virtual server usage measures performance capabilities. Cloud providers of IaaS and PaaS environments tend to provision virtual servers with a range of performance attributes that are generally determined by CPU and RAM consumption and the amount of available dedicated allocated storage.

Cloud Storage Device Usage

Cloud storage is generally charged by the amount of space allocated within a predefined period, as measured by the *on-demand storage allocation* metric. Similar to IaaS-based cost metrics, on-demand storage allocation fees are usually based on short time increments (such as on an hourly basis). Another common cost metric for cloud storage is *I/O data transferred*, which measures the amount of transferred input and output data.

On-Demand Storage Space Allocation Metric

- *Description* – duration and size of on-demand storage space allocation in bytes
- *Measurement* – Σ, date of storage release / reallocation to date of storage allocation (resets upon change in storage size)
- *Frequency* – continuous
- *Cloud Delivery Model* – IaaS, PaaS, SaaS
- *Example* – $0.01/GB per hour (typically expressed as GB/month)

I/O Data Transferred Metric

- *Description* – amount of transferred I/O data
- *Measurement* – Σ, I/O data in bytes
- *Frequency* – continuous
- *Cloud Delivery Model* – IaaS, PaaS
- *Example* – $0.10/TB

Note that some cloud providers do not charge for I/O usage for IaaS and PaaS implementations, and limit charges to storage space allocation only.

Cloud Service Usage

Cloud service usage in SaaS environments is typically measured using the following three metrics:

Application Subscription Duration Metric

- *Description* – duration of cloud service usage subscription
- *Measurement* – Σ, subscription start date to expiry date

- *Frequency* – daily, monthly, yearly

- *Cloud Delivery Model* – SaaS

- *Example* – $69.90 per month

Number of Nominated Users Metric

- *Description* – number of registered users with legitimate access

- *Measurement* – number of users

- *Frequency* – monthly, yearly

- *Cloud Delivery Model* – SaaS

- *Example* – $0.90/additional user per month

Number of Transactions Users Metric

- *Description* – number of transactions served by the cloud service

- *Measurement* – number of transactions (request-response message exchanges)

- *Frequency* – continuous

- *Cloud Delivery Model* – PaaS, SaaS

- *Example* – $0.05 per 1,000 transactions

15.3 Cost Management Considerations

Cost management is often centered around the lifecycle phases of cloud services, as follows:

- *Cloud Service Design and Development* – During this stage, the vanilla pricing models and cost templates are typically defined by the organization delivering the cloud service.

- *Cloud Service Deployment* – Prior to and during the deployment of a cloud service, the backend architecture for usage measurement and billing-related data collection is determined and implemented, including the positioning of pay-per-use monitor and billing management system mechanisms.

- *Cloud Service Contracting* – This phase consists of negotiations between the cloud consumer and cloud provider with the goal of reaching a mutual agreement on rates based on usage cost metrics.

- *Cloud Service Offering* – This stage entails the concrete offering of a cloud service's pricing models through cost templates, and any available customization options.

- *Cloud Service Provisioning* – Cloud service usage and instance creation thresholds may be imposed by the cloud provider or set by the cloud consumer. Either way, these and other provisioning options can impact usage costs and other fees.

- *Cloud Service Operation* – This is the phase during which active usage of the cloud service produces usage cost metric data.

- *Cloud Service Decommissioning* – When a cloud service is temporarily or permanently deactivated, statistical cost data may be archived.

Both cloud providers and cloud consumers can implement cost management systems that reference or build upon the aforementioned lifecycle phases. It is also possible for the cloud provider to carry out some cost management stages on behalf of the cloud consumer and to then provide the cloud consumer with regular reports.

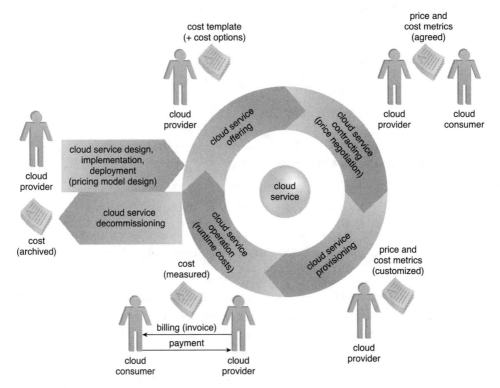

Figure 15.1

Common cloud service lifecycle stages as they relate to cost management considerations.

Pricing Models

The pricing models used by cloud providers are defined using templates that specify unit costs for fine-grained resource usage according to usage cost metrics. Various factors can influence a pricing model, such as:

- market competition and regulatory requirements

- overhead incurred during the design, development, deployment, and operation of cloud services and other IT resources

- opportunities to reduce expenses via IT resource sharing and data center optimization

Most major cloud providers offer cloud services at relatively stable, competitive prices even though their own expenses can be volatile. A price template or pricing plan contains a set of standardized costs and metrics that specify how cloud service fees are measured and calculated. Price templates define a pricing model's structure by setting various units of measure, usage quotas, discounts, and other codified fees. A pricing model can contain multiple price templates, whose formulation is determined by variables like:

- *Cost Metrics and Associated Prices* – These are costs that are dependent on the type of IT resource allocation (such as on-demand versus reserved allocation).

- *Fixed and Variable Rates Definitions* – Fixed rates are based on resource allocation and define the usage quotas included in the fixed price, while variable rates are aligned with actual resource usage.

- *Volume Discounts* – More IT resources are consumed as the degree of IT resource scaling progressively increases, thereby possibly qualifying a cloud consumer for higher discounts.

- *Cost and Price Customization Options* – This variable is associated with payment options and schedules. For example, cloud consumers may be able to choose monthly, semi-annual, or annual payment installments.

Price templates are important for cloud consumers that are appraising cloud providers and negotiating rates, since they can vary depending on the adopted cloud delivery model.

For example:

- *IaaS* – Pricing is usually based on IT resource allocation and usage, which includes the amount of transferred network data, number of virtual servers, and allocated storage capacity.

- *PaaS* – Similar to IaaS, this model typically defines pricing for network data transferred, virtual servers, and storage. Prices are variable depending on factors such as software configurations, development tools, and licensing fees.

- *SaaS* – Because this model is solely concerned with application software usage, pricing is determined by the number of application modules in the subscription, the number of nominated cloud service consumers, and the number of transactions.

It is possible for a cloud service that is provided by one cloud provider to be built upon IT resources provisioned from another cloud provider. Figures 15.2 and 15.3 explore two sample scenarios.

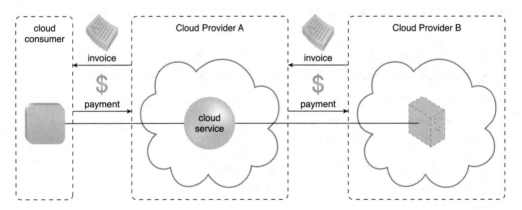

Figure 15.2

An integrated pricing model, whereby the cloud consumer leases a SaaS product from Cloud Provider A, which is leasing an IaaS environment (including the virtual server used to host the cloud service) from Cloud Provider B. The cloud consumer pays Cloud Provider A. Cloud Provider A pays Cloud Provider B.

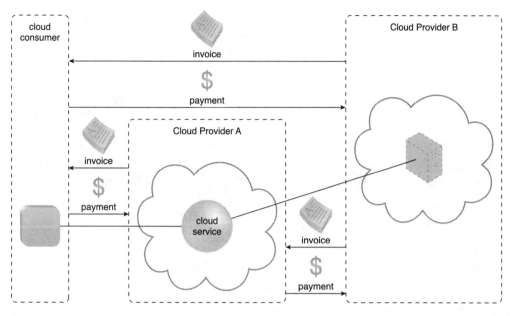

Figure 15.3

Separate pricing models are used in this scenario, whereby the cloud consumer leases a virtual server from Cloud Provider B to host the cloud service from Cloud Provider A. Both leasing agreements may have been arranged for the cloud consumer by Cloud Provider A. As part of this arrangement, there may still be some fees billed directly by Cloud Provider B to Cloud Provider A.

Additional Considerations

- *Negotiation* – Cloud provider pricing is often open to negotiation, especially for customers willing to commit to higher volumes or longer terms. Price negotiations can sometimes be executed online via the cloud provider's Web site by submitting estimated usage volumes along with proposed discounts. There are even tools available for cloud consumers to help generate accurate IT resource usage estimates for this purpose.

- *Payment Options* – After completing each measurement period, the cloud provider's billing management system calculates the amount owed by a cloud consumer. There are two common payment options available to cloud consumers: pre-payment and post-payment. With pre-paid billing, cloud consumers are provided with IT resource usage credits that can be applied to future usage bills. With the post-payment method, cloud consumers are billed and invoiced for each IT resource consumption period, which is usually on a monthly basis.

- *Cost Archiving* – By tracking historical billing information both cloud providers and cloud consumers can generate insightful reports that help identify usage and financial trends.

CASE STUDY EXAMPLE

DTGOV structures their pricing model around leasing packages for virtual servers and block-based cloud storage devices, with the assumption that resource allocation is performed either on-demand or based on already reserved IT resources.

On-demand resource allocation is measured and charged back by the hour, while reserved resource allocation requires a one to three-year commitment from the cloud consumer, with fees billed monthly.

As IT resources can scale up and down automatically, any additional capacity used is charged on a pay-per-use basis whenever a reserved IT resource is scaled beyond its allocated capacity. Windows and Linux-based virtual servers are made available in the following basic performance profiles:

- *Small Virtual Server Instance* – 1 virtual processor core, 4 GB of virtual RAM, and 320 GB of storage space in the root file system.

- *Medium Virtual Server Instance* – 2 virtual processor cores, 8 GB of virtual RAM, and 540 GB of storage space in the root file system.

- *Large Virtual Server Instance* – 8 virtual processor cores, 16 GB of virtual RAM, and 1.2 TB of storage space in the root file system.

- *Memory Large Virtual Server Instance* – 8 virtual processor cores, 64 GB of virtual RAM, and 1.2 TB of storage space in the root file system.

- *Processor Large Virtual Server Instance* – 32 virtual processor cores, 16 GB of virtual RAM, and 1.2 TB of storage space in the root file system.

- *Ultra-Large Virtual Server Instance* – 128 virtual processor cores, 512 GB of virtual RAM, and 1.2 TB of storage space in the root file system.

Virtual servers are also available in "resilient" or "clustered" formats. With the former option the virtual servers are replicated in at least two different data centers. In the latter case, the virtual servers are run in a high-availability cluster that is implemented by the virtualization platform.

The pricing model is further based on the capacity of the cloud storage devices as expressed by multiples of 1 GB, with a minimum of 40 GB. Storage device capacity can be fixed and administratively adjusted by the cloud consumer to increase or decrease by increments of 40 GB, while the block storage has a maximum capacity of 1.2 TB. I/O transfers to and from cloud storage devices are also subject to charges in addition to pay-per-use fees applied to outbound WAN traffic. Inbound WAN and intra-cloud traffic are free of charge.

A complimentary usage allowance permits cloud consumers to lease up to three small virtual server instances and a 60 GB block-based cloud storage device, 5 GB of I/O transfers monthly, as well as 5 GB of WAN outbound traffic monthly, all in the first 90 days. As DTGOV prepares their pricing model for public release, they realize that setting cloud service prices is more challenging than they expected because:

- Their prices need to reflect and respond to marketplace conditions while staying competitive with other cloud offerings and remaining profitable to DTGOV.

- The client portfolio has not been established yet, as DTGOV is expecting new customers. Their non-cloud clients are expected to progressively migrate to the cloud, although the actual rate of migration is too difficult to predict.

After performing further market research, DTGOV settles on the following price template for virtual server instance allocation:

Virtual Server On-Demand Instance Allocation

- Metric: on-demand instance allocation

- Measurement: pay-per-use charges calculated for total service consumption for each calendar month (hourly rate is used for the actual instance size when the instance has been scaled up)

- Billing Period: monthly

The price template is outlined in Table 15.3.

Instance Name	Instance Size	Operating System	Hourly
Small Virtual Server Instance	1 virtual processor core 4 GB of virtual RAM 20 GB of storage	Linux Ubuntu	$0.06
		Linux Red Hat	$0.08
		Windows	$0.09
Medium Virtual Server Instance	2 virtual processor cores 8 GB of virtual RAM 20 GB of storage	Linux Ubuntu	$0.14
		Linux Red Hat	$0.17
		Windows	$0.19
Large Virtual Server Instance	8 virtual processor cores 16 GB of virtual RAM 20 GB of storage	Linux Ubuntu	$0.32
		Linux Red Hat	$0.37
		Windows	$0.39
Memory Large Virtual Server Instance	8 virtual processor cores 64 GB of virtual RAM 20 GB of storage	Linux Ubuntu	$0.89
		Linux Red Hat	$0.95
		Windows	$0.99
Processor Large Virtual Server Instance	32 virtual processor cores 16 GB of virtual RAM 20 GB of storage	Linux Ubuntu	$0.89
		Linux Red Hat	$0.95
		Windows	$0.99
Ultra-Large Virtual Server Instance	128 virtual processor cores 512 GB of virtual RAM 20 GB of storage	Linux Ubuntu	$1.29
		Linux Red Hat	$1.69
		Windows	$1.89

Table 15.3
The price template for virtual server on-demand instance allocation.

Surcharge for clustered IT resources: 120%

Surcharge for resilient IT resources: 150%

Virtual Server Reserved Instance Allocation

- Metric: reserved instance allocation

- Measurement: reserved instance allocation fee charged up-front with pay-per-use fees calculated based on the total consumption during each calendar month (additional charges apply for periods when the instance is scaled up)

- Billing Period: monthly

The price template is outlined in Table 15.4.

Instance Name	Instance Size	Operating System	1-Year Term Pricing		3-Year Term Pricing	
			Up-Front	Hourly	Up-Front	Hourly
Small Virtual Server Instance	1 virtual processor core 4 GB of virtual RAM 20 GB of storage	Linux Ubuntu	$57.10	$0.032	$87.97	$0.026
		Linux Red Hat	$76.14	$0.043	$117.30	$0.034
		Windows	$85.66	$0.048	$131.96	$0.038
Medium Virtual Server Instance	2 virtual processor cores 8 GB of virtual RAM 20 GB of storage	Linux Ubuntu	$133.24	$0.075	$205.27	$0.060
		Linux Red Hat	$161.79	$0.091	$249.26	$0.073
		Windows	$180.83	$0.102	$278.58	$0.081

continues

Instance Name	Instance Size	Operating System	1-Year Term Pricing		3-Year Term Pricing	
			Up-Front	Hourly	Up-Front	Hourly
Large Virtual Server Instance	8 virtual processor cores 16 GB of virtual RAM 20 GB of storage	Linux Ubuntu	$304.55	$0.172	$469.19	$0.137
		Linux Red Hat	$352.14	$0.199	$542.50	$0.158
		Windows	$371.17	$0.210	$571.82	$0.167
Memory Large Virtual Server Instance	8 virtual processor cores 64 GB of virtual RAM 20 GB of storage	Linux Ubuntu	$751.86	$0.425	$1158.30	$0.338
		Linux Red Hat	$808.97	$0.457	$1246.28	$0.363
		Windows	$847.03	$0.479	$1304.92	$0.381
Processor Large Virtual Server Instance	32 virtual processor cores 16 GB of virtual RAM 20 GB of storage	Linux Ubuntu	$751.86	$0.425	$1158.30	$0.338
		Linux Red Hat	$808.97	$0.457	$1246.28	$0.363
		Windows	$847.03	$0.479	$1304.92	$0.381
Ultra-Large Virtual Server Instance	128 virtual processor cores 512 GB of virtual RAM 20 GB of storage	Linux Ubuntu	$1132.55	$0.640	$1744.79	$0.509
		Linux Red Hat	$1322.90	$0.748	$2038.03	$0.594
		Windows	$1418.07	$0.802	$2184.65	$0.637

Table 15.4

The price template for virtual server reserved instance allocation.

Surcharge for clustered IT resources: 100%

Surcharge for resilient IT resources: 120%

DTGOV further provides the following simplified price templates for cloud storage device allocation and WAN bandwidth usage:

Cloud Storage Device

- Metric: on-demand storage allocation, I/O data transferred

- Measurement: pay-per-use charges calculated based on total consumption during each calendar month (storage allocation calculated with per hour granularity and cumulative I/O transfer volume)

- Billing Period: monthly

Price Template: $0.10/GB per month of allocated storage, $0.001/GB for I/O transfers

WAN Traffic

- Metric: outbound network usage

- Measurement: pay-per-use charges calculated based on total consumption for each calendar month (WAN traffic volume calculated cumulatively)

- Billing Period: monthly

- Price Template: $0.01/GB for outbound network data

Chapter 16

Service Quality Metrics and SLAs

S ervice-level agreements (SLAs) are a focal point of negotiations, contract terms, legal obligations, and runtime metrics and measurements. SLAs formalize the guarantees put forth by cloud providers, and correspondingly influence or determine the pricing models and payment terms. SLAs set cloud consumer expectations and are integral to how organizations build business automation around the utilization of cloud-based IT resources.

The guarantees made by a cloud provider to a cloud consumer are often carried forward, in that the same guarantees are made by the cloud consumer organization to its clients, business partners, or whomever will be relying on the services and solutions hosted by the cloud provider. It is therefore crucial for SLAs and related service quality metrics to be understood and aligned in support of the cloud consumer's business requirements, while also ensuring that the guarantees can, in fact, be realistically fulfilled consistently and reliably by the cloud provider. The latter consideration is especially relevant for cloud providers that host shared IT resources for high volumes of cloud consumers, each of which will have been issued its own SLA guarantees.

16.1 Service Quality Metrics

SLAs issued by cloud providers are human-readable documents that describe quality-of-service (QoS) features, guarantees, and limitations of one or more cloud-based IT resources.

SLAs use service quality metrics to express measurable QoS characteristics.

For example:

- *Availability* – up-time, outages, service duration
- *Reliability* – minimum time between failures, guaranteed rate of successful responses
- *Performance* – capacity, response time, and delivery time guarantees
- *Scalability* – capacity fluctuation and responsiveness guarantees
- *Resiliency* – mean-time to switchover and recovery

SLA management systems use these metrics to perform periodic measurements that verify compliance with SLA guarantees, in addition to collecting SLA-related data for various types of statistical analyses.

Each service quality metric is ideally defined using the following characteristics:

- *Quantifiable* – The unit of measure is clearly set, absolute, and appropriate so that the metric can be based on quantitative measurements.

- *Repeatable* – The methods of measuring the metric need to yield identical results when repeated under identical conditions.

- *Comparable* – The units of measure used by a metric need to be standardized and comparable. For example, a service quality metric cannot measure smaller quantities of data in bits and larger quantities in bytes.

- *Easily Obtainable* – The metric needs to be based on a non-proprietary, common form of measurement that can be easily obtained and understood by cloud consumers.

The upcoming sections provide a series of common service quality metrics, each of which is documented with description, unit of measure, measurement frequency, and applicable cloud delivery model values, as well as a brief example.

Service Availability Metrics

Availability Rate Metric

The overall availability of an IT resource is usually expressed as a percentage of up-time. For example, an IT resource that is always available will have an up-time of 100%.

- *Description* – percentage of service up-time

- *Measurement* – total up-time / total time

- *Frequency* – weekly, monthly, yearly

- *Cloud Delivery Model* – IaaS, PaaS, SaaS

- *Example* – minimum 99.5% up-time

Availability rates are calculated cumulatively, meaning that unavailability periods are combined in order to compute the total downtime (Table 16.1).

Availability (%)	Downtime/Week (Seconds)	Downtime/Month (Seconds)	Downtime/Year (Seconds)
99.5	3024	216	158112
99.8	1210	5174	63072
99.9	606	2592	31536
99.95	302	1294	15768
99.99	60.6	259.2	3154
99.999	6.05	25.9	316.6
99.9999	0.605	2.59	31.5

Table 16.1
Sample availability rates measured in units of seconds.

Outage Duration Metric

This service quality metric is used to define both maximum and average continuous outage service-level targets.

- *Description* – duration of a single outage
- *Measurement* – date/time of outage end – date/time of outage start
- *Frequency* – per event
- *Cloud Delivery Model* – IaaS, PaaS, SaaS
- *Example* – 1 hour maximum, 15 minute average

NOTE

In addition to being quantitatively measured, availability can be described qualitatively using terms such as high-availability (HA), which is used to label an IT resource with exceptionally low downtime usually due to underlying resource replication and/or clustering infrastructure.

Service Reliability Metrics

A characteristic closely related to availability, reliability is the probability that an IT resource can perform its intended function under pre-defined conditions without experiencing failure. Reliability focuses on how often the service performs as expected, which requires the service to remain in an operational and available state. Certain reliability metrics only consider runtime errors and exception conditions as failures, which are commonly measured only when the IT resource is available.

Mean-Time Between Failures (MTBF) Metric

- *Description* – expected time between consecutive service failures

- *Measurement* – Σ normal operational period duration / number of failures

- *Frequency* – monthly, yearly

- *Cloud Delivery Model* – IaaS, PaaS

- *Example* – 90 day average

Reliability Rate Metric

Overall reliability is more complicated to measure and is usually defined by a reliability rate that represents the percentage of successful service outcomes. This metric measures the effects of non-fatal errors and failures that occur during up-time periods. For example, an IT resource's reliability is 100% if it has performed as expected every time it is invoked, but only 80% if it fails to perform every fifth time.

- *Description* – percentage of successful service outcomes under pre-defined conditions

- *Measurement* – total number of successful responses / total number of requests

- *Frequency* – weekly, monthly, yearly

- *Cloud Delivery Model* – SaaS

- *Example* – minimum 99.5%

Service Performance Metrics

Service performance refers to the ability on an IT resource to carry out its functions within expected parameters. This quality is measured using service capacity metrics, each of which focuses on a related measurable characteristic of IT resource capacity. A set of common performance capacity metrics is provided in this section. Note that different metrics may apply, depending on the type of IT resource being measured.

Network Capacity Metric

- *Description* – measurable characteristics of network capacity
- *Measurement* – bandwidth / throughput in bits per second
- *Frequency* – continuous
- *Cloud Delivery Model* – IaaS, PaaS, SaaS
- *Example* – 10 MB per second

Storage Device Capacity Metric

- *Description* – measurable characteristics of storage device capacity
- *Measurement* – storage size in GB
- *Frequency* – continuous
- *Cloud Delivery Model* – IaaS, PaaS, SaaS
- *Example* – 80 GB of storage

Server Capacity Metric

- *Description* – measurable characteristics of server capacity
- *Measurement* – number of CPUs, CPU frequency in GHz, RAM size in GB, storage size in GB
- *Frequency* – continuous
- *Cloud Delivery Model* – IaaS, PaaS
- *Example* – 1 core at 1.7 GHz, 16 GB of RAM, 80 GB of storage

Web Application Capacity Metric

- *Description* – measurable characteristics of Web application capacity
- *Measurement* – rate of requests per minute
- *Frequency* – continuous

- *Cloud Delivery Model* – SaaS

- *Example* – maximum 100,000 requests per minute

Instance Starting Time Metric

- *Description* – length of time required to initialize a new instance

- *Measurement* – date/time of instance up – date/time of start request

- *Frequency* – per event

- *Cloud Delivery Model* – IaaS, PaaS

- *Example* – 5 minute maximum, 3 minute average

Response Time Metric

- *Description* – time required to perform synchronous operation

- *Measurement* – (date/time of request – date/time of response) / total number of requests

- *Frequency* – daily, weekly, monthly

- *Cloud Delivery Model* – SaaS

- *Example* – 5 millisecond average

Completion Time Metric

- *Description* – time required to complete an asynchronous task

- *Measurement* – (date of request – date of response) / total number of requests

- *Frequency* – daily, weekly, monthly

- *Cloud Delivery Model* – PaaS, SaaS

- *Example* – 1 second average

Service Scalability Metrics

Service scalability metrics are related to IT resource elasticity capacity, which is related to the maximum capacity that an IT resource can achieve, as well as measurements of its ability to adapt to workload fluctuations. For example, a server can be scaled up to a maximum of 128 CPU cores and 512 GB of RAM, or scaled out to a maximum of 16 load-balanced replicated instances.

The following metrics help determine whether dynamic service demands will be met proactively or reactively, as well as the impacts of manual or automated IT resource allocation processes.

Storage Scalability (Horizontal) Metric

- *Description* – permissible storage device capacity changes in response to increased workloads

- *Measurement* – storage size in GB

- *Frequency* – continuous

- *Cloud Delivery Model* – IaaS, PaaS, SaaS

- *Example* – 1,000 GB maximum (automated scaling)

Server Scalability (Horizontal) Metric

- *Description* – permissible server capacity changes in response to increased workloads

- *Measurement* – number of virtual servers in resource pool

- *Frequency* – continuous

- *Cloud Delivery Model* – IaaS, PaaS

- *Example* – 1 virtual server minimum, 10 virtual server maximum (automated scaling)

Server Scalability (Vertical) Metric

- *Description* – permissible server capacity fluctuations in response to workload fluctuations

- *Measurement* – number of CPUs, RAM size in GB

- *Frequency* – continuous

- *Cloud Delivery Model* – IaaS, PaaS

- *Example* – 512 core maximum, 512 GB of RAM

Service Resiliency Metrics

The ability of an IT resource to recover from operational disturbances is often measured using service resiliency metrics. When resiliency is described within or in relation to SLA resiliency guarantees, it is often based on redundant implementations and resource replication over different physical locations, as well as various disaster recovery systems.

The type of cloud delivery model determines how resiliency is implemented and measured. For example, the physical locations of replicated virtual servers that are implementing resilient cloud services can be explicitly expressed in the SLAs for IaaS environments, while being implicitly expressed for the corresponding PaaS and SaaS environments.

Resiliency metrics can be applied in three different phases to address the challenges and events that can threaten the regular level of a service:

- *Design Phase* – Metrics that measure how prepared systems and services are to cope with challenges.

- *Operational Phase* – Metrics that measure the difference in service levels before, during, and after a downtime event or service outage, which are further qualified by availability, reliability, performance, and scalability metrics.

- *Recovery Phase* – Metrics that measure the rate at which an IT resource recovers from downtime, such as the meantime for a system to log an outage and switchover to a new virtual server.

Two common metrics related to measuring resiliency are as follows:

Mean-Time to Switchover (MTSO) Metric

- *Description* – the time expected to complete a switchover from a severe failure to a replicated instance in a different geographical area

- *Measurement* – (date/time of switchover completion – date/time of failure) / total number of failures

- *Frequency* – monthly, yearly

- *Cloud Delivery Model* – IaaS, PaaS, SaaS

- *Example* – 10 minute average

Mean-Time System Recovery (MTSR) Metric

- *Description* – time expected for a resilient system to perform a complete recovery from a severe failure

- *Measurement* – (date/time of recovery – date/time of failure) / total number of failures

- *Frequency* – monthly, yearly

- *Cloud Delivery Model* – IaaS, PaaS, SaaS

- *Example* – 120 minute average

16.2 CASE STUDY EXAMPLE

After suffering a cloud outage that made their Web portal unavailable for about an hour, Innovartus decides to thoroughly review the terms and conditions of their SLA. They begin by researching the cloud provider's availability guarantees, which prove to be ambiguous because they do not clearly state which events in the cloud provider's SLA management system are classified as "downtime." Innovartus also discovers that the SLA lacks reliability and resilience metrics, which had become essential to their cloud service operations.

In preparation for a renegotiation of the SLA terms with the cloud provider, Innovartus decides to compile a list of additional requirements and guarantee stipulations:

- The availability rate needs to be described in greater detail to enable more effective management of service availability conditions.

- Technical data that supports service operations models needs to be included in order to ensure that the operation of select critical services remains fault-tolerant and resilient.

- Additional metrics that assist in service quality assessment need to be included.

- Any events that are to be excluded from what is measured with availability metrics need to be clearly defined.

After several conversations with the cloud provider sales represenatative, Innovartus is offered a revised SLA with the following additions:

- The method by which the availability of cloud services are to be measured, in addition to any supporting IT resources on which ATN core processes depend.

- Inclusion of a set of reliability and performance metrics approved by Innovartus.

Six months later, Innovartus performs another SLA metrics assessment and compares the newly generated values with ones that were generated prior to the SLA improvements (Table 16.2).

SLA Metrics	Statistics of Previous SLA	Statistics of Revised SLA
Average Availability	98.10%	99.98%
High-Availability Model	Cold-Standby	Hot-Standby
Average Service Quality *based on customer satisfaction surveys.*	52%	70%

Table 16.2
The evolution of Innovartus' SLA evaluation, as monitored by their cloud resource administrators.

16.3 SLA Guidelines

This section provides a number of best practices and recommendations for working with SLAs, the majority of which are applicable to cloud consumers:

- *Mapping Business Cases to SLAs* – It can be helpful to identify the necessary QoS requirements for a given automation solution and to then concretely link them to the guarantees expressed in the SLAs for IT resources responsible for carrying out the automation. This can avoid situations where SLAs are inadvertently misaligned or perhaps unreasonably deviate in their guarantees, subsequent to IT resource usage.

- *Working with Cloud and On-Premise SLAs* – Due to the vast infrastructure available to support IT resources in public clouds, the QoS guarantees issued in SLAs for cloud-based IT resources are generally superior to those provided for on-premise IT resources. This variance needs to be understood, especially when building hybrid distributed solutions that utilize both on on-premise and cloud-based services or when incorporating cross-environment technology architectures, such as cloud bursting.

- *Understanding the Scope of an SLA* – Cloud environments are comprised of many supporting architectural and infrastructure layers upon which IT resources reside and are integrated. It is important to acknowledge the extent to which a given IT resource guarantee applies. For example, an SLA may be limited to the IT resource implementation but not its underlying hosting environment.

- *Understanding the Scope of SLA Monitoring* – SLAs need to specify where monitoring is performed and where measurements are calculated, primarily in relation to the cloud's firewall. For example, monitoring within the cloud firewall is not always advantageous or relevant to the cloud consumer's required QoS guarantees. Even the most efficient firewalls have a measurable degree of influence on performance and can further present a point of failure.

- *Documenting Guarantees at Appropriate Granularity* – SLA templates used by cloud providers sometimes define guarantees in broad terms. If a cloud consumer has specific requirements, the corresponding level of detail should be used to describe the guarantees. For example, if data replication needs to take place across particular geographic locations, then these need to be specified directly within the SLA.

- *Defining Penalties for Non-Compliance* – If a cloud provider is unable to follow through on the QoS guarantees promised within the SLAs, recourse can be formally documented in terms of compensation, penalties, reimbursements, or otherwise.

- *Incorporating Non-Measurable Requirements* – Some guarantees cannot be easily measured using service quality metrics, but are relevant to QoS nonetheless, and should therefore still be documented within the SLA. For example, a cloud consumer may have specific security and privacy requirements for data hosted by the cloud provider that can be addressed by assurances in the SLA for the cloud storage device being leased.

- *Disclosure of Compliance Verification and Management* – Cloud providers are often responsible for monitoring IT resources to ensure compliance with their own SLAs. In this case, the SLAs themselves should state what tools and practices are being used to carry out the compliance checking process, in addition to any legal-related auditing that may be occurring.

- *Inclusion of Specific Metric Formulas* – Some cloud providers do not mention common SLA metrics or the metrics-related calculations in their SLAs, instead focusing on service-level descriptions that highlight the use of best practices and customer support. Metrics being used to measure SLAs should be part of the SLA document, including the formulas and calculations that the metrics are based upon.

- *Considering Independent SLA Monitoring* – Although cloud providers will often have sophisticated SLA management systems and SLA monitors, it may be in the best interest of a cloud consumer to hire a third-party organization to perform independent monitoring as well, especially if there are suspicions that SLA guarantees are not always being met by the cloud provider (despite the results shown on periodically issued monitoring reports).

- *Archiving SLA Data* – The SLA-related statistics collected by SLA monitors are commonly stored and archived by the cloud provider for future reporting purposes. If a cloud provider intends to keep SLA data specific to a cloud consumer even after the cloud consumer no longer continues its business relationship with the cloud provider, then this should be disclosed. The cloud consumer may have data privacy requirements that disallow the unauthorized storage of this type of information. Similarly, during and after a cloud consumer's engagement with a cloud provider, it may want to keep a copy of historical SLA-related data as well. It may be especially useful for comparing cloud providers in the future.

- *Disclosing Cross-Cloud Dependencies* – Cloud providers may be leasing IT resources from other cloud providers, which results in a loss of control over the guarantees they are able to make to cloud consumers. Although a cloud provider will rely on the SLA assurances made to it by other cloud providers, the cloud consumer may want disclosure of the fact that the IT resources it is leasing may have dependencies beyond the environment of the cloud provider organization that it is leasing them from.

16.4 CASE STUDY EXAMPLE

DTGOV begins its SLA template authoring process by working with a legal advisory team that has been adamant about an approach whereby cloud consumers are presented with an online Web page outlining the SLA guarantees, along with a "click-once-to-accept" button. The default agreement contains extensive limitations to DTGOV's liability in relation to possible SLA non-compliance, as follows:

- The SLA defines guarantees only for service availability.

- Service availability is defined for all of the cloud services simultaneously.

- Service availability metrics are loosely defined to establish a level of flexibility regarding unexpected outages.

- The terms and conditions are linked to the Cloud Services Customer Agreement, which is accepted implicitly by all of the cloud consumers that use the self-service portal.

- Extended periods of unavailability are to be recompensed by monetary "service credits," which are to be discounted on future invoices and have no actual monetary value.

Provided here are key excerpts from DTGOV's SLA template:

Scope and Applicability

This Service Level Agreement ("SLA") establishes the service quality parameters that are to be applied to the use of DTGOV's cloud services ("DTGOV cloud"), and is part of the DTGOV Cloud Services Customer Agreement ("DTGOV Cloud Agreement").

The terms and conditions specified in this agreement apply solely to virtual server and cloud storage device services, herein called "Covered Services." This SLA applies separately to each cloud consumer ("Consumer") that is using the DTGOV Cloud. DTGOV reserves the right to change the terms of this SLA in accordance with the DTGOV Cloud Agreement at any time.

Service Quality Guarantees

The Covered Services will be operational and available to Consumers at least 99.95% of the time in any calendar month. If DTGOV does not meet this SLA requirement while the Consumer succeeds in meeting its SLA obligations, the Consumer will be eligible to receive Financial Credits as compensation. This SLA states the Consumer's exclusive right to compensation for any failure on DTGOV's part to fulfill the SLA requirements.

Definitions

The following definitions are to be applied to DTGOV's SLA:

- "Unavailability" is defined as the entirety of the Consumer's running instances as having no external connectivity for a duration that is at least five consecutive minutes in length, during which the Consumer is unable to launch commands against the remote administration system through either the Web application or Web service API.

- "Downtime Period" is defined as a period of five or more consecutive minutes of the service remaining in a state of Unavailability. Periods of "Intermittent Downtime" that are less than five minutes long do not count towards Downtime Periods.

- "Monthly Up-time Percentage" (MUP) is calculated as: (total number of minutes in a month – total number of downtime period minutes in a month) / (total number of minutes in a month)

- "Financial Credit" is defined as the percentage of the monthly invoice total that is credited towards future monthly invoices of the Consumer, which is calculated as follows:

  99.00% < MUP % < 99.95% – 10% of the monthly invoice is credited in favor of the Consumer's invoice

  89.00% < MUP % < 99.00% – 30% of the monthly invoice is credited in favor of the Consumer's invoice

  MUP % < 89.00% – 100% of the monthly invoice is credited in favor of the Consumer's invoice

Usage of Financial Credits

The MUP for each billing period is to be displayed on each monthly invoice. The Consumer is to submit a request for Financial Credit in order to be eligible to redeem

Financial Credits. For that purpose, the Consumer is to notify DTGOV within thirty days from the time the Consumer receives the invoice that states the MUP beneath the defined SLA. Notification is to be sent to DTGOV via e-mail. Failure to comply with this requirement forfeits the Consumer's right to the redemption of Financial Credits.

SLA Exclusions

The SLA does not apply to any of the following:

- Unavailability periods caused by factors that cannot be reasonably foreseen or prevented by DTGOV.

- Unavailability periods resulting from the malfunctioning of the Consumer's software and/or hardware, third party software and/or hardware, or both.

- Unavailability periods resulting from abuse or detrimental behavior and actions that are in violation of the DTGOV Cloud Agreement.

- Consumers with overdue invoices or are otherwise not considered in good standing with DTGOV.

Part V

Appendices

Appendix A

Case Study Conclusions

This appendix briefly concludes the storylines of the three case studies that were first introduced in Chapter 2.

A.1 ATN

The cloud initiative necessitated migrating selected applications and IT services to the cloud, allowing for the consolidation and retirement of solutions in a crowded application portfolio. Not all of the applications could be migrated, and selecting appropriate applications was a major issue. Some of the chosen applications required significant re-development effort to adapt to the new cloud environment.

Costs were effectively reduced for most of the applications that were moved to the cloud. This was discovered after six months of expenditures were compared with the costs of the traditional applications over a three year period. Both capital and operational expenses were used in the ROI evaluation.

ATN's level of service has improved in business areas that use cloud-based applications. In the past, most of these applications showed a noticeable performance deterioration during peak usage periods. The cloud-based applications can now scale out whenever a peak workload arises.

ATN is currently evaluating other applications for potential cloud migration.

A.2 DTGOV

Although DTGOV has been outsourcing IT resources for public sector organizations for more than 30 years, establishing the cloud and its associated IT infrastructure was a major undertaking that took over two years. DTGOV now offers IaaS services to the government sector and is building a new cloud service portfolio that targets private sector organizations.

Diversification of its client and service portfolios is the next logical step for DTGOV, after all of the changes they made to their technology architecture to produce a mature cloud. Before proceeding with this next phase, DTGOV produces a report to document aspects of its completed transition to cloud adoption. A summary of the report is documented in Table A.1.

Pre-Cloud Status	Required Change	Business Benefit	Challenges
The data center and related IT resources were not completely standardized.	The standardization of IT resources, including servers, storage systems, network devices, virtualization platform, and management systems.	Required investment costs are reduced by making bulk IT infrastructure acquisitions. Operational costs are reduced by optimizing the IT infrastructure.	Establishing new practices for IT procurement, technology lifecycle management, and data center management.
IT resources were deployed reactively due to long-term client commitment.	Deployment of IT resources supported by infrastructure with large-scale computing capacity.	Investments are reduced by making bulk IT infrastructure acquisitions and scaling IT resources to client demands.	Capacity planning and related ROI calculations are challenging tasks that require ongoing training.
IT resources were provisioned through long-term commitment contracts.	Flexible allocation, reallocation, release, and control of available IT resources by comprehensively applying virtualization.	Cloud service provisioning is agile and on-demand for clients, and carried out via flexible (software-based) allocation and management of IT resources.	Establishing the virtualization platform related to IT resource provisioning.
Monitoring capabilities were basic.	Detailed monitoring of cloud service usage and QoS.	Service provisioning is on-demand and pay-per-use for clients. Service charges are proportional to actual IT resource consumption. Service quality management uses business-relevant SLAs.	Establishing SLA monitors, billing monitors, and management mechanisms, which were all new to DTGOV's architecture.

continues

Pre-Cloud Status	Required Change	Business Benefit	Challenges
The resiliency of the overall IT architecture was basic.	Enhanced resiliency of IT architecture, with fully interconnected data centers and cooperative IT resource allocation and management.	Computational resiliency is improved for clients.	Governance and management efforts to regulate and administer large-scale resiliency are significant.
Outsourcing contracts and related provisions were followed on a "per-contract" and "per-client" basis.	New pricing and SLA contracts for cloud service provisioning.	Rapid (agile), on-demand, and scalable services (computational capacity) for clients.	Negotiating contracts with existing clients in the new cloud-based contracting model.

Table A.1
The results of an analysis of DTGOV's cloud initiative.

A.3 Innovartus

The business objective of increasing company growth required the original cloud to undergo major modifications, since they needed to move from their regional cloud provider to a large-scale global cloud provider. Portability issues were discovered only after the move, and a new cloud provider procurement process had to be created when the regional cloud provider was unable to meets all of their needs. Data recovery, application migration, and interoperability issues were also addressed.

Highly available computing IT resources and the pay-per-use feature were key in developing Innovartus' business feasibility, since access to funding and investment resources were not initially available.

Innovartus has defined several business goals they plan to achieve over the next couple of years:

- Additional applications will be migrated to different clouds, using multiple cloud providers in order to improve resiliency and reduce dependency on individual cloud provider vendors.

- A new mobile-only business area is to be created, since mobile access to their cloud services has experienced 20% growth.

- The application platform developed by Innovartus is being evaluated as a value-added PaaS to be offered to companies that require enhanced and innovative UI-centric features for both Web-based and mobile application development.

Appendix B

Industry Standards Organizations

This appendix provides an overview of industry standards development organizations and their contributions to the standardization of the cloud computing industry.

B.1 National Institute of Standards and Technology (NIST)

NIST is a federal agency within the US Department of Commerce that promotes standards and technology in order to improve the general public's security and quality of life. One of NIST's projects is to lead federal government efforts on standards for data portability, cloud interoperability, and cloud security.

This agency has developed several standards and recommendations related to cloud computing that include:

- NIST Definition of Cloud Computing (Special Publication 800-145): Provides broad cloud computing definitions in terms of characteristics and models. The aim is to develop industry standards with minimal restrictions to avoid specifications that inhibit innovation.

- NIST Guidelines on Security and Privacy in Public Cloud Computing (Special Publication 800-144): Provides an overview of the security and privacy challenges pertinent to public cloud computing and points out considerations organizations should take when outsourcing data, applications, and infrastructure to a public cloud environment.

- NIST Cloud Computing Standards Roadmap (Special Publication 500-291): Surveys the existing standards landscape for security, portability, and interoperability standards, models, and use cases that are relevant to cloud computing, as well as identifying current standards, gaps, and priorities.

- NIST Cloud Computing Reference Architecture (Special Publication 500-292): Describes a cloud computing reference architecture, designed as an extension to the NIST Cloud Computing Definition, that depicts a generic high-level conceptual model for discussing the requirements, structures, and operations of cloud computing.

Official Web site: www.nist.gov

B.2 Cloud Security Alliance (CSA)

The CSA is a member-driven organization that was formed in December 2008 and chartered with promoting the use of best practices to enable security assurance in the field of cloud computing. CSA corporate membership is comprised of many of the industry's large-scale vendors and suppliers.

This alliance considers itself to be a standards incubator rather than a standards developing organization, having published the following cloud security-related best practice guides and checklists:

- Security Guidance for Critical Areas of Focus in Cloud Computing (Version 3): This document describes security concerns and foundational best practices that are organized into 14 domains (Cloud Architecture, Governance and Enterprise Risk, Legal: Contracts and Electronic Discovery, Compliance and Audit, Information Lifecycle Management and Data Security, Portability and Interoperability, Traditional Security, Business Continuity and Disaster Recovery, Data Center Operations, Incident Response, Application Security, Encryption and Key Management, Identity and Access Management, Virtualization, and Security-as-a-Service).

- Cloud Controls Matrix (CCM) (Version 2.1): Provides a security controls list and framework that enables detailed understanding of security concepts and principles.

Official Web site: www.cloudsecurityalliance.org

B.3 Distributed Management Task Force (DMTF)

The DMTF focuses on developing standards to enable interoperable IT management and promote worldwide multi-vendor interoperability. DMTF's board of members are representatives from companies such as Advanced Micro Devices (AMD), Broadcom Corporation, CA, Inc., Cisco, Citrix Systems, Inc., EMC, Fujitsu, HP, Huawei, IBM, Intel Corporation, Microsoft Corporation, NetApp, Oracle, RedHat, SunGard, and VMware, Inc.

The cloud computing standards that were developed by the DMTF include the Open Virtualization Format (OVF) (DMTF Standard Version 1.1), an industry standard that aims at enabling interoperability between virtualized environments.

Official Web site: www.dmtf.org

B.4 Storage Networking Industry Association (SNIA)

The main objective of the SNIA is to develop and promote standards, technologies, and educational services for the management of information. The SNIA developed a Storage Management Initiative Specification (SMI-S) that was adopted by the ISO (International Standards Organization). The SNIA further established an intermediary council known as the Cloud Storage Initiative (CSI) that promotes the adoption of the Storage-as-a-Service cloud delivery model to provide elastic, on-demand storage on a pay-as-you-go basis.

The SNIA standards portfolio includes the Cloud Data Management Interface (CDMI), an industry standard that defines a functional interface that allows for interoperable data transfer and management in cloud storage, as well as discovery of various cloud storage capabilities. Cloud consumers that use CDMI can exploit the capabilities of standardized cloud storage devices that are offered by different cloud providers.

Official Web site: www.snia.org

B.5 Organization for the Advancement of Structured Information Standards (OASIS)

OASIS is a consortium of vendors and users that is devoted to developing guidelines for IT product interoperability, so that the global information society can establish and adopt open standards. This organization produces standards in fields such as security, cloud computing, service-oriented architecture, Web services, and smart grids, and has put forth numerous service technology recommendations that include UDDI, WS-BPEL, SAML, WS-SecurityPolicy, WS-Trust, SCA, and ODF.

Official Web site: www.oasis-open.org

B.6 The Open Group

The Open Group is a consortium that works together with other standards bodies such as the Cloud Security Alliance and the Cloud Computing Interoperability Forum. Its mission is to enable access to integrated information both within and between enterprises, based on open standards and global interoperability.

The Open Group has a dedicated Cloud Working Group that was created to educate cloud providers and cloud consumers on the ways in which cloud technologies can be used to fully achieve benefits such as cost reduction, scalability, and agility.

Official Web site: www.opengroup.org

B.7 Open Cloud Consortium (OCC)

The OCC is a not-for-profit organization that manages and operates cloud infrastructure in support of scientific, environmental, medical, and healthcare research. This organization assists in the development of cloud computing industry standards, with a heightened focus on data-intensive cloud-based environments.

Contributions from the OCC include the development of reference implementations, benchmarks, and standards that include the MalGen Benchmark, a tool for testing and benchmarking data-intensive cloud implementations. The OCC also established a number of cloud test beds, such as the OCC Virtual Network Testbed and Open Cloud Testbed.

The OCC's membership includes organizations and universities such as Cisco, Yahoo, Citrix, NASA, Aerospace Corporation, John Hopkins University, and the University of Chicago.

Official Web site: www.opencloudconsortium.org

B.8 European Telecommunications Standards Institute (ETSI)

The ETSI is recognized as an official industry standards body by the European Union that develops globally applicable standards for information and communications technologies. The main focus of this organization is to support interoperability via standardization in multi-vendor, multi-network, and multi-service environments.

The ETSI is comprised of a number of technical committees, such as a body called the TC CLOUD that focuses on building standardized solutions for using, integrating, and deploying cloud computing technology. This committee is particularly focused on the telecommunications industry's interoperable solutions, and emphasizes the IaaS delivery model.

Official Web site: www.etsi.org

B.9 Telecommunications Industry Association (TIA)

A trade association founded in 1988 that represents the global information and communications technology (ICT) industry, the TIA is responsible for standards development, policy initiatives, business opportunities, market intelligence, and networking events.

The TIA develops standards for telecommunications and data center technologies, such as the Telecommunications Infrastructure Standard for Data Centers (TIA-942 Standard, published in 2005, latest amendment in 2010). This standard outlines the minimum requirements for infrastructure redundancy on four different tiers, as well as those for data center and computer room telecommunications infrastructures. The latter includes single-tenant enterprise data centers and multitenant Internet-hosting data centers.

Official Web site: www.tiaonline.org

B.10 Liberty Alliance

The Liberty Alliance develops open standards for protecting the privacy and security of identity information. This body published the Liberty Identity Assurance Framework (LIAF) to facilitate trusted identity federation and promote uniformity and interoperability among identity service providers, including cloud providers. The main building blocks of the LIAF are assurance level criteria, service assessment criteria, and accreditation and certification rules.

Official Web site: www.projectliberty.org

B.11 Open Grid Forum (OGF)

The OGF launched the Open Cloud Computing Interface (OCCI) working group to deliver an API specification for the remote management of cloud infrastructure. The OCCI specification assists in the development of interoperable tools for common tasks that include deployment, automated scaling, and monitoring. The specification consists of core models, infrastructure models, XHTML5 rendering, and HTTP header rendering.

Official Web site: www.ogf.org

Appendix C

Mapping Mechanisms to Characteristics

The following table summarizes the direct relationships between the cloud characteristics introduced in Chapter 4 and cloud computing mechanisms covered in Chapters 7, 8, and 9.

Cloud Characteristics	Cloud Mechanisms
On-Demand Usage	Hypervisor
	Virtual Server
	Ready-Made Environment
	Resource Replication
	Remote Administration Environment
	Resource Management System
	SLA Management System
	Billing Management System
Ubiquitous Access	Logical Network Perimeter
	Multi-Device Broker
Multitenancy/Resource Pooling	Logical Network Perimeter
	Hypervisor
	Resource Replication
	Resource Cluster
	Resource Management System

Cloud Characteristics	Cloud Mechanisms
Elasticity	Hypervisor
	Cloud Usage Monitor
	Automated Scaling Listener
	Resource Replication
	Load Balancer
	Resource Management System
Measured Usage	Hypervisor
	Cloud Usage Monitor
	SLA Monitor
	Pay-Per-Use Monitor
	Audit Monitor
	SLA Management System
	Billing Management System
Resiliency	Hypervisor
	Resource Replication
	Failover System
	Resource Cluster
	Resource Management System

Table C.1

Cloud characteristics are mapped to cloud computing mechanisms. Essentially, the use of the listed cloud computing mechanisms supports the realization of the corresponding cloud characteristics.

Appendix D

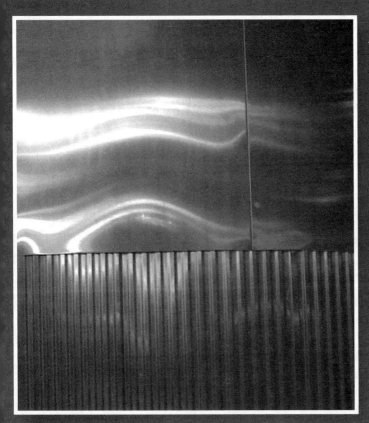

Data Center Facilities (TIA-942)

This appendix acts as a continuation of the *Data Center Technology* section from Chapter 5 by describing common parts of data center facilities, in reference to the Telecommunications Industry Association's TIA-942 Telecommunications Infrastructure Standard for Data Centers. It can be helpful to have an understanding of these details to better appreciate the complexity of data center infrastructure.

D.1 Primary Rooms

Electrical Room

Reserved for electrical equipment and installations, such as power distribution and bypasses, this space is divided into individual rooms dedicated to housing power generators for temporary emergency use, UPS, battery banks, and other electrical subsystems.

Mechanical Room

This space houses mechanical equipment, such as air conditioning and cooling engines.

Storage and Staging

This space is dedicated to safely storing both new and used consumables, such as removable media used for backups.

Offices, Operations Center, and Support

A building space that is usually isolated from the computer room for the placement of personnel involved in data center operations.

Telecommunications Entrance

Typically located outside of the computer room, this space functions as a demarcated area that houses telecommunications equipment and the ends of the external cabling that enter the data center boundaries.

Computer Room

A highly critical zone with strict environmental control and access that is limited to authorized personnel, this room usually has raised floors and safety vaults that are designed to protect the data center equipment from physical hazards. The computer room is subdivided into the following specialized areas:

- *Main Distribution Area (MDA)* – Encloses backbone-level telecom and network equipment, such as core switches, firewalls, PBX, and multiplexers.

- *Horizontal Distribution Area (HDM)* – Encloses network, storage, and keyboard, video, and mouse (KVM) switches.

- *Equipment Distribution Area (EDM)* – This is where computing and storage equipment is installed on standardized rack cabinets. Cabling subsystems, usually divided into backbone cabling (main interconnects) and horizontal cabling (individual equipment connects), interconnect all of the data center equipment, as illustrated in Figure D.1.

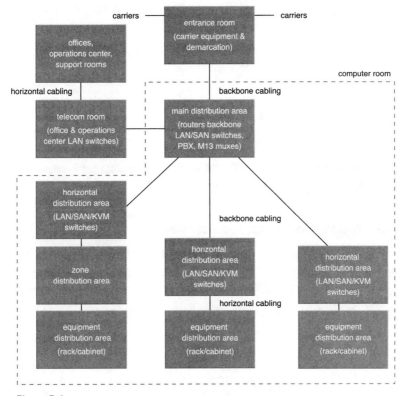

Figure D.1

A data center's internetworking regions, divided into backbone and horizontal cablings (adapted from TIA-942).

D.2 Environmental Controls

Environmental control subsystems include fire suppression, humidification/dehumidi-fication, and heating, ventilation, and air conditioning (HVAC). Figure D.2 depicts three rack cabinets that are placed so as to enable cold/hot air circulation that optimally uti-lizes the HVAC subsystems. Controlling this airflow is crucial in order to handle the significant amounts of heat generated by the server racks.

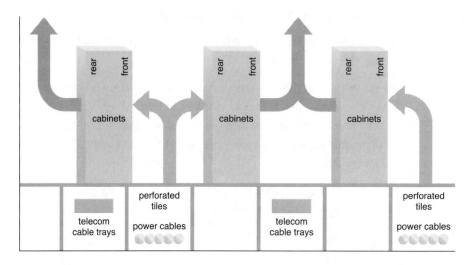

Figure D.2
A depiction of the flow of cold and hot air that accommodates server racks in a typical data center design. The hot air generally leaves the room through ceiling air ducts (adapted from TIA-942).

The power supply system is a complex electrical engineering installation encompassing several subsystems that include:

External Electrical Power Provider Interconnection

Utility power infrastructure interconnects with external power utility providers, and is usually supplied by high-voltage power lines in larger data centers. Voltage conversion requires the use of on-site utility power stations, while redundant interconnections are required for electrical grid configurations.

Power Distribution

An electrical subsystem that traditionally uses low-voltage alternating current (AC) for its operations, the power distribution system comprises power distribution units that provide electrical power to all data center equipment. The power supplies that are embedded in the computer equipment can require an AC/DC conversion, since some electronic circuits in IT equipment run on DC power. The common inefficiencies of both voltage and AC/DC conversions are notorious for causing power outages.

Uninterruptible Power Source (UPS)

Many IT resources, most notably physical servers, undergo data loss and other types of malfunctioning if they are unexpectedly shut off. This subsystem is comprised of equipment dedicated to powering the data center during temporary primary power source failures. Multiple UPS devices can operate alongside other power sources to quickly fulfill the data center's power requirements. The UPS subsystems are also responsible for removing voltage flow fluctuations in order to normalize the incoming current and prevent undue strain on the IT infrastructure. UPS equipment usually relies on DC battery banks, which provide only a few hours' worth of backup power.

Power Engine-Generator

Gas generators are standard combustion engines that are used by larger data centers to sustain operations during natural disasters and power-grid failures. Energy efficiency is commonly measured by the power usage effectiveness (PUE) metric, which is expressed as the ratio of the total facility power entering a data center to the power used by its IT equipment, as follows:

$$PUE = \frac{\text{total data center power}}{\text{power used by IT equipment}}$$

The PUE is determined by the power required by the IT equipment's supporting subsystems and should ideally be a ratio of 1.0. An average data center would have a PUE over 2.0, while the PUE of a more complex and efficient data center would be closer to 1.2.

D.3 Infrastructure Redundancy Summary

The TIA-942 classification specifies the minimum requirements for infrastructure redundancy in four tiers, an approach that is useful for comparing and evaluating data center facilities (briefly described in Table D.1).

Tier	Characteristics
1	Basic Data Center • single path for power and cooling distribution systems • non-redundant components (power, cooling equipment) • optional raised flooring, UPS, and/or generator • subject to disruption of IT hardware operations • average availability (uptime): 99.671%
2	Redundant Components Data Center • single path for power and cooling distribution systems • redundant components (multiple power and cooling backups) • mandatory raised flooring, UPS, and/or generator • power path failure may result in disruption of IT hardware operations • average availability (uptime): 99.741%
3	Concurrently Maintainable Data Center • multiple paths for power and cooling distribution systems • maintenance activities can be carried out without disruption of IT hardware operations • average availability (uptime): 99.982%
4	Fault-Tolerant Data Center • fault-tolerant components • planned activity does not affect the critical load • one unplanned worst-case failure during maintenance can be sustained without disruption of IT hardware operations • average availability (uptime): 99.995%

Table D.1
The four tiers of data center component redundancy, with availability averages.

Cloud-Adapted Risk Management Framework

R isk management was introduced in Chapter 6 as a cyclically executed process comprising a set of coordinated activities for overseeing and controlling risks. This set of activities is composed of risk assessment, risk treatment, and risk control tasks that collectively target the enhancement of strategic and tactical security.

How confident cloud consumers feel about whether the amount of risk related to using cloud services is acceptable depends on how much trust they place on those involved in the surrounding cloud ecosystem's orchestration. The risk management process ensures that issues are identified and mitigated early on in the investment cycle and followed by periodic reviews. Since cloud consumers, cloud carriers, and other types of actors (such as cloud brokers), in a cloud ecosystem all have differing degrees of control over cloud-based IT resources, they need to share the responsibility of implementing the security requirements.

The Special Publication (SP) 500-299: NIST Cloud Computing Security Reference Architecture specification discusses several key aspects of managing risks associated with a cloud environment. The document highlights the high-level steps of the Cloud-Adapted Risk Management Framework (CRMF) and stresses the importance of adhering to the security conservation principle.

NOTE

Further details about the NIST Cloud Reference Architecture can be found in the NIST Special Publication 500-292: NIST Cloud Computing Reference Architecture.

Figure E.1 depicts the NIST Cloud Reference Architecture in the background, over which a graphical representation (as presented in NIST SP 500-299) of the secure orchestration of a cloud ecosystem is layered. This illustrates how secure orchestration encompasses all of the cloud actors and depicts their shared responsibilities in orchestrating and operating a cloud ecosystem.

Secure orchestrations typically have two intrinsic considerations. The first is the cloud delivery model (SaaS, PaaS, or IaaS), whose correlation can be depicted by building blocks. The second is the cloud deployment model (public, private, hybrid, or community) that can most successfully fulfill the cloud consumer's business objectives and security requirements.

For each cloud-based solution, cloud consumers need to identify the threats, perform a risk assessment, and evaluate the security requirements of their individual cloud architectural context. The requirements also need to be mapped to the proper security controls and practices in the technical, operational, and management classes.

The type of cloud delivery model that is chosen for adoption does not impact the security posture of the cloud-based system. The overall security requirements either remain unchanged or at a logical constant, and are, at minimum, equivalent to the security requirements of an on-premise technology architecture or solution. Conversely, the type of deployment model that is selected does have an impact on the distribution of security responsibilities among the cloud actors, which relates to the security conservation principle as discussed in the NIST Special Publication 500-299.

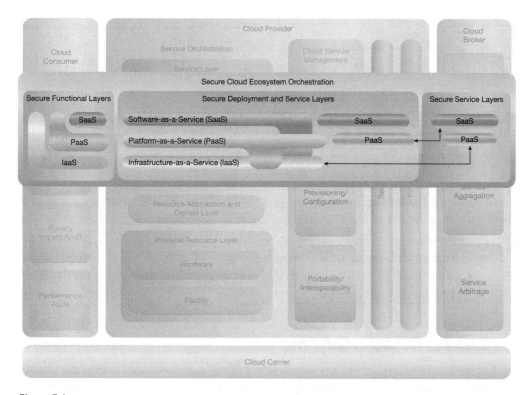

Figure E.1
A visual representation of the NIST Cloud Computing Reference Architecture and ecosystem orchestration.

When adopting cloud-based solutions, cloud consumers need to exercise due diligence in fully grasping the distinct security requirements that can be triggered, such as:

- broad network access

- data residency

- measured usage

- multitenancy

- dynamic system boundaries

- shared roles and responsibilities between the cloud consumer and cloud provider

- decrease in cloud consumer visibility

- decrease in cloud consumer control

- significant increase in scale (on demand)

- significant increase in dynamics (elasticity, cost optimization)

- significant increase in complexity (automation, virtualization)

These issues often present cloud consumers with security risks that are greater than or different from those in traditional on-premise solutions.

The key element to the successful adoption of a cloud-based system solution is the cloud consumer's full understanding of the cloud-specific traits and characteristics, the architectural components for each cloud service type and deployment model, and each cloud actor's role in orchestrating a secure ecosystem.

Furthermore, it is essential for the cloud consumers' business and mission-critical processes that they be able to identify all cloud-specific risk-adjusted security controls. The cloud consumers need to leverage their contractual agreements to hold the cloud providers (and cloud brokers) accountable for the implementation of the security controls. They also need to be able to assess the correct implementation and continuously monitor all identified security controls.

E.1 Security Conservation Principle

The core concept of the security conservation principle is that a cloud service's full set of security controls needs to remain unchanged or, in a logical sense, at a constant. The responsibility of fulfilling security requirements and implementing mitigatory actions dynamically shifts between cloud actors according to the dynamics that occur within a cloud. Figure E.2 depicts the security conservation principle for the cloud ecosystem:

For simplicity's sake, this diagram identifies only the cloud consumer and cloud provider roles. It highlights the responsibility of implementing security controls being shared between the cloud consumer and cloud provider to different degrees, depending on which deployment model is adopted. The level of responsibility of either cloud actor fundamentally correlates to each cloud actor's level of control over certain "layers" of the cloud.

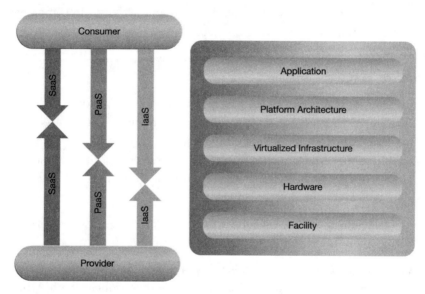

Figure E.2
A visual representation of the security conservation principle (courtesy of NIST, SP 500-299).

In SaaS clouds, the cloud provider assumes most of the responsibility for security controls implementation since the cloud consumer only controls the application layer. Conversely, cloud consumers of IaaS clouds may control everything except the hardware on which the cloud service runs and the facility storing the hardware, meaning they are primarily accountable.

NOTE
See NIST SP 500-299: "NIST Cloud Computing Security Reference Architecture" and NIST 800-144: "Guidelines on Security and Privacy in Public Cloud Computing" for further information.

E.2 The Risk Management Framework

A risk-based approach of managing information systems is a holistic activity that should be fully integrated into every aspect of the organization, from planning and system development lifecycle processes to security controls allocation and continuous monitoring. The selection and specification of security controls support effectiveness, efficiency, and constraints via appropriate laws, directives, policies, standards, and regulations.

The NIST Special Publication 800-37: Guide for Applying the Risk Management Framework to Federal Information Systems provides a disciplined and structured process that integrates information security and risk management activities into the development lifecycle by identifying the following six steps:

- *Step 1* – Use an impact analysis to categorize the system and the information it processes, stores, and transmits.

- *Step 2* – Select the set of initial or baseline security controls for the system based on the security categorization. Tailor and supplement the set of baseline security controls according to the organizational assessment of the risk and the conditions of the operational environment. Develop a strategy for continuous monitoring to achieve security control effectiveness. Document all the controls in the security plan. Review and approve the security plan.

- *Step 3* – Implement the security controls and describe how the security controls are employed within the system and its environment of operation.

- *Step 4* – Assess the security controls using the appropriate procedures as documented in the assessment plan. This assessment determines whether the security controls have been implemented correctly and will effectively produce the intended outcome.

- *Step 5* – Authorize information system operation if the estimated risk resulting from the operation is acceptable. The assessment considers risk to organizational assets and operations (including mission, functions, image, or reputation), individuals, and other organizations.

- *Step 6* – Monitor the security controls on an ongoing basis. Monitoring includes assessing control effectiveness, documenting changes to the system or its environment of operation, conducting security impact analyses of these changes, and reporting the security state of the system to designated officials.

While the risk management framework is adaptable to most scenarios, it defaults to the traditional IT environment and requires customization to successfully address the unique characteristics of cloud-based services and solutions. The CRMF closely follows the original RMF approach. Table E.1 shows the aforementioned six steps listed in the right column, with each step grouped into one of the three main activities in the left column that collectively comprise the risk management process:

CRMF	CRMF Steps
Risk Assessment	*Step 1* – Use an impact analysis to categorize the information system that has been migrated to the cloud, and the information that is processed, stored, and transmitted by that system. (This step is very similar to Step 1 of the traditional RMF.)
	Step 2 – Identify the security requirements of the system by performing a risk assessment (the Confidentiality, Integrity, and Availability (CIA) analysis is recommended). Select the baseline and tailored supplemental security controls.
Risk Treatment	*Step 3* – Select the cloud ecosystem architecture that best suits the assessment results for the system.
	Step 4 – Assess your service provider options. Identify the security controls needed for the system the cloud provider has implemented. Negotiate the implementation of any additional security controls that are identified. Identify any remaining security controls that fall under the cloud consumer's responsibility for their implementation.
Risk Control	*Step 5* – Select and authorize a cloud provider to host the cloud consumer's information system. Draft up a service agreement and SLA that list the negotiated contractual terms and conditions.
	Step 6 – Monitor the cloud provider to ensure that all service agreement and SLA terms are being met. Ensure that the cloud-based system maintains the necessary security posture. Monitor the security controls that fall under the cloud consumer's responsibility.

Table E.1
The six steps are mapped to each of the three activities comprising the CRMF.

Adopting the approach outlined by these steps enables organizations to systematically identify their common, hybrid, and system-specific security controls and other security requirements for procurement officials, cloud providers, cloud carriers and cloud brokers alike.

The CRMF can be used to address the security risks associated with cloud-based systems by incorporating possible outcomes into the cloud provider's contractual terms. Performance aspects of these terms and conditions also need to be represented in the SLA, which is an intrinsic part of the service agreement between the cloud consumer and cloud provider. Contractual terms should, for example, include guarantees concerning the cloud consumer's timely access to cloud audit logs and the details pertaining to the continuous monitoring of the logs.

If permitted by the adopted deployment model, the organization should implement both the cloud consumer's set of identified security controls and the specifically tailored supplemental security controls. Cloud consumers are advised to request that cloud providers (and cloud brokers) provide sufficient evidence to demonstrate that the security controls being used to protect their IT assets have been correctly implemented.

Appendix F

Cloud Provisioning Contracts

A *cloud provisioning contract* is the fundamental agreement between the cloud consumer and cloud provider that encompasses the contractual terms and conditions of their business relationship. This appendix drills down into the common parts and sections of a generic cloud provisioning contract and further provides guidelines for choosing a cloud provider (partially based on the contents of cloud provisioning contracts).

F.1 Cloud Provisioning Contract Structure

A cloud provisioning contract is a legally binding document that defines rights, responsibilities, terms, and conditions for a scope of provisioning by a cloud provider to a cloud consumer.

As shown in Figure F.1, this document is typically comprised of the following parts:

- *Technical Conditions* – specifies the IT resources being provided and their corresponding SLAs

- *Economic Conditions* – defines the pricing policy and model with cost metrics, established pricing, and billing procedures

- *Terms of Service* – provides the general terms and conditions of the service provision, which are usually composed of the following five elements:

  - *Service Usage Policy* – defines acceptable service usage methods, usage conditions, and usage terms, as well as suitable courses of action in response to violations

  - *Security and Privacy Policy* – defines terms and conditions for security and privacy requirements

  - *Warranties and Liabilities* – describes warranties, liabilities, and other risk reduction provisions including compensation for SLA non-compliance

  - *Rights and Responsibilities* – outlines the obligations and responsibilities of the cloud consumer and cloud provider

  - *Contract Termination and Renewal* – defines the terms and conditions of terminating and renewing the contract

Figure F.1

A sample cloud provisioning contract table of contents.

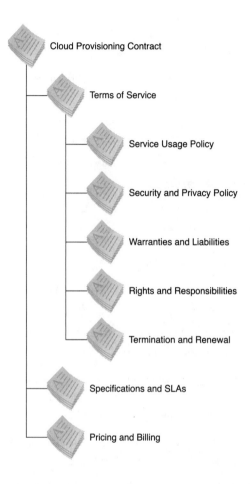

Cloud provisioning contracts are usually based on templates and provided online, where they can be accepted by cloud consumers with the click of a button. These contracts are, by default, generally geared to limiting the cloud provider's risk and liability. For example, common clauses that specify the provisioning and responsibilities in contract templates include:

- Cloud services are provided "as is" without warranty.

- Liability limitations do not offer compensation for most kinds of damage.

- Warranties are not provided for performance metrics.

- Warranties are not provided to guarantee service continuity.

- The cloud provider has minimal to no responsibility for data security breaches and damages incurred from these events.

- The cloud provider can unilaterally modify the terms and conditions without prior notice.

Furthermore, typically slack data privacy warranties and clauses permit the "sharing" of cloud-based data and other potential threats to data privacy.

Terms of Service

This part defines the general terms and conditions that can be broken down into the following sub-sections:

Service Usage Policy

A service usage policy, or acceptable use policy (AUP), comprises definitions of acceptable methods of cloud service usage, including clauses with stipulations such as:

- The cloud consumer shall be solely responsible for the content of the transmissions made through cloud services.

- Cloud services shall not be used for illegal purposes, and any transmitted materials shall not be unlawful, defamatory, libelous, abusive, harmful, or otherwise deemed objectionable by third parties or legal regulations.

- Cloud service usage shall not infringe on any party's intellectual property rights, copyrights, or any other right.

- Transmitted and stored data shall not contain viruses, malware, or any other harmful content.

- Cloud services shall not be used for the unsolicited mass distribution of e-mail.

Some elements of the service usage policy that cloud consumers may need to review and negotiate include:

- *Mutuality of Conditions* – Conditions should be identically applicable to the cloud consumer and cloud provider, since the actions and business operations of one party directly impact the operations of the other.

- *Policy Update Conditions* – Even though many contract templates state that policy updates do not require advance notice, unilateral modifications to cloud service usage terms and conditions can be detrimental for cloud consumers. Cloud consumers should formally acknowledge any changes before they are applied to the policy, especially for larger contracts.

- *Actions in Response to Violation* – Specifications on how violations are detected and notified, how much time is allowed to issue and carry out corrective responses, and cloud service termination conditions in the event of non-compliance.

Security and Privacy Policy

Conditions pertaining to security and privacy can be complex and difficult to define in measurable terms. Therefore, these issues are commonly isolated in a dedicated section of the cloud provisioning contract.

Many contract templates are designed to favor the cloud provider by limiting their liability and warranties in the event of data breaches and other security violations. It is not uncommon to have loose or vaguely defined security and privacy specifications that oblige the cloud consumers to be responsible for security-related cloud service configuration and usage. Some contract templates even contain policies that grant the cloud provider the right to share cloud consumer data with third parties using generalized, subjective, and/or ambiguous terms, under conditions that were deemed necessary to:

- prevent fraud and/or other illegal activities

- prevent imminent bodily harm

- protect other cloud consumers from security and privacy policy violation

An important policy criterion is making sure that the multiple levels of the cloud architecture are differentiated, since policies often need to encompass and address a broad range of data security concerns.

Common issues that require additional consideration when assessing and negotiating security and privacy policies include:

- *Security Measures* – Policies need to clearly describe the cloud provider's measures for protecting cloud service operations and cloud consumer data, and further identify those that are the cloud consumer's responsibility.

- *Access Control* – The different ways of accessing cloud services, the cloud mechanisms that control and monitor usage, and any data the cloud services manipulate all need to be well-defined.

- *Vulnerability Control* – The cloud provider's methods for handling security vulnerabilities and any patching approaches required by the cloud consumer need to be documented.

- *Data Transfer* – Security policies on data entering and leaving the cloud need to address how the cloud provider intends to defend against insider and external threats during data transmission.

- *Data Security* – Policies need to clearly define the management of data ownership and the warranties that protect information security, which pertain to issues concerning:

  - *Data Access* – when and how to access data, and the optimal format for reducing the risk of cloud provider lock-in

  - *Data Blocking Conditions* – conditions for blocking data access

  - *Data Classification* – ownership and confidentiality requirements that differentiate between public and private data

  - *Technical and Organizational Measures* – controls to ensure the confidentiality and integrity of data in cloud storage, transmission, and processing

- *Disclosure of Data* – Conditions for disclosing cloud consumer data to the cloud provider and third parties, including:

  - *Law Enforcement Access*

  - *Confidentiality and Non-Disclosure*

- *Intellectual Property Rights and Preservation* – Original software that is created on IaaS and PaaS platforms can be exposed to and potentially exploited by cloud providers and third parties.

- *Data Backup and Disaster Recovery Procedures* – This policy needs to outline the terms to adequately provision for disaster recovery and business continuity planning to preserve service continuity. These provisions should be detailed and specified at lower levels. Most often, these are related to the use of data replication and resilient implementations in different geographical locations.

- *Change of Control* – This policy needs to clearly define how the cloud provider will honor contractual obligations in the event of a change of control and/or ownership, as well as terms of contract termination.

Warranties and Liabilities

Many contract templates state that services are to be provided "as is" without any guarantees. The limitation of liability excludes most forms of monetary damage, with little or no cloud provider responsibility for data security breaches. Measurable terms of compensation are also typically absent in contract templates, while conditions of service failure and unavailability periods may be vaguely defined. One of the only recourses for cloud consumers that are receiving unsatisfactory service is to terminate the cloud provisioning contract prematurely, usually resulting in monetary penalties.

Cloud consumers can attempt to negotiate an arragement whereby part of the payment is due only when other terms of service and the SLAs are being complied with, which is an awards-based approach. This "at-risk" payment can be an effective way of ensuring that risk is being shared with or transferred to the cloud provider.

Rights and Responsibilities

This section establishes the legal duties and rights of both parties in the agreement.

The duties of the cloud consumer are generally to:

- comply with the terms of service and associated policies
- pay for the cloud services being used, in accordance with the pricing model and rates

The rights of the cloud consumer are to:

- access and use the IT resources as stated in the cloud provisioning contract
- receive reports on IT resource usage, SLA compliance, and billing
- receive due compensation in the event of cloud provider SLA non-compliance
- terminate or renew IT resource usage terms, as per the agreement

The duties of the cloud provider are to:

- comply with the terms of service and associated polices
- provide IT resources in compliance with predefined conditions

- accurately manage and report SLAs, IT resource usage, and billing costs

- compensate the cloud consumer in the event of SLA non-compliance

The rights of the cloud provider are to:

- receive payment for the IT resource usage provided, in accordance with the pricing model and rates

- terminate IT resources in the event of breach of contract by the cloud consumer, after sufficient review of the agreement stipulations

Termination and Renewal

This sub-section addresses the following:

- *Renewal Conditions* – The conditions for agreement renewal, including the maximum prices applicable to a renewed agreement.

- *Termination of Initial Term* – The expiration date for the contract, after which access to IT resources is discontinued if the contract is not renewed.

- *Termination for Convenience* – The condition for contract termination, usually as requested by the cloud consumer, without requiring the cloud provider to have been at fault or breach.

- *Termination with Cause* – The terms and conditions for contract termination due to a party's breach of the terms of service.

- *Payment on Termination* – The payment conditions for contract termination.

- *Period for Data Recovery After Termination* – The duration for which data needs to remain restorable by the cloud provider after contract termination.

Specifications and SLAs

This part of the contract provides a detailed description on the IT resources and QoS guarantees. A large section of the SLA deals with monitoring and measuring service quality metrics, with its benchmarks and targets identified.

Many SLAs that are based off of SLA templates are incomplete and use vague definitions for QoS guarantees, such as service availability. Besides clearly identifying metrics and measurement procedures, the specifications for availability also should allow for the definition of:

- *Recovery Point Objective (RPO)* – A description of how an IT resource resumes operation after a failure, and an identification of possible types of resultant loss.

- *Recovery Time Objective (RTO)* – A definition of how long an IT resource remains non-operational upon failure.

Pricing and Billing

In addition to providing the details of the pricing structure, models, and applicable fees, the following are fundamental billing types:

- *Free of Charge*

- *Billing in Arrears/Post-Payment* (charges are issued after IT resource usage has commenced)

- *Billing in Advance/Pre-Payment* (charges are issued prior to IT resource usage)

Other Issues

Legal and Compliance Issues

When laws and regulations are applicable to how a cloud consumer will use provisioned IT resources, the cloud provisioning contract needs to provide sufficient warranties so that both the cloud consumer and cloud provider can fulfill legal and regulatory requirements. Some cloud providers use contract templates that are customizable using pre-defined criteria. For example, they may already have templates for when the physical location or geographic area proposed for the hosting of cloud consumer data raises legal concerns.

Auditability and Accountability

Auditing applications, systems, and data enables research and investigation into failure instances, causes for failure, and the parties involved. Auditability and accountability requirements are commonly present in cloud provisioning contracts and need to be assessed and discussed during contract negotiations.

Changes in the Contract Terms and Conditions

Contracts signed with large-scale cloud providers are often subject to adjustments over time, especially since these cloud providers may include a generalized clause that allows contractual modifications to be made without prior notice.

F.2 Cloud Provider Selection Guidelines

Choosing a cloud provider can be one of the most important strategic decisions made by a cloud consumer organization. Depending on the extent to which cloud-based IT resources are adopted and relied upon, the success of a cloud consumer's business automation can be heavily dependent on the extent to which its cloud provider follows through on commitments made in the cloud provisioning contract.

This section contains a checklist of questions and considerations that can be used for evaluating cloud providers.

Cloud Provider Viability

- How long has the cloud provider been in business and how have its service offerings evolved over time?

- Is the cloud provider financially stable?

- Does the cloud provider have a proven backup and recovery strategy?

- How transparently are the cloud provider's business strategy and financial status communicated to its clients?

- Is the cloud provider subject to acquisition by another company?

- What are the cloud provider's current practices and vendor partnerships with regards to its infrastructure?

- What are the cloud provider's current and projected services and products?

- Are reviews on the cloud provider's past provisions available online?

- What type of technical certifications does the cloud provider have?

- How does the cloud provider's security and privacy policy support the cloud consumer's requirements?

- What are the capabilities of its security and management tools? (And, how mature are these tools compared to the rest of the market?)

- Is the cloud provider supporting the development or application of any relevant cloud computing industry standards?

- Does the cloud provider support auditability and security laws, certifications, and programs? These can include industry standards, such as the Payment Card Industry Data Security Standard (PCI DSS), Cloud Controls Matrix (CCM), and Statement on Auditing Standards No. 70 (SAS 70).

Negotiating multiple cloud provisioning contracts and SLAs with different cloud providers may be necessary to meet all of an organization's specific business requirements.

Appendix G

Cloud Business Case Template

This appendix presents a generic template for building a business case for the adoption of cloud computing models, environments, and technologies. This type of template is intended as a generic starting point that needs further customization to better match organizational requirements and preferences.

The cloud business case template also acts as an effective checklist of considerations that pertain to cloud adoption. A draft business case based on this template can be used to promote discussion around the legitimacy of cloud adoption during preliminary planning stages.

G.1 Business Case Identification

This section provides information that specifies the details of the business case, such as the following:

- *Business Case Name*
- *Description* – A brief summary of the business case's purpose and goals.
- *Sponsor* – Identification of business case stakeholders.
- *List of Revisions (optional)* – Revisions by date, author, and approval if control or historical logging is required.

G.2 Business Needs

The expected benefits and requirements that are to be addressed and fulfilled by cloud adoption are detailed in this part of the template:

- *Background* – A description of relevant historical information that spurred on the motivation for the business case.
- *Business Goals* – A list of the tactical and strategic business objectives that are associated with the business case.

- *Business Requirements* – A list of the business requirements that are expected to be fulfilled by the achievement of the business goals.

- *Performance Objectives* – A list of any relevant performance objectives related to the business goals and business requirements.

- *Priorities* – Business goals, business requirements, and performance objectives listed in order of priority.

- *Affected On-Premise Solutions (optional)* – A detailed description of current and planned on-premise solutions that are to be migrated, or that will otherwise be affected by the adoption effort.

- *Target Environment* – A description of the anticipated outcome of the adoption of the project, including a high-level overview of cloud-based solutions that are to be built in support of the business case.

G.3 Target Cloud Environment

The cloud deployment and delivery models expected to be utilized as part of the cloud adoption effort are listed and briefly described, along with other available information regarding planned cloud services and cloud-based solutions:

- *Cloud Deployment Model* – Reasons for the choice of models, advantages, and disadvantages are provided to help communicate the rationale.

- *Cloud Characteristics* – A description of how the planned target state relates to and supports cloud characteristics.

- *Cloud Service Candidates (optional)* – A list of candidate cloud services and corresponding usage estimates.

- *Cloud Provider Candidates (optional)* – A list of potential cloud providers and a comparison of costs and features.

- *Cloud Delivery Model* – The cloud delivery model that is presumably required to meet the business goals of the business case is documented.

G.4 Technical Issues

This section highlights requirements and limitations related to common technical concerns:

- *Solution Architecture*
- *SLA*
- *Security Requirements*
- *Governance Requirements*
- *Interoperability Requirements*
- *Portability Requirements*
- *Regulatory Compliance Requirements*
- *Migration Approach (optional)*

G.5 Economic Factors

This section comprises considerations related to the economics of the business case, involving the pricing, costs, and formulaic tools that are used for calculation and analysis. See Chapter 15 for a broad range of financial metrics, formulas, and considerations that can be incorporated into this section.

About the Authors

Thomas Erl

Thomas Erl is a top-selling IT author, founder of Arcitura Education, editor of the *Service Technology Magazine* and series editor of the *Prentice Hall Service Technology Series from Thomas Erl*. With more than 175,000 copies in print world-wide, his books have become international bestsellers and have been formally endorsed by senior members of major IT organizations, such as IBM, Microsoft, Oracle, Intel, Accenture, IEEE, HL7, MITRE, SAP, CISCO, HP, and many others. As CEO of Arcitura Education Inc. and in cooperation with CloudSchool.com™ and SOASchool.com®, Thomas has led the development of curricula for the internationally recognized Cloud Certified Professional (CCP) and SOA Certified Professional (SOACP) accreditation programs, which have established a series of formal, vendor-neutral industry certifications obtained by thousands of IT professionals around the world. Thomas has toured more than 20 countries as a speaker and instructor and regularly participates in international conferences, including Service Technology Symposium and Gartner events. More than 100 articles and interviews by Thomas have been published in numerous publications, including *The Wall Street Journal* and *CIO Magazine*.

Zaigham Mahmood

Dr. Zaigham Mahmood is a published author of six books, four of which are dedicated to cloud computing. He acts as a technology consultant at Debesis Education UK and a Researcher at the University of Derby, UK. He further holds positions as a foreign professor and professor extraordinaire with international educational institutions. Professor Mahmood is a certified cloud trainer and a regular speaker at the International SOA, Cloud + Service Technology Symposium, and he has published more than 100 articles. His specialized areas of research include distributed computing, project management, and e-government.

Ricardo Puttini

Professor Ricardo Puttini has 15 years of field experience as a senior IT consultant at major government organizations in Brazil. He has taught several undergraduate and graduate-level courses in service orientation, service-oriented architecture, and cloud computing. Ricardo was the general chair of the 4th International SOA Symposium and 3rd International Cloud Symposium that was held in the spring of 2011. He holds a Ph.D. in Communication Networks (2004) from the University of Brasília, where he has taught in the Electrical Engineering department since 1998. Ricardo spent 18 months at the L'Ecole Supérieure d'Électricité (Supelec) in Rennes, France, during his Ph.D., where he started researching distributed system architecture and security.

About the Contributors

Pamela J. Wise-Martinez, MSc

Pamela is chief architect of the Department of Energy and National Nuclear Security Administration (NNSA). She is a strategic C-level advisor, inventor, business analyst, and information engineer with more than 20 years of experience in systems engineering, as well as business application development, networks, enterprise strategies, and implementations. A published inventor, Pamela has performed extensive research in security, expert systems, NANO technology, and mobile infrastructure. She holds a patent for secure biometric financial payments via mobile, contactless, and smart payment technology from the United States Patents and Trademark Office. Another patent for secure handheld device technology, business methods, and apparatus based on secure mobile financial markets and a third patent for service technology are currently pending. As an emerging technology leader and futurist, she has delivered leading-edge, high-profile national systems to form collaborative partnerships with numerous government and private organizations. Pamela has performed as a senior network analyst on the performance of event and service-driven architectures and is responsible for technical and business alignment with emerging service-oriented technologies at her current role at the NNSA. She has created an innovative service-layered approach for modeling network and provisioning segments for enterprise components and SOA planning and design and is currently leading the OneArchitecture-SmartPath approach. Pamela received a Master of Science degree in Engineering Management and Technology at George Washington University and is certified in the Governance of Enterprise Information Technology (CGEIT) with ISACA.

Gustavo Azzolin, BSc, MSc

Gustavo is a senior IT consultant with 10 years of professional experience in the IT, tele-communications, public sector, and media industries. Gustavo has delivered technical and management consulting services to global market leaders and major governmental organizations alike and holds several IT certifications in technical and service management. He has worked with the product portfolios of cloud computing giants such as Microsoft, Cisco, and VMware. Gustavo graduated from the University of Brasília with a Bachelor of Science degree, followed by a Master of Science degree from the KTH Royal Institute of Technology in Stockholm, Sweden.

Dr. Michaela Iorga, Ph.D.

Dr. Michaela Iorga serves as senior security technical lead for cloud computing with the National Institute of Standards and Technology (NIST), Computer Security division. She also chairs the NIST Cloud Computing Public Security Working Group and co-chairs the recently-established NIST Cloud Computing Public Forensic Science Working Group. Having previously served in a wide range of consulting positions in both government and private sector industries before joining NIST, Dr. Iorga, a recognized expert in information security, risk assessment, information assurance, and cloud computing security, has a deep understanding of cybersecurity, identity and credential management, and cyberspace privacy issues, as well as an extensive knowledge base in the development of complex security architectures. In her role as senior security technical lead at NIST and chair of the NIST Public Security Working Group, Dr. Iorga supports the development and dissemination of cybersecurity standards and guidelines that meet national priorities and promote American innovation and industrial competitiveness. Dr. Iorga is particularly focused on working with industrial, academic, and other government stakeholders to develop a high-level, vendor-neutral cloud computing security reference architecture under the NIST Strategy for Developing a US Government Cloud Computing Technology Roadmap. A proven leader and expert in problem-solving and analysis, Dr. Iorga is also managing several other NIST efforts that include the development of the Federal Information Processing Standard 140-3: "Security Requirements for Cryptographic Modules" and the implementation of a NIST public, secure randomness source. She also contributes to the NIST efforts in developing the security testing requirements for electrical smart meters. Dr. Iorga received her Ph.D. from Duke University in North Carolina, USA.

Disclaimer: Any mention of commercial products or reference to commercial organizations is for information only; it does not imply recommendation or endorsement by NIST nor does it imply that the products mentioned are necessarily the best available for the purpose.

Amin Naserpour

A certified IT professional with more than 14 years of experience in solution architecture and design, engineering, and consultation, Amin specializes in designing medium- to enterprise-level complex solutions for partially to fully virtualized front-end infrastructures. His portfolio includes clients such as VMware, Microsoft, and Citrix, and his work consists of integrating front-ends with back-end infrastructure-layer solutions. Amin designed a unified, vendor-independent cloud computing framework that he presented at the 5th International SOA, Cloud + Service Technology Symposium in 2012. Certified in cloud computing, virtualization, and storage, Amin currently holds technical consultant and cloud operations lead positions for Hewlett-Packard, Australia.

Vinícius Pacheco, MSc

Vinícius has more than 13 years of IT experience in network management, network security, convergence, and IT governance from working in multiple federal public departments in Brazil. He has been the chief information officer of Brazil's Ministry of National Integration for two years and recently published several academic papers focused on enabling privacy in the cloud computing paradigm. Vinícius is currently pursuing a Ph.D. in cloud security and holds a Master of Science degree in Telecommunications (2007) from the University of Brasília.

Matthias Ziegler

Dr. Matthias Ziegler leads the Emerging Technology Innovation practice and is responsible for cloud computing at Accenture in Austria, Switzerland, and Germany. He is part of an international team that is looking at emerging technologies in areas such as cloud computing, Big Data, analytics, and social media and develops innovative solutions for clients that create business value. His work spans from conducting innovation workshops with clients' senior leadership, to discussing architecture alternatives with enterprise architects, to leading teams that bring emerging technology solutions successfully to production. He is a requested speaker at conferences such as the SOA, Cloud + Service Technology Symposium. Dr. Ziegler holds a diploma in Computer Science from the University of Würzburg and a Ph.D. from the Technical University of Munich and teaches Management Information Systems at the University of Applied Management in Erding. He lives with his wife and three children near Munich, Germany.

Index

X-Z

PRENTICE HALL

REGISTER

THIS PRODUCT

informit.com/register

Register the Addison-Wesley, Exam Cram, Prentice Hall, Que, and Sams products you own to unlock great benefits.

To begin the registration process, simply go to **informit.com/register** to sign in or create an account. You will then be prompted to enter the 10- or 13-digit ISBN that appears on the back cover of your product.

Registering your products can unlock the following benefits:

- Access to supplemental content, including bonus chapters, source code, or project files.
- A coupon to be used on your next purchase.

Registration benefits vary by product. Benefits will be listed on your Account page under Registered Products.

About InformIT — THE TRUSTED TECHNOLOGY LEARNING SOURCE

INFORMIT IS HOME TO THE LEADING TECHNOLOGY PUBLISHING IMPRINTS
Addison-Wesley Professional, Cisco Press, Exam Cram, IBM Press, Prentice Hall Professional, Que, and Sams. Here you will gain access to quality and trusted content and resources from the authors, creators, innovators, and leaders of technology. Whether you're looking for a book on a new technology, a helpful article, timely newsletters, or access to the Safari Books Online digital library, InformIT has a solution for you.

THE TRUSTED TECHNOLOGY LEARNING SOURCE

Addison-Wesley | Cisco Press | Exam Cram
IBM Press | Que | Prentice Hall | Sams

SAFARI BOOKS ONLINE

informIT.com THE TRUSTED TECHNOLOGY LEARNING SOURCE

PEARSON

InformIT is a brand of Pearson and the online presence for the world's leading technology publishers. It's your source for reliable and qualified content and knowledge, providing access to the top brands, authors, and contributors from the tech community.

✦Addison-Wesley   **Cisco Press**   EXAM/**CRAM**   **IBM Press.**   **que**   **PRENTICE HALL**   **SAMS**   │ Safari Books Online

LearnIT at InformIT

Looking for a book, eBook, or training video on a new technology? Seeking timely and relevant information and tutorials? Looking for expert opinions, advice, and tips? **InformIT has the solution.**

- Learn about new releases and special promotions by subscribing to a wide variety of newsletters.
  Visit **informit.com/newsletters**.

- Access FREE podcasts from experts at **informit.com/podcasts**.

- Read the latest author articles and sample chapters at **informit.com/articles**.

- Access thousands of books and videos in the Safari Books Online digital library at **safari.informit.com**.

- Get tips from expert blogs at **informit.com/blogs**.

Visit **informit.com/learn** to discover all the ways you can access the hottest technology content.

Are You Part of the **IT** Crowd?

Connect with Pearson authors and editors via RSS feeds, Facebook, Twitter, YouTube, and more! Visit **informit.com/socialconnect**.

informIT.com THE TRUSTED TECHNOLOGY LEARNING SOURCE   **PEARSON**

✦Addison-Wesley   **Cisco Press**   EXAM/**CRAM**   **IBM Press.**   **que**   **PRENTICE HALL**   **SAMS**   │ Safari Books Online

Try Safari Books Online FREE for 15 days

Get online access to Thousands of Books and Videos

Safari Books Online — FREE 15-DAY TRIAL + 15% OFF*
informit.com/safaritrial

> **Feed your brain**
> Gain unlimited access to thousands of books and videos about technology,
> digital media and professional development from O'Reilly Media,
> Addison-Wesley, Microsoft Press, Cisco Press, McGraw Hill, Wiley, WROX,
> Prentice Hall, Que, Sams, Apress, Adobe Press and other top publishers.

> **See it, believe it**
> Watch hundreds of expert-led instructional videos on today's hottest topics.

WAIT, THERE'S MORE!

> **Gain a competitive edge**
> Be first to learn about the newest technologies and subjects with Rough Cuts
> pre-published manuscripts and new technology overviews in Short Cuts.

> **Accelerate your project**
> Copy and paste code, create smart searches that let you know when new
> books about your favorite topics are available, and customize your library
> with favorites, highlights, tags, notes, mash-ups and more.

* Available to new subscribers only. Discount applies to the Safari Library and is valid for first
12 consecutive monthly billing cycles. Safari Library is not available in all countries.

FREE
Online Edition

Your purchase of **Cloud Computing** includes access to a free online edition for 45 days through the **Safari Books Online** subscription service. Nearly every Prentice Hall book is available online through **Safari Books Online**, along with thousands of books and videos from publishers such as Addison-Wesley Professional, Cisco Press, Exam Cram, IBM Press, O'Reilly Media, Que, Sams, and VMware Press.

Safari Books Online is a digital library providing searchable, on-demand access to thousands of technology, digital media, and professional development books and videos from leading publishers. With one monthly or yearly subscription price, you get unlimited access to learning tools and information on topics including mobile app and software development, tips and tricks on using your favorite gadgets, networking, project management, graphic design, and much more.

Activate your FREE Online Edition at
informit.com/safarifree

STEP 1:   Enter the coupon code: VCWGXBI.

STEP 2:   New Safari users, complete the brief registration form.
Safari subscribers, just log in.

If you have difficulty registering on Safari or accessing the online edition,
please e-mail customer-service@safaribooksonline.com

Prentice Hall Service Technology Series

THE WORLD'S TOP-SELLING SERVICE TECHNOLOGY TITLES WITH OVE

ABOUT THE SERIES

The Prentice Hall Service Technology Series from Thomas Erl aims to provide the IT industry with a consistent level of unbiased, practical, and comprehensive guidance and instruction in the areas service technology application and innovation. Each title in this book series is authored in relation other titles so as to establish a library of complementary knowledge. Although the series covers a spectrum of service technology-related topics, each title is authored in compliance with common language, vocabulary, and illustration conventions so as to enable readers to continually explore cross-topic research and education.

www.servicetechbooks.com/community

ABOUT THE SERIES EDITOR

Thomas Erl is a best-selling IT author, the series editor of the Prentice Hall Service Technology Series from Thomas Erl, and the editor of the Service Technology Magazine. As CEO of Arcitura Education Inc. and in cooperation with CloudSchool.com™ and SOASchool.com®, Thomas has led the development of curricula for the internationally recognized SOA Certified Professional (SOACP) and Cloud Certified Professional (CCP) accreditation programs, which have established a series of formal, vendor-neutral industry certifications. Thomas has toured over 20 countries as a speaker and instructor. Over 100 articles and interviews by Thomas have been published in numerous publications, including the Wall Street Journal and CIO Magazine.

 | 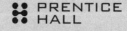 |

homas Erl

COPIES IN PRINT

A Design Patterns
Thomas Erl

N: 0136135161
dcover, Full-Color,
pages

SOA Governance:
Governing Shared
Services On-Premise
& in the Cloud
by S. Bennett, T. Erl,
C. Gee, R. Laird,
A. T. Manes,
R. Schneider, L. Shuster,
A. Tost, C. Venable

ISBN: 0138156751
Hardcover, 675 pages

SOA with REST:
Principles, Patterns &
Constraints for Building
Enterprise Solutions
with REST
by Raj Balasubramanian,
Benjamin Carlyle,
Thomas Erl,
Cesare Pautasso

ISBN: 0137012519
Hardcover, 577 pages

Cloud Computing:
Concepts, Technology
& Architecture
by Thomas Erl,
Zaigham Mahmood,
Ricardo Puttini

ISBN: 9780133387520
Hardcover, 528 pages

Cloud Computing
Design Patterns
by Thomas Erl,
Amin Naserpour

Coming Soon

vice-Oriented
rchitecture:
ield Guide to
egrating XML and
b Services
Thomas Erl

N: 0131428985
perback, 534 pages

Service-Oriented
Architecture:
Concepts, Technology
and Design
by Thomas Erl

ISBN: 0131858580
Hardcover, 760 pages

SOA Principles of
Service Design
by Thomas Erl

ISBN: 0132344823
Hardcover, Full-Color,
573 pages

Web Service Contract
Design and Versioning
for SOA
by T. Erl, H. Haas,
A. Karmarkar, C. K. Liu,
D. Orchard, J. Pasley,
A. Tost, P. Walmsley,
U. Yalcinalp

ISBN: 013613517X
Hardcover, 826 pages

SOA with .NET &
Windows Azure:
Realizing Service-
Orientation with the
Microsoft Platform
by D. Chou, J. de
Vadoss, T. Erl, N. Gandhi
H. Kommalapati,
B. Loesgen, C. Schittko
H. Wilhelmsen, M. Williams

ISBN: 0131582313
Hardcover, 893 pages

ming Soon:
ervice Infrastructure: On-Premise and in the Cloud
Next Generation Service Technology
OA with Java

www.servicetechbooks.com

Cloud Computing Training & Certification

The CloudSchool.com Cloud Certified Professional (CCP) program from Arcitura Education establishes a series of vendor-neutral industry certifications, each dedicated to an area of specialization in the field of cloud computing. Founded by author Thomas Erl, the CCP program is comprised of 8 certifications and 21 courses and labs. For an overview of the program, visit: **www.cloudschool.com**

Each of the 21 CCP courses has a corresponding exam. To complete a given CCP certification requires passing grades in a specific combination of exams. To view a matrix that shows how CCP courses and exams are associated with certification tracks, visit: **www.cloudschool.com/matrix**

CCP exams can be taken world-wide through Prometric testing centers. To view testing center locations or to schedule exams, visit: **www.prometric.com/arcitura**

Both public and private workshops taught by Certified Cloud Trainers are available for the delivery of courses for both general training and exam preparation purposes. To inquire about private workshops, contact **info@cloudschool.com**. To view the public workshop calendar, visit: **www.cloudworkshops.com**

Each CCP course and exam also has a corresponding CCP Self-Study Kit that contains the materials provided in the workshops in addition to a series of supplements, resources, and CDs designed for self-study and self-paced exam preparation. Different bundles of CCP Self-Study Kits are available for the individual certification tracks. To learn more, visit: **www.cloudselfstudy.com**

Individuals that pass CCP exams with honors are eligible to become Certified Cloud Trainers. For more information regarding CCP trainer development programs, visit: **www.arcitura.com/trainerdevelopment**

Arcitura Education has a range of partner licensing and reseller programs for public and private educational institutions, resellers, and distributors. To learn more, visit: **www.arcitura.com/programs**

CloudSchool.com™
CLOUD CERTIFIED
Professional

CloudSchool.com™
CLOUD CERTIFIED
Technology Professional

CloudSchool.com™
CLOUD CERTIFIED
Architect

CloudSchool.com™
CLOUD CERTIFIED
Security Specialist

CloudSchool.com™
CLOUD CERTIFIED
Governance Specialist

CloudSchool.com™
CLOUD CERTIFIED
Storage Specialist

CloudSchool.com™
CLOUD CERTIFIED
Virtualization Specialist

CloudSchool.com™
CLOUD CERTIFIED
Capacity Specialist

PROMETRIC

www.arcitura.com/community

Arcitura
the IT education company